DAILY
MEDITATIONS

POPE JOHN PAUL II

DAILY
MEDITATIONS

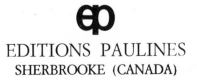

EDITIONS PAULINES
SHERBROOKE (CANADA)

Imprimatur
Casali, 15 iulii 1984
† CAROLUS CAVALLA, *Episcopus*

Editors:

Valeria Caprioglio
Francesco Massola
Alfredo Ferrari

Photographs:

by Arturo Mari
photographer of « Osservatore Romano »

Jacket:
Studio Aemme

English edition for: Canada, United States and New Zeland
ⓒ 1985 EDITIONS PAULINES
    250, boul. St-François Nord
    Sherbrooke, Qué, CANADA J1E 2B9

ISBN 2-89039-066-7

ⓒ 1984 LIBRERIA EDITRICE VATICANA
    Città del Vaticano - Roma

ⓒ 1984 EDIZIONI PIEMME DI PIETRO MARIETTI
    Via Paleologi 45 - 15033 Casale Monferrato - Italy
    (for international rights)

Printed in Italy

*Today like never before
man is realizing
how important and necessary it is
to get deeply and radically to the heart
of christian doctrine.
Our keen need and desire
of knowing and living that Truth
Jesus Christ gave us that day in Bethlehem
and assured by his death on the Cross
and his Resurrection,
have to be freed
from the stifling caused by routine
and everyday troubles and worries.
Truth only
can bring great joy and support
in spite of the crisis it may cause,
for all its constant request
of courageous and final choices,
even if indulging in the current of doubts,
opinions, hypotheses,
emotions and questions
of a certain "convenient" culture
created by a number of hidden thinkers,
might seem much easier to reach.
A deep and complete religious culture,
a continuous and honest pursuit
of the good and the truth
closely linked
with personal and liturgical prayers
are nowadays of primary importance.
Here lies the source
of the greatest decisions
in christian life.*

Joannes Paulus PP. II

SEASON OF ADVENT

THE EXPECTATION OF CHRIST

Human history is woven with this expectation, which in the most aware men and women becomes a cry, a request, an invocation. Man, created in Christ and through Christ, can attain his truth and his fullness only in him. Here is disclosed the meaning of the search for salvation which underlies every human experience. Here is explained that yearning for the infinite which, aside from God's merciful initiative in Christ, would remain frustrated.

The expectation of Christ is part of the mystery of Christ. If it is true that man of himself, despite his good will, cannot achieve salvation, the one who seriously and alertly faces his human experience finally discovers within himself the "urgent need for an encounter" which is marvellously satisfied by Christ.

He who has placed in man's heart the yearning for Redemption has also taken the initiative to satisfy it.

The words, « for us men and for our salvation », in which the Creed presents to us the significance of Christ's Redemption, assume, in the light of the mystery of the Incarnation, a truly resolutive concreteness: « By his incarnation the Son of God has united himself in some fashion "with every man" » (Const. GS, 22).

Christian Tradition calls a supernatural mystery that initiative of Christ, who enters into history in order to redeem it and to point out to man the way to return to his original intimacy with God. This initiative is a mistery also because it is unthinkable as such, on man's part, in so far as it is totally gratuitous, the result of God's free initiative. Nevertheless, this mystery has the surprising ability to grasp man at his roots, to respond to his aspiration for the infinite, to satisfy his thirst for being, for good, for truth and beauty, which burns within him.

HARMONY BETWEEN MAN AND CHRIST

« What you are thus worshipping in ignorance I intend to make known to you » (Acts 17:23). The explicit proclamation of the Redemption brought by Christ, which Paul dares to make in the Areopagus in Athens, the city where philosophical and doctrinal arguments were traditionally the most sophisticated, is among the most significant documents of early catechesis.

The instinctive religiousness of the Athenians is seized upon by Paul as an unintentional prophecy of the true Body in whom « ...we live and move and have our being » (Acts 17:28).

Similarly, the Athenians' thirst for knowledge is seen by him as the natural shoot on which he can graft the message of truth and justice that the death, resurrection and "parousia" of Christ introduce into the world.

There is evidenced in this way the affirmation dear to the great Christian tradition according to which the Redemption event turns out as befitting and reasonable for man, who keeps himself open to God's unpredictable initiatives.

« There is a profound harmony between man and Christ the Redeemer ». Truly the living God is close to man, and man, without realizing it, awaits him as the one who will disclose to him the full meaning of himself.

The Second Vatican Council strongly reproposed this conviction of faith and ecclesial doctrine when, in that precious twenty-second paragraph of "Gaudium et Spes" it affirmed: « The truth is that only in the mystery of the Incarnate Word does the mystery of man take on light... Christ... fully reveals man to man himself...''

THE BOOK OF EMMANUEL

One collection of Isaiah's predictions and prophecies is commonly called the « Book of Emmanuel » (chapters 6-12) because there stands out the figure of a marvellous child, whose name « Emmanuel » is full of mystery in so far as it means « God with us ». This child is proclaimed as a sign by the Prophet Isaiah to King Ahaz at a time of extreme danger for the ruling house and for the people, while the king and the nation are about to be overwhelmed by enemies.

The king is distrustful and does not intend to address God; he has human plans he wants to carry out: « I will not ask (for a sign)! I will not tempt the Lord! ». Then God announces a punishment for Ahaz, but at the same time he confirms his fidelity to the promises to David's descendants: « The Lord himself will give you this sign: the virgin shall be with child, and bear a son, and shall name him Emmanuel » (Is 7:12-14).

It is a sign of salvation and a pledge of liberation for believers. In fact, we read in the Book of Isaiah: « The people who walked in darkness have seen a great light; upon those who dwell in the land of gloom a light has shone. You have brought them abundant joy and great rejoicing » (Is 9:1-2). « For a child is born to us, a son is given to us; upon his shoulder dominion rests. They name him Wonder-Counsellor, God-Hero, Father-Forever, Prince of Peace » (Is 9:5-7).

And the prophecy continues in a crescendo: « But a shoot shall sprout from the stump of Jesse, and from his roots a bud shall blossom. The Spirit of the Lord shall rest upon him, a spirit of wisdom and of understanding, a spirit of counsel and of strength, a spirit of knowledge and of fear of the Lord » (Is 11:1-2).

THE NEW EARTH, IN WHICH JUSTICE WILL DWELL

The eschatological perspective of the Apostle's letter: « new heavens and a new earth in which justice dwells » (2 Pt 3:13), speaks of the Creator's definitive meeting with creation in the kingdom of the age to come, for which every man must become ready through the interior advent of faith, hope and charity.

The witness to this truth is John the Baptist, who in the region of the Jordan preaches « a baptism of repentance for the forgiveness of sins » (Mk 1:4). Thus there are fulfilled in him the words of the first reading from the Book of Isaiah. John, in fact, preached:

« After me comes he who is mightier than I, the thong of whose sandals I am not worthy to stoop down and untie. I have baptized you with water; but he will baptize you with the Holy Spirit » (Mk 1:7-8).

THE ADVENT OF MEETING

John distinguishes clearly the « advent of preparation » from the « advent of meeting ». The advent of meeting is the work of the Holy Spirit, it is baptism with the Holy Spirit. It is God himself who goes to meet man; he wants to meet him at the very heart of his humanity, thus confirming this humanity as the eternal image of God and at the same time making it « new ».

John's words about the Messiah, about Christ: « He will baptize you with the Holy Spirit », reach the very root of man's meeting with the living God, a meeting that is carried out in Jesus Christ and is part of the process of the expectation of new heavens and a new earth, in which justice will dwell: the advent of the « future world ». In him, in Christ, God assumed the concrete figure of the Shepherd foretold by the prophets, and at the same time he became the Lamb who takes away the sin of the world.

« BEHOLD, THE LORD GOD COMES »

« Comfort, comfort my people... Speak tenderly to Jerusalem, and cry to her that her warfare is ended, that her iniquity is pardoned... Get you up to a high mountain, O Zion, herald of good tidings... Lift up your voice... fear not; say... "Behold our God!" Behold, the Lord God comes with him... He will feed his flock like a shepherd » (Is 40:1-2; 9-11). Together with this message, there is the call to « prepare » and to « level the way », the same call that John the Baptist, the last prophet of the Lord's coming, will make his own at the Jordan. In short, Isaiah states: The Lord is coming... as a shepherd...; it is necessary to create the conditions required for the meeting with him. It is necessary to prepare.

« Behold, the Lord God comes », we are told, but at the same time the voice cries: « In the wilderness prepare the way of the Lord... every mountain and hill shall be made low; the uneven ground shall become level, and the rough places a plain. And the glory of the Lord shall be revealed... » (Is 40:3-5).

Let us accept joyfully, therefore, both the good news and the tasks it sets befor us. God wants to be with us; he comes as a ruler, « his arm rules for him », but above all he comes as a shepherd and as such « he will feed his flock, he will gather the lambs in his arms, he will carry them in his bosom, and gently lead those that are with young » (Is 40:11).

We are here to strengthen ourselves in our joy and in our hope, and at the same time we are here that, guided by the conviction about the presence of God on our paths, we may again prepare the way for him, removing from it everything that makes the meeting difficult or even impossible; that we can always return to him!

THE LORD KEEPS FAITH FOREVER

The fact that the messianic promises were fulfilled in Jesus of Nazareth is the proof that God is Faithful to his word. We can truly repeat with the Psalmist: « The Lord keeps faith forever! » (Ps 146 [145]:6).

Every year Advent reminds us of the fulfilment of the messianic promises regarding Christ, for the purpose of orienting our souls toward those promises, whose fulfilment we have received in Christ and through Christ. These promises lead towards the last "destinies" of man.

In Christ and through Christ « the Lord keeps faith forever! » From generation to generation, in him and through him "the second" Advent opens up, which is the « time of the Church ». Through Christ the Church lives the advent of every day—that is, its own faith in the fidelity of God, who « keeps faith forever ». In this way, Advent always reconfirms the "eschatological" dimension of hope in the life of the Church. For this reason St James advises us: « Be patient, brothers, until the coming of the Lord » (Jas 5:7).

In this perspective, the Liturgy of Advent is not only an invitation to joy, but also to courage. If, in fact, we must rejoice in the serene hope of the future fullness of messianic goods, we must also pass with courage through and above "temporary and transitory reality with our glance and commitment turned toward what is eternal and unchangeable". This courage is born of Christian hope and, in a certain sense, is Christian hope itself.

THE SOURCE OF OUR JOY

Advent brings with it a pressing "invitation to joy" and is called, because of the first word of the Latin text of the entrance antiphon, "Gaudete" Sunday (Phil 4:4-5). Nature itself is invited by the Prophet to manifest signs of exultation with lively rejoicing: « The desert and the parched land will exult; the steppe will rejoice and bloom" (Is 35:1), because they will soon see "the glory of the Lord". It is the joy of Advent, which in the faithful is accompanied by the humble and intense invocation to God: « Come! » It is the ardent supplication which serves as a refrain to the Responsorial Psalm of the Liturgy: « Lord, come and save us! » Here is your God, / he comes with vindication; / With divine recompense he comes to save you. / Then will the eyes of the blind be opened, / the ears of the deaf be cleared; / Then will the lame leap like a stag, / then the tongue of the dumb will sing. / Streams will burst forth in the desert, / and rivers in the steppe... / A highway will be there, / called the holy way;... / It is for those with a journey to make, / and on it the redeemed will walk, / Those whom the Lord has ransomed will return / and enter Zion singing, / crowned with everlasting joy; / They will meet with joy and gladness, / sorrow and mourning will flee » (Is 35:4-10).

So, therefore, Christ answers John the Baptizer: Aren't the messianic promises being fulfilled? Therefore, "the time of the first Advent has come!" We already have this time behind us and, at the same time, we continue to persevere in it. In fact, the Liturgy makes it present every year. And this "is the source of our joy".

MESSIANIC PROMISES

The Advent joy finds its source "in the answer" which the messengers sent by John the Baptizer received "from Christ".

While he was in prison, having heard talk about Jesus' works, he sent him his disciples, bearers of the crucial question which awaited a definitive answer: « Are you "He who is to come" or do we look for another? » (Mt 11:3).

And here is Christ's answer: « Go back and report to John what you hear and see: the blind recover their sight, cripples walk, lepers are cured, the deaf hear, dead men are raised to life, and the poor have the good news preached to them. Blest is the man who finds no stumbling block in me" » (Mt 11:4-6).

Jesus of Nazareth, in his solemn reply to John the Baptizer, refers, with evidence, to the fulfilment of the "messianic promises". And they are those promises which are found prophesied in the Book of Isaiah:

« Say to those whose hearts are frightened:
Be strong, fear not! »

LET US VENERATE THE REDEMPTION WHICH WAS ACCOMPLISHED IN YOU

Blessed be the God and Father of Our Lord Jesus Christ, who has filled you, Virgin of Nazareth, with every spiritual blessing in Christ.

In him you were conceived immaculate! Chosen to be his mother, in him and through him you were redeemed more than any other human being! Preserved from inheriting original sin, you were conceived and came into the world in the state of sanctifying grace.

Full of grace! Today we venerate this mystery of the faith.

Today, together with the whole Church, we venerate the redemption of world and of man, which was reserved only to you: only to you.

Hail, Mary, « Alma Redemptoris Mater »! Today, the Roman Church presents to you a particular request: help us to prepare ourselves worthly for the Holy Year which will be a new Jubilee of our Redemption.

You who are the first among the redeemed, help us, people of the twentieth century, which is drawing to its close, and at the same time, people of the second millennium after Christ; help us to rediscover our part of the mystery of redemption; help us to understand more deeply the divine and at the same time human dimension of that mystery, and to draw more fully from its inexhaustible resources;

– help us, who belong to the community of the Roman Church and all the pilgrims who will come here to pray at the tombs of the Apostles and Martyrs

– and all the brothers and sisters of the world, redeemed by the most precious Blood of Christ. All this we ask of you. O clement, O loving, O sweet Virgin Mary. Amen.

THE EXALTED DAUGHTER OF SION

Mary, if she is considered in the fullness of the Church's mystery and its mission, expresses not only its autonomous personality, at the vertex and the beginning of the Church, but in the dynamics of the history of salvation, she is also so intimately joined with the Church that she seems to be an embodiment and a living image of the mystical personality of the Church itself, the Spouse of Christ, signifying from the first moment of her existence all the wealth of grace that animates the Church. With regard to this, there comes to mind the precious information in the eighth chapter of « Lumen Gentium » which, interpreting St Luke's perception, tell us: « ...With her, the exalted Daughter of Sion, and after a long expectation of the promise, the times were at lenght fulfilled and the new dispensation established ».

That is, after the meeting between the Old and the New Covenant, Mary is the end of the messianic Church of Israel and the beginning of the newborn Church of Christ. It is she who is the ultimate and perfect expression of the ancient People of God, born of Abraham, and the first, sublime realization of the new People of children of God born of Christ.

TEMPLE AND SPOUSE

With Mary, therefore, the promises, the prefigurations, the prophecies and the spirituality of the Old Testament Church come to an end and there begins the New Testament Church, without stain or wrinkle, in the fullness of the grace of the Holy Spirit. It is this ecclesiological dimension, proclaimed by the Second Vatican Council, that is the new itinerary that allows us to read and to understand in all its width and depth the mystery of Mary. Considered in this dimension, the Immaculate Conception of the Mother of God and our Mother acquires a richer ecclesial significance. With her, the masterpiece of God the Father and the purest reflection of the grace of the Holy Spirit, the Church of Christ begins. In Mary we see the immaculate conception of the Church, the temple and the spouse without stain or wrinkle. It is in her that the Church feels it has attained its highest perfection, without a shadow of sin; and it is in her as the prototype, sign and help, that the ecclesial community, still a pilgrim on earth, is inspired and strengthened to advance in sanctity and in the struggle against sin.

THE IMMACULATE ONE IS THE
FIRST MARVEL OF THE REDEMPTION

The perfection accorded to Mary must not produce in us the impression that her life on earth was a kind of heavenly life, very different from ours. In reality, Mary had a life like ours. She knew the daily difficulties and trials of human life; she lived in the darkness that faith involves. No less than Jesus, she experienced the temptation and the suffering of inner struggles. We can imagine how stricken she was by the drama of her Son's Passion. It would be a mistake to think that the life of her who was full of grace was an easy and comfortable life. Mary shared everything that pertains to our earthly condition, with all that is demanding and painful.

We must above all note that Mary was created immaculate in order to be better able to act on our behalf. The fullness of grace allowed her to fulfil perfectly her mission of collaboration with the work of salvation: it gave the maximum value to her cooperation in the sacrifice. When Mary presented to the Father her Son nailed to the cross, her painful offering was entirely pure.

And now the Immaculate Virgin, still in virtue of the purity of her heart, helps us to strive for the perfection realized in her. It is for sinners, that is, for all of us, that she received an exceptional grace. In her role as mother, she strives to make all her earthly children sharers in some way in the favour with which she was personally enriched.

Mary intercedes with her Son to obtain mercy and forgiveness for us. She invisibly stoops to all who are in spiritual anguish in order to comfort them and lead them to reconciliation. The unique privilege of her Immaculate Conception puts her at the service of everyone and constitutes a joy for all who call her their mother.

FULL OF GRACE

In a special way, Advent is Mary's time. In fact, through Mary, the Son of God entered into the expectation of all humanity. Thus in her is found the "apex and the synthesis of Advent". The Solemnity of the Immaculate Conception, which we celebrate liturgically during the season of Advent, testifies to this very eloquently.

And although every year on 8 September the Church venerates Mary's birth with a special feast, nevertheless the solemnity of Immaculate Conception at the beginning of Advent introduces us even more deeply into the sacred mystery of her birth. Before coming into the world she was conceived in her mother's womb and at that moment she was born "of God himself" who accomplished the mystery of the Immaculate Conception: "full of grace".

And so we repeat with the Apostle of the Gentiles: "Praised be the God and Father of our Lord Jesus Christ, who has bestowed on us in Christ every spiritual blessing in the heavens » (Eph 1:3). And she, Mary, has been blessed in an altogether special way: unique and unrepeatable. In him, in fact, in Christ, God chose her before the world began to be holy and blameless in his sight (Eph 1:4).

Yes. The Eternal Father chose Mary in Christ; he chose her for Christ. He made her holy, rather, most holy. And the first fruit of this choice and divine vocation was the "Immaculate Conception". This is her « origin » in God's eternal thought: in the Eternal Word: and this together with her origin on earth. Her birth. Her birth "in the splendour" of the Immaculate Conception.

MARY, MOTHER AND VIRGIN

Mary, as the Immaculate Conception, "more than any other among men", bears in herself the mystery of those divine eternal destinies, with which man has been embraced in God's chosen Son,

– the destiny "to the grace" and the holiness of divine sonship,

– the destiny to glory in the God of infinite majesty.

And so she, Mary, "precedes" us all in the great procession of faith, hope and charity.

In fact, as the Second Vatican Council said so well, « in the mystery of the Church, herself rightly called mother and virgin, the Blessed Virgin "stands out" in eminent and singular fashion as exemplar of both virginity and motherhood » (LG 63).

She illuminates the People of God with the divine light, which more fully reflects the light of the Eternal Word. « The Mother of Jesus – the Council further stresses – shines forth on earth as a sign of sure hope and solace for the pilgrim People of God » (LG, 68).

When this light began to shine on the "horizon of man's history" through Mary – when with Mary's birth there appeared in the world she who was the Immaculate Conception – then "there began", in the history of salvation, the dawn of the Advent of God's Son. And then the work of Redemption took on its eternally designed shape.

THE THEOLOGICAL DIMENSION
OF MARY'S IMMACULATE CONCEPTION

The feast of Mary's Immaculate Conception, assumes a totally special theological and liturgical dimension. In fact, Mary's preservation from original sin from the first moment of her existence represents the first and radical effect of Christ's redemptive work, and links the Virgin, with a tight and indissoluble bond, to the Incarnation of the Son, who, before being born of her, redeems her in the most sublime way. This great Marian mystery, with which man's redemption begins in history, was already foreseen in that eternal plan of God the Father, in which Mary, preserved free from original sin in view of Christ's merits, was predestined to become in time the worthy mother of the same Saviour. Besides being a sublime privilege that exalts Mary among all human creatures and the choirs of angels themselves, her sinless conception was the eminent condition of grace so that her whole person, from the very first instant, would be disposed in the most complete freedom, the freedom from original sin, to the service of Christ and his redemptive work, for all mankind.

In this truth that closely unites Mary to Christ, our faith very joyfully perceives a richness and variety of significance.

— Seen in God's eternal plan for man, Mary is closely united to the Incarnate Word by an indissoluble bond of motherhood and is associated, from all eternity, to his redemptive work. For this mission of hers, it was fitting that there not be any stain of original sin in her from the first moment of her existence.

— In the history of human generations, her Immaculate Conception represents the most perfect result of the gratuitous action of the Holy Spirit who forms her and makes her a new creation, virgin soil, a temple of the Spirit, from her very first moment.

MAXIMILIAN KOLBE,
THE APOSTLE OF A NEW « MARIAN ERA »

With the intuition of a saint and the refinement of a theologian, Maximilian Kolbe meditated with extraordinary insight on the mystery of Mary's Immaculate Conception in the light of Sacred Scripture, the Magisterium, and the Liturgy of the Church, drawing from them wonderful lessons for life. He has appeared in our times as a prophet and an apostle of a new « Marian era », destined to make Jesus Christ and his Gospel shine with a bright light in the entire world.

This mission that he carried out with ardour and dedication « classified him », as Paul VI stated in the homily at his beatification, « among the great saints and clairvoyant minds that have understood, venerated and sung the mystery of Mary » (Insegnamenti di Paolo VI, IX, 1971, p. 909). **Though** he was aware of the inexhaustible depths of the mystery of the Immaculate Conception, for which « human words are not able to describe her who became the Mother of God » (Writings of Maximilian Kolbe, III, 1975, p. 690), his greatest regret was that Mary Immaculate was not sufficiently known and loved after the example of Jesus Christ and how the Tradition of the Church and the examples of the saints teach us. Indeed, in loving Mary we honour God, who raised her to the dignity of the Mother of his Son made man, and we unite ourselves with Jesus Christ who loved her as a mother. We will never love her as he loved her: « Jesus was the first to honour her as his mother, and we must imitate him in this also. We will never be able to equal the love with which Jesus loved her » (Writings of Maximilian Kolbe, II, p. 351). Love for Mary, Father Maximilian states, is the simplest and easiest way to sanctify ourselves, fulfilling our Christian vocation.

IMMACULATE
BECAUSE MOTHER OF GOD

St. Maximilian Kolbe's attention was incessantly concentrated on Mary's Immaculate Conception in order to be able to gather the marvellous wealth contained in the name that she herself revealed and that constitues the explanation of what today's Gospel teaches us in the words of the Angel Gabriel: « Hail, full of grace, the Lord is with you » (Lk 1:28). Recalling the apparitions at Lourdes – which for him were a stimulus and an incentive to better understand the fonts of Revelation – he observes: « To Saint Bernadette, who had questioned her many times, the Virgin answered, "I am the Immaculate Conception". With these words she clearly revealed that she not only is conceived without sin, but she is moreover the very "Immaculate Conception", just as a white object is one thing and whiteness something else; a perfect thing is one thing, perfection is something else". The Immaculate Conception is the name which reveals with precision who Mary is: it not only affirms a quality, but it exactly defines her person: Mary is radically holy in the totality of her existence, from the very beginning.

The sublime supernatural grandeur was granted to Mary with regard to Jesus Christ; it is in him and through him that God shared with her the fullness of sanctity. Mary is Immaculate because she is the Mother of God, and she became the Mother of God because she is Immaculate, Maximilian Kolbe states in clear-cut terms. Mary's Immaculate Conception manifests in a unique and sublime way the absolute centrality and the universal salvific role of Jesus Christ.

« THERE IS LOVE EVERYWHERE »

Investigating with ecstatic admiration the divine plan of salvation, which has its source in the Father who willed to communicate freely to creatures the divine life of Jesus Christ, and which was manifested in Mary Immaculate in a marvellous way, Father Kolbe, fascinated and enraptured, exclaims: « There is love everywhere ». The gratuitous love of God is the answer to all questions. « God is love », St John affirms (1 Jn 4:8).

Everything that exists is a reflection of the free love of God, and therefore every creature expresses in some way its infinite splendour. In a particular way, love is the centre and vertex of the human person, made in the image and likeness of God.

Mary Immaculate, the highest and most perfect of human persons, eminently reproduces the image of God and is therefore made capable of loving him with incomparable intensity as the Immaculate, without distractions or slackening. She is the unique handmaid of the Lord (Lk 1:38) who with her free and personal « fiat » responds to God's love by always doing what he asks of her. As the response of every other creature, hers is not an autonomous response, but it is a grace and a gift of God. In this response there is involved all of her freedom, the freedom of the Immaculate. « In the union of the Holy Spirit with Mary, love does not join only these two persons, but the first love is all the love of the Most Holy Trinity, while the second, Mary's love, is all the love of creation, and so in this union heaven is united to earth, all the uncreated Love with all created love... It is the vertex of love ».

THE DUTY OF « ACCEPTANCE »

The One who comes – the Christ – is sent « to accept you for the glory of God » (Rom 15:7). He comes to show the « faithfulness of God in fulfilling the promises to the patriarchs... » (Rom 15:8). He comes to reveal that the Lord is the « God of patience and encouragement » (Rom 15:5). He comes to « accept you for the glory of God » (Rom 15:7). And therefore the One who is to come enables you « to accept one another » (Rom 15:7). He indeed points out the true and authentic moral conduct which consists in giving glory to God the Father, following his example and with his same sentiments, and in loving one's neighbour. St Paul, writing to the Romans, had in mind both the converts from Judaism and those from paganism. But for everyone he spoke of the duty of « acceptance »: the Word of God, who comes, is to enable you to « have "the same sentiments" towards one another after the example of Christ Jesus » (Rom 15:5); « so that with one heart and voice you may "glorify God" the Father » (Rom 15:6).

In this way, therefore, the « making straight the paths », preached by John the Baptist, becomes in the light of St Paul's teaching in the Letter to the Romans, "accepting the whole messianic programme of the Gospel": the programme of adoring God – glory! – through the love of man, reciprocal love. In this spirit the Church announces Advent as the "continual dimension of man's existence towards God": towards that God « who is, who was, and who is to come » (Rv 1:4). This essential dimension of man's Christian existence corresponds to the « preparation » taught by today's liturgy. Man must always return to his heart, to his conscience, in order to live in the perspective of the « Coming ».

MISSION OF THE MESSIAH

Who is that Lord who must come? From his very words we can identify the person, the mission and the authority of the Messiah.

John the Baptist first of all clearly pictures the "person": the Baptist says, « He is more powerful than I. I am not even fit to carry his sandals » (Mt 3:11).

With this typically oriental expression he acknowledges the infinite distance that lies between him and the One who is to come, and he also emphasizes his own role in the immediate preparation for the great event.

He then points out the « mission » of the Messiah: « He it is who will baptize you in the Holy Spirit and fire » (Mt 3:11). This is the first time after the Angel's announcement to Mary that there appears the striking expression « Holy Spirit », which will then become part of Jesus' fundamental Trinitarian teaching. John the Baptist, divinely enlightened, announces that Jesus, the Messiah, will continue to confer baptism, but this rite will give God's « grace », the Holy Spirit, biblically understood as a mystical « fire » that cancels (burns away) sin and incorporates one into the divine life itself (it enkindles with love).

Finally, the Baptist clarifies the "authority" of the Messiah: « His winnowing-fan is in his hand. He will clear the threshing floor and gather his grain into the barn, but the chaff he will burn in unquenchable fire » (Mt 3:12). According to the words of John's teaching, the One who is to come is the « judge of consciences »; in other words, it is he who establishes what is good and what is evil (the grain and the chaff), truth and error; it is he who determines which trees bear good fruit and which instead bear bad fruit and must be cut down and burned! With these statements John the Baptist announces the « divinity » of the Messiah, because only God can be the supreme judge of good, indicate with absolute certainty the positive way for moral conduct, judge consciences, reward or condemn.

« INTERMEDIARY ADVENT »

Before the manger of Bethlehem — as later before the cross on Golgotha — mankind already makes a basic choice in regard to Jesus; a choice which in the last analysis, is that which man is called to make definitely day after day, in regard to God, Creator and Father. And this takes place, especially and above all, within the sphere of the depths of personal conscience. It is here that the meeting between man and God occurs. This is the "third coming" of which the Fathers speak, or the « intermediary Advent » analysed theologically and ascetically by St Bernard: « In the first coming the Word was seen on earth and he spoke with man when, as he himself stated, they saw him and they hated him. In the final coming "everyone shall see the salvation of God" and "they shall look on him whom they pierced". The third coming is however hidden: it is the coming in which only the elects see him within themselves and their souls are thereby saved ». (Sermo V, De medio adventu).

This Advent – in which man is inserted under the impulse of grace, by imitating the interior attitudes of those who awaited, sought, believed and loved Jesus – is made alive by the constant meditation and assimilation of the Word of God, who for the Christian, remains the first and fundamental point of reference for his spiritual life. It is made fruitful and animated by the "prayer of adoration and praise to God". This interior Advent is strengthened by the constant reception of the sacraments, in particular those of Reconciliation and the Eucharist, which, by purifying us and enriching us with Christ's grace, make us « new men », in harmony with the pressing invitation of Jesus: « Be converted! » (Mt 3:2; 4:17; Lk 5:32; Mk 1:15).

ADVENT: A TIME OF CONVERSION

Advent is « a time particularly suited to devotion to the Mother of the Lord » (Marialis Cultus, 4) and to a suitable catechesis. This is an orientation that I hope will be « accepted and followed everywhere » (Marialis Cultus, 4).

Joy is a fundamental element of this sacred season. Advent is a time of vigilance, prayer and conversion, in addition to being a season of fervent and joyful expectation. The reason is clear: the Lord is near (Phil 4:5), the Lord is with you or in your midst, as was announced to Mary (Lk 1:28) and to the daughter of Sion (Zep 3:15). The first word addressed to Mary in the New Testament is a joyful invitation: exult, rejoice! This greeting is linked to the coming of the Saviour. To Mary first is announced a joy that later will be proclaimed to all the people. She shares in this joy in an extraordinary manner and degree. In her, the joy of ancient Israel is concentrated and reaches its fullness, and the happiness of messianic times bursts forth unrestrainably. The Virgin's joy is particularly the joy of the « remnant » of Israel, the poor who awaits God's salvation and experiences his fidelity. To share in this feast it is necessary to await the Saviour with humility and to welcome him with confidence. « The faithful, living in the liturgy the spirit of Advent, by thinking about the inexpressible love with which the Virgin Mother awaited her Son, are invited to take her as a model and to prepare themselves to meet the saviour who is to come. They must be vigilant in prayer and joyful in praise » (Marialis Cultus, 4).

« A CLEAN HEART CREATE FOR ME »

The Church calls upon us to implore the mercy of God, revealed to us in the person of Jesus Christ the Redeemer. And so we repeat: "Regem venturum Dominum venite adoremus": Come, let us go to meet the King and Saviour who is coming, and

« Sing a new song to the Lord »
(Ps 149:1)

let us adore him. Let us place ourselves before him like the sick before the doctor, like the poor before one who has a plenitude of goods, like the sinner before sanctity and justice. A very well-known Psalm, the 50th, which biblical tradition attributes to David, « when the prophet Nathan came to him because of his sin with Bathsheba », existentially outlines the marvellous event of the encounter between the mercy of God and the innate weakness of the sinner, the tendency to sin. The humble and sincere acknowledgement of his moral infirmity gushes into a confident prayer, and the expectation of interior rebirth is so alive and certain that it overflows, as it were, into feelings of interior happiness and gratitude: « Have mercy on me, O God, in your compassion wipe out my offense... Cleanse me of sin with hyssop, that I may be purified; wash me, and I shall be whiter than snow... A clean heart create for me, O God, and a steadfast spirit renew within me... Give me back the joy of your salvation, and a willing spirit sustain in me ».

And the liberating experience of interior rebirth, the experience of the encounter with the merciful love of God, is translated into resolutions and plans for a new life, committed to the service of God and to witnessing his message among men: « I will teach transgressors your ways, and sinners shall return to you... O Lord, open my lips, and my mouth shall proclaim your praise ».

« YOU KNOW THE TIME »

« You know the time »: what does this mean? « Put on the Lord Jesus Christ » (Rom 13:14). — The way of Advent leads towards "man's

interior", which in various ways is weighed down by sin, as the reading attests.
– The encounter is not brought about only « from without », but also « from within », and it consists in such a "transformation of man's interior" as to correspond to the sanctity of the One whom we encounter: in this way it consists in « putting on the Lord Jesus Christ ».
– The "historical" meaning of Advent is "penetrated" by the "spiritual" meaning. In fact, Advent is not intended to be merely a remembering of the historical period that preceded the birth of the Saviour, even if so understood it already has « per sè » a very great spiritual significance. Beyond that, and more profoundly, Advent means to remind us that the history of man and of each one of us is understood as a great « Advent », as an expectation, moment by moment of the Lord's coming, so that he will find us ready and alert in order to be able to welcome him worthily.
« You know the time » means: « Stay awake... you cannot know the day your Lord is coming » (Mt 24:32).
This linking of God, of the divine Reality, with human time, on one hand confirms the limitation of this "time", which has an end! On the other hand, it "opens this time" to the eternity of God and to the « last things » "connected" with it.
Advent has an « eschatological » meaning, inasmuch as it recalls our thoughts and our intentions to future realities. It reminds us of the ultimate goal of our journey and urges us to be committed to earthly realities without letting ourselves be submerged in them, but on the contrary, leading them towards heavenly realities. It exhorts us to prepare well for these last things in such a way that the Lord's coming will not find us unprepared or ill disposed.

SALVATION COMES FROM GOD

In prophetic preaching, the announcement and promise of salvation and redemption come to "coincide ever more clearly with a person": he will be the new David, the good shepherd of his people. This is how Jeremiah speaks of it: « Behold, the days are coming, says the Lord, when I will raise up a righteous shoot to David; as king he shall reign and govern wisely, he shall do what is just and right in the land. In his days Judah shall be saved, Israel shall dwell in security. This is the name they give him: The Lord our justice » (Jer 23:5-6). There also progressively takes shape the idea that redemption "will be above all a spiritual happening". It will touch the people in their inmost being, purify them, transform them in mind and heart. « I will sprinkle clean water upon you to cleanse you from all your impurities, and from all your idols I will cleanse you. I will give you a new heart and place a new spirit within you... » (Ez 36:25-26).

The great messianic hope is thus expressed in terms of redemption, justice, a gift of the Spirit, purification of hearts, liberation from personal and social sins. In the course of the centuries, under God's guidance, the people's expectation therefore became more detailed in the hope of a definitive liberation capable of reaching the deepest roots of the human being and leading him into a new life of « justice and peace in the Holy Spirit » (Rm 14:17). In the Psalms, and in the whole prayer of the People of God, the plea for this salvation becomes a daily experience. Salvation comes from God; it is futile and harmful to nurture a presumptuous confidence in human powers; the Lord himself is salvation; he will free his people from all their sins.

SALVATION
IS MAN'S GREAT ASPIRATION

The season of Advent which we are living makes spontaneously rise to our lips this plea for salvation in which the prayerful expectation that runs through the whole Old Testament and continues into the New comes to life again.

Because we have been saved in hope, Saint Paul says (Rm 8:24), and « in the Spirit we eagerly await the justification we hope for, and only faith can yield it » (Gal 5:5).

Salvation!

It is man's great aspiration.

Sacred Scripture attests to this on every page and calls upon us to discover where man's true salvation lies, who his liberator and redeemer is.

THE FIRST EXPERIENCE
OF SALVATION

"The first and fundamental experience of salvation" was experienced by the People of God in the liberation from slavery in Egypt.

The Bible calls it redemption, ransom, liberation, salvation.

« I am the Lord.

I will free you from the forced labour of the Egyptians and will deliver you from their slavery.

I will rescue you by my outstretched arm...

I will take you as my own people, and you shall have me as your God » (Ex 6:6-7).

This was the first form of redemption-salvation collectively experienced in history by the People of God.

It is the memory of this salvation that will be the distinctive trait of Israel's faith.

For this reason, Israel has always seen it as the guarantee of all the promises of salvation made by God to his people, and the early Christian community immediately related it to the person and the work of Christ.

It is he who will be the great liberator, the new Moses who leads from slavery to the freedom of the children of God, from death to life, from sin to reconciliation and the fullness of divine mercy.

SEASON OF CHRISTMAS

FOR THAT WORD
WHO WAS MADE FLESH...

We thank you, our Father, for « that Word who was made flesh » and, on Bethlehem night, came to dwell among us (Jn 1:14).

We thank you for the Word, to whom you eternally communicate the most holy reality of your very godhead.

We thank you for the Word, in whom from all eternity you resolved to create the world, that it might bear witness to you.

We thank you, for in your Word you have loved man « before the foundation ot the world » (Eph 1:4).

We thank you, for in him, your Beloved Son, you resolved "to renew the whole of creation"; you resolved "to redeem man".

We thank you, eternal Father, for Bethlehem night of the birth of God, when the Word was made flesh "and the power of the Redemption" came to dwell among us.

« We thank you, our Father, for the holy vine of David, your servant, whom you revealed to us through Jesus, your Son » (Didache, IX, 2), born of the Virgin and laid in a manger.

In this « vine of David », in the heritage of Abraham, you promised "your salvation" and "your eternal covenant" to all men and women, to all the peoples of the earth.

We thank you for "the heritage of your grace", which you did not take away from man's heart, but which you renewed through the earthly birth of your Son, so that we, through his Cross and Resurrection, might regain, from generation to generation, "the dignity of children of God", lost through sin, the dignity of adopted brothers and sisters of your eternal Son.

We give you thanks, holy Father, "for your holy name" (Didache, X, 2), which you have caused to blossom anew in our hearts, through the Redemption of the world.

WE THANK YOU FOR THE CHILD
LAID IN A MANGER...

We thank you, eternal Father, for « the motherhood of the Virgin Mary », who under the protection of Joseph, the carpenter of Nazareth, brought your Son into the world, in utter poverty.
« He came to his own home, and his own people received him not » (Jn 1:11).
And yet, he « received all of us, from his very birth », and embraced each one of us with the eternal love of the Father, with the love that saves man, that raises the human conscience from sin: in him we have "reconciliation and the forgiveness of sins". We thank you, heavenly Father, for the Child laid in a manger: in him « the goodness and loving-kindness of God our Saviour appeared » (Ti 3:4).
We thank you, eternal Father, "for this love", which comes down "like a frail Infant into the history of each human being".
We thank you, because, though he was rich, yet for our sake he became poor, so that by his poverty we might become rich (2 Cor 8:9).
We thank you for the wonderful "economy of the Redemption" of man and of the world, revealed for the first time in the night of the birth in Bethlehem.

GOD AND MAN

The event which gives a God Saviour to mankind greatly surpasses the expectations of the Jewish people. This people expected salvation, was waiting for the Messiah, an ideal king for the future who was to establish the kingdom of God on earth. As high as the Jewish hope had placed this Messiah, he was only a man.

The great news of the coming of the Saviour consists in the fact that he is both God and man. What Judaism was not able to conceive nor hope for, that is, a Son of God become man, is achieved in the mystery of the Incarnation. "The fulfilment is far more wonderful than the promise".

This is the reason why we cannot measure Jesus' greatness only with the prophetic oracles in the Old Testament. When he fulfils these prophecies, it is on a transcendental level. All attempts to place Jesus within the limits of a human personality fail to recognize what is essential in the revelation of the New Covenant: the divine person of the Son who became man, or, according to the word of St. John, of the « Word who became flesh and made his dwelling among us » (Jn 1:14). Here appears the generous grandeur of the divine plan of salvation. The Father sent his own Son, who is God as he is.

He did not limit himself to send servants, men who would speak in his name, like the prophets. He wanted to witness the maximum of love to mankind, and surprised it by giving it a Saviour who possessed divine omnipotence.

NOTHING IS LOST IN MAN

In the unique person of Jesus, divinity and humanity are united in the most complete way. The one who is perfectly God is perfectly man. He has achieved in himself this union between divinity and humanity in order to enable all men to share in it. Perfectly man, he who is God wants to transmit to his human brothers a divine life which enables them to be perfectly men, reflecting divine perfection in themselves.

An aspect of reconciliation deserves to be emphasized here. While sinful man could fear for his future the consequences of his guilt and expect a diminished human life, instead he receives "the possibility of complete human development" from Christ the Saviour. Not only is he freed from the slavery in which his guilt imprisoned him, but he can acquire "a human perfection superior" to that which he possessed before sinning. Christ offers him a more abundant and more elevated life because of the fact that, in Christ, divinity has not repressed humanity in any way but brought it to a high level of development. With his divine life he transmits to men a deeper and more complete human life. That Jesus is the God Saviour become man therefore means that now "nothing is lost in man". All that had been wounded, stained, by sin can live again and flourish. This explains how Christian grace fosters the full exercise of all the human faculties, as well as the affirmation of every personality, both the female and male.

CHRISTMAS

The feast of Christmas has entered custom as an undisputed occasion of joy and goodness and as the occasion and stimulus for a kind thought, an act of altruism and love. This blossoming of generosity and courtesy, attention and thoughtfulness, puts Christmas among the most beautiful moments of the year, of life, in fact, impressing itself also on those who have no faith and yet are unable to resist the fascination that springs from this magic word: Christmas.

42   *SEASON OF CHRISTMAS*

That also explains the lyrical and poetic aspect which surrounds this event: how many pastoral melodies, how many sweet songs have bloomed around it! And what a surge of feeling or, sometimes, nostalgia it is able to arouse! Nature around us acquires on this day a sweet and innocent language of its own, which makes us appreciate the joy of simple, true things, to which our heart aspires, even without knowing it.

But behind this inspiring aspect, others show themselves at once, spoiling its clarity and jeopardizing its authenticity. These are the purely exterior and consumerist aspects of the feast, which threaten to empty the event of its real meaning, when they appear not as expressions of the interior joy that characterizes it, but as its main elements, or almost as its only "raison d'être".

Christmas then loses its authenticity, its religious meaning, and becomes an opportunity for dissipation and waste, slipping into unseemly and vulgar exterior expressions, which are an offence to those condemned by poverty to content themselves with the crumbs.

LET US RECOVER
THE TRUTH OF CHRISTMAS

It is necessary to recover the truth about Christmas in the authenticity of historical fact and in the fullness of the meaning it bears.

The historical fact is that at a given moment of history, in a certain area of the earth, there was born, of a humble woman of the race of David, the Messiah, announced by the Prophets: Jesus Christ the Lord.

The meaning is that, with the coming of Christ, the whole of human history found its outlet, its explanation, its dignity. God came to meet us in Christ, in order that we might have access to Him. On careful examination, human history is an uninterrupted aspiration to joy, beauty, justice and peace. They are realities which can be found fully only in God. Well, Christmas brings us the announcement that God has decided to overcome distances, to cross the ineffable abysses of his transcendence, to approach us, to the extent of making our life his, to the extent of becoming our brother.

So this is how things stand: are you looking for God? Find Him in your brother, because Christ has identified Himself, as it were, in every man. Do you want to love Christ? Love Him in your brother, because what you do to any one of your fellowmen, Christ considers it done to Himself. If, therefore, you endeavour to open your heart lovingly to your neighbour, if you try to establish relations of peace with him, if you want to share your resources with your neighbour, so that your joy, being shared, may become more real, you will have Christ at your side, and with Him you will be able to reach the goal of which your heart dreams: a world which is more just, and therefore more human.

THE « POWER » OF THE NEW-BORN

On Christmas night we wonder about the « power » that the New-born brings into the world. Do the words of Isaiah perhaps speak of the future of this Child born on Christmas night, seeing in him an earthly sovereign of the people?

So what power is it that is placed upon his shoulders on the night of his birth? And also what will it be in the hours of Golgotha?

The answer to these questions is "contained" in the liturgical text taken as a whole. It enters into the very heart of the events of Christmas night, but surpasses their purely human dimension.

Behold, we hear that with that angel who announced to the shepherds the birth of the Saviour there appeared « a multitude of the heavenly host praising God and saying, Glory to God in the highest, and on earth peace "among men with whom he is pleased" » (Lk 2:13).

This truth, which Christmas night contains as an integral part of itself, could not be pronounced by purely human lips. It could not be "pronounced", but only "announced" – the same as the truth about the conception of God the Son in the womb of the Virgin of Nazareth.

And behold, in that announcement at Bethlehem we find an answer to our question. What power was placed upon the shoulders of Christ that night? A "unique power". The power that he alone possesses. In fact only he has the power to permeate the soul of every human being with the peace of the "divine pleasure".

Only he has the power to enable human beings to become children of God.

CHRIST IS OUR PEACE

Let us rediscover the power of "prayer": to pray is to be reconciled with him whom we invoke, whom we meet, who makes us live. To experience prayer is to accept the grace which changes us: the Spirit, united to our spirit, commits us to conform our life with the Word of God. To pray is to enter into the action of God upon history: he, the sovereign actor of history, has wished to make people his collaborators.

Paul says to us about Christ: « For he is our peace, who has made us both one, and has broken down the dividing wall of hostility » (Eph 2:14). We know what a great power of mercy transforms us in "the Sacrament of Reconciliation". This gift overwhelms us: in that case, in all loyalty, we cannot remain resigned to the divisions and confrontations which set us against one another even though we share the same faith; we cannot accept, without reacting, the fact that conflicts are dragging on which are destroying the unity of humanity, which is called to become one single body. If we celebrate forgiveness, can we fight one another endlessly?

TO BE BLESSED BY GOD IS TO BE HAPPY

In the expectation of this Virgin « blessed among women » (Lk 1:42), there is contained all the hope that the People of God had placed in the promises made by God to their patriarchs, and, through the People of Israel, there is gathered the hope of all mankind.

We too try to make our own this awareness of Mary's faith, so deeply rooted in the history of her people and of all mankind, so as to grasp the essential meaning of its journey in the centuries and in the millenniums as a journey based on the hope of a salvation that comes from God.

Mary is happy because she believed that the Lord's words to her would be fulfilled (Lk 1:45), knowing that God does not go back on his promises. She is « happy » and at the same time « blessed » by God. The two terms cannot be separated, and the first is the result of the second. Spoken by God, the word of blessing is always a source of life and therefore of happiness. For Scripture, happiness lies in generating and communicating life, physical or spiritual. For this reason, whoever is « blessed » by God is « happy ».

Mary's expectation is the expectation of generating life, but a life by which she herself is at the same time saved and made happy, because it is the Son of God himself.

MARY « OUR MOTHER » IN THE FAITH

Mankind's response of faith must follow God's creative and salvific word. This logic is present to the greatest extent in the fundamental event of salvation, the Incarnation of the Son of God. Just as in Christ Jesus, the Word of the Father, all of God's saving acts are summed up, so in Mary's response the adherence of faith of God's people and all its members is summed up and reaches completion.

Mary, in particular, is the heiress and the completion of the faith of Abraham. Just as the patriarch is considered « our father » in the faith, so Mary, for all the more reason, must be claimed as « our mother » in the faith. Abraham is at the beginning, Mary at the summit of the generations of Israel. He anticipates and represents before God the people of the promise; she, a descendent of Abraham and a privileged heiress of his faith, receives the fruit of the promise. Through Mary's faith and obedience, all the families of the earth are blessed, according to the promise made to Abraham (Gn 12:3). The Virgin's words, « I am the servant of the Lord. Let it be done to me as you say » (Lk 1:38), evoke not only the figure and attitude of Abraham, but the picture of all the servants of the Lord who have collaborated with him in the history of salvation. More generally, Mary's words recall the words of the children of Israel at the foot of Sinai on the day of the covenant: « We will do everything that the Lord has told us! » (Ex 24:3).

« NOT KNOWING MAN »

"The motherhood" of Mary is "virginal". Through the power of the Holy Spirit she conceived and gave to the world the Son of God, « not knowing man ».

Paul explains this mystery of the divine motherhood of Mary, making reference "to the eternal fatherhood of God":

« When the time had fully come, God sent forth his Son, born of a woman » (Gal 4:4).

The virginal maternity of the Mother of God is related to the eternal fatherhood of God. It is, "in a certain sense", along the way of the "mission of the Son", who comes to humanity from the Father through the Mother. The motherhood of Mary opens this way — "it opens the way of God to humanity".

In a certain sense, it is the culminating point of this way.

We know that the way of this mission — once opened in man's history — remains forever. It always makes possible, throughout the history of humanity, the saving mission of the Son of God: "the mission", which is consummated with the Cross and the Resurrection. And together with the Son's mission there remains in the history of humanity "the saving motherhood" of his earthly mother: Mary of Nazareth.

In his earthly birth, Christ has brought us the same divine fatherhood: he has directed it to all people and has given it to everyone as an inviolable gift.

In reference to all of us the maternity of the Virgin Mother of God bears a particularly eloquent witness of this fatherhood of God.
The fatherhood of God tells us that we are all brothers and sisters.

MARY AND THE CHURCH, LIVING TEMPLES

Mary is the prototype of the Church in her virginal motherhood, an essential mystery which unites her to the Church in a common vocation and mission. Christ, as the Second Vatican Council states, was born of the Virgin Mary through the work of the Holy Spirit in order to be able to continue in a certain sense to be born and to grow in the Church, always through the work of the Holy Spirit. Both Mary and the Church are living temples, sanctuaries and instruments through which and in which the Holy Spirit is manifested. In a virginal way, they give birth to the same Saviour: Mary bears life in her womb and gives birth virginally; the Church gives life in the baptismal water and in the proclamation of the faith, giving it birth in the hearts of the faithful.
In the mystery of the Church, which in turn is rightly called Mother-Virgin, the Blessed Virgin Mary, first and in an eminent way, gives the example of the virgin and of the mother. In this close typological relationship, Mary's motherhood receives light and significance from the motherhood of the Church, of which she is a member and figure, and the Church's motherhood receives light and begins truly from Mary's motherhood, in which it already feels completely and perfectly realized. Like Mary, the Church too is a virgin and, in giving birth to the children of God, wholly preserves faith, hope and charity.

The virginal motherhood which Mary and the Church have in common makes of them an indivisible and indissoluble unit, as in a sole sacrament of salvation for all men.

MARY: « THEOTOKOS »

When at the Council of Ephesus the title of "Theotokos", Mother of God, was applied to Mary, the intention of the Council Fathers was to guarantee "the truth of the mystery of the Incarnation".

They wanted to affirm the personal unity of Christ, God and man, a unity such that Mary's motherhood in regard to Jesus was for that very reason motherhood in regard to the Son of God. Mary is « Mother of God » because her Son is God; she is mother only in the order of human generation, but since the infant conceived and brought into the world by her is God, she must be called « Mother of God ».

The affirmation of divine motherhood enlightens us about the "meaning of the Incarnation". It shows how the Word, a divine person, became man: he became so through a woman's participation in the work of the Holy Spirit. In a singular way, a woman was associated with the mystery of the Saviour's coming into the world. Through this woman, Jesus joins the human generations which preceded his birth.

Thanks to Mary, he has a "true birth" and his life on earth begins in a way similar to that of all other men. Through her motherhood, Mary enables the Son of God to have — after the extraordinary conception by the work of the Holy Spirit — a human development and a normal introduction into the society of men.

While it emphasizes the humanity of Jesus in the Incarnation, the title of « Mother of God » also calls attention to the "highest dignity granted to a creature".

MARY, THE « SERVANT » OF THE LORD

In this period we Christians are invited to meditate on the marvellous and mysterious events of the Incarnation of the Son of God, who becomes humble, poor, weak, fragile, in the moving reality of a child wrapped in swaddling clothes and laid in a manger.

But it is this very Child who guides, directs and makes an impression on the behaviour, the choices and the lives of persons who are near to him and who are involved in his appearance upon the scene. There is Elizabeth advanced in age who felt miraculously developing in her womb the life of a child expected for years as a grace of the Lord: John the Baptist, the precursor of the Messiah. Then there is her husband, Zechariah, whose tongue is loosed to sing the great deeds of God for his people. There are the shepherds who can contemplate the Saviour; there are the Magi searching for years for the Absolute in the signs of the heavens and the stars, and who will prostrate themselves in adoration before the newborn Babe. There is old Simeon who has also for a long time awaited the Messiah « the light of the Gentiles and the glory of his people Israel » (Lk 2:32); there is Anna, the venerable prophetess, who rejoices for the « redemption of Jerusalem » (Lk 2:38). There is Joseph, silent, watchfull, attentive, tender, the paternal guardian and protector of the Child in his weakness; and lastly, and above all, there is his Mother, Mary Most Holy, who in the presence of the ineffable design of God humbled herself in her littleness, calling herself the « servant » of the Lord and placing herself fully at the service of the divine plan.

THE MOTHER OF THE REDEEMER

In the liturgy the figure of Mary is traced in two selections from Scripture: as a prefiguration, in the Old Testament, in the text of Isaiah (Is 7:10-14); as fulfilment, in the New Testament, in the text of Matthew (Mt 1:18-24).

The books of the Old Testament, in describing for us the history of salvation, gradually bring out more clearly — as the Council observes (LG, 55) — the Mother of the Redeemer. Under this beam of light, she is already prophetically sketched in the image of the Virgin who will conceive and bear a Son, whose name will be Emmanuel, which means « God with us ». It is just an anticipation, effective in prefiguring a being without equal, predestined by God, who, already several centuries beforehand, begins to project to us some marks of his greatness. This text of Isaiah, in the course of the centuries, has been read in the Church and understood in the light of further revelation. What in the Old Testament, with its messianic overtones, was a beginning, in the New Testament becomes clarity. Saint Matthew recognizes in Isaiah's words the woman who through the work of the Holy Spirit virginally conceives without any human intervention. Jesus is the one who will save the people from their sins. And she, Mary, is the mother of Jesus. The Son of God « comes » into her womb to become man. She welcomes him. God has never so closely approached a human being as in this case of establishing the relationship between Son and Mother.

PEACE ON EARTH IS PROCLAIMED

The mystery of Christmas makes resound in our ears the canticle with which the heavenly host wants to make the earth participate in the great event of the Incarnation: « Glory to God in high heaven, peace on earth to those on whom his favour rests » (Lk 2:14).

"Peace on earth is proclaimed". It is not a peace which men are able to achieve through their efforts. It "comes from above", like a wonderful gift from God to mankind. We cannot forget that, if all of us must work for the establishment of peace in the world, we must first of all open ourselves to the divine gift of peace, placing our complete faith in the Lord.

According to the Christmas canticle, the peace promised to earth "is bound to God's love for men". Men are called « men of goodwill », because now divine goodwill belongs to them. The birth of Jesus is the irrefutable and definitive testimony of this goodwill, which will never be taken away from mankind.

This birth manifests "the divine will for reconciliation".

God desires to reconcile with himself the sinful world, forgiving and removing sins.

When announcing the birth, the angel had already expressed this reconciliatory will by indicating the name that the infant was to bear: Jesus, or rather « God saves ».

In fact, the angel says « he will save his people from their sins » (Mt 1:21).

The name reveals the infant's destiny and mission, along with his personality: he is the God who saves, the one who frees mankind from the slavery of sin and who therefore re-establishes man's friendly relations with God.

FROM A NEW HEART PEACE IS BORN

If the present systems generated by the « heart » of man turn out to be incapable of ensuring peace, then it is the « heart » of man that must be renewed, in order to renew systems, institutions and methods. Christian faith has a word for this fundamental change of heart: it is « conversion ». Speaking generally, it is a matter of rediscovering clearsightedness and impartiality with freedom of spirit, the sense of justice with respect for the rights of man, the sense of equity with global solidarity between the rich and the poor, mutual trust and fraternal love. In the first place individuals and nations must acquire a true "freedom of spirit" in order to become conscious of the sterile attitudes of the past, of the biased and partial character of philosophical and social systems which begin from debatable premises and which reduce man and history to a closed system of materialistic forces, which rely on nothing but the force of arms and the power of the economy, which shut human beings into categories in opposition to each other, which present onesided solutions, which ignore the complex reality of the life of nations and hinder their being treated as free. So a re-examination is needed of these systems that manifestly lead to deadlock, that freeze dialogue and understanding, develop mistrust, increase threats and dangers, without resolving the real problems, without offering true security, without making people truly happy, peaceful and free.

EPIPHANY MEANS MANIFESTATION

In the Church's liturgy the solemnity bears the name of the "Epiphany of the Lord". Epiphany means manifestation.

This expression invites us to think not only of the star that appeared before the eyes of the Magi, not only of the way these men of the East pursued, following the sign of the star. The Epiphany invites us "to think of the inner way", at whose beginning is found the mysterious encounter of the human intellect and will "with the light of God himself". « The real light which gives light to every man was coming into the world » (Jn 1:9).

The three personages from the East followed this light with certainty even before the appearance of the star.

God spoke to them "with the eloquence of all creation": he said that he is, he exists; that he is the Creator and Lord of the world.

At a certain moment, beyond the veil of created things, he drew them still closer to himself. And at the same time, he began to entrust them with "the truth of his coming" into the world. They, in some way, were made aware of the divine plan of salvation.

The Magi "responded with faith" to that inner Epiphany of God.

This faith enabled them to recognize the meaning of the star. This faith also compelled them to set out on their journey.

They went toward Jerusalem, the capital of Israel, where the truth of the coming of the Messiah was handed down from generation to generation. The prophets had preached it and the holy books had written about it.

THE INNER STRENGTH OF THE EPIPHANY

God, who hides himself from the eyes of men who live close to him, "reveals" himself to men who come from afar.

The Prophet says to Jerusalem: « Nations shall walk by your light, and kings by your shining radiance. Raise your eyes and look about; they all gather and come to you: Your sons "come from afar" » (Is 60:3-4).

"Faith" guides them. The "inner strength of the Epiphany" guides them.

Of this strength the Second Vatican Council says: « In his goodness and wisdom God chose to reveal himself and to make known to us the hidden purpose of his will (Eph 1:9) by which through Christ, the Word made flesh, man has access to the Father in the Holy Spirit and comes to share in the divine nature (Eph 2:18; 2 Pt 1:4). Through this revelation, therefore, the invisible God out of the abundance of his love speaks to men as friends (Ex 33:11; Jn 15:14-15) and lives among them (Bar 3:38), so that he may invite and take them into fellowship with himself » (DV, 2).

The Magi of the East bear in themselves that inner strength of the Epiphany. This "enables them to recognize the Messiah" in the Baby lying in the manger. This power disposes them to prostrate themselves before him and to offer gifts: gold, frankincense and myrrh (Mt 2:11).

At the same time, the Magi are a foreshadowing that the inner strength of the Epiphany will be widely spread among the peoples of the earth.

THE ATTITUDE
OF ST. JOHN THE BAPTIST

Since the image of the "Lamb of God" is closely connected with that of the suffering servant described by the Prophet Isaiah as the « lamb led to the slaughter » (Is 53:7) and as the paschal lamb (Ex 12), which is the symbol of Israel's redemption,

SEASON OF CHRISTMAS

with this image John points out Christ to us as the
"Redeemer". Jesus must pass through the passion,
death and resurrection in order to baptize « in the
Holy Spirit » and bring about salvation as the
« Son of God ». The attitude of the Baptist in this
passage is that of one who by stages progresses in
faith and in the knowledge of Christ: at first he says
that he does not know him (Jn 1:31), then he sees
in him the "suffering Messiah" (v. 29), and finally
the "Sanctifier" (v. 31) and the "Son of God" (v.
34). This attitude is an example for us, since it
teaches us to welcome Christ as the one who by
Baptism introduces into us a new reality, a « new
creation », a new reign: the one which is given life
by the Holy Spirit; but it also teaches us to begin a
journey of faith in which we feel ever more
committed to bear witness to Christ, not only as
"Son of man", but also as the "Son of God" who
came to remove from man's heart the root of every
evil, that is, sin. All of this evokes the delicate and
moving image of the Lamb, with which John the
Baptist « manifested » Christ to the world that day
long ago along the banks of the Jordan.
We must have our minds and hearts open to receive
this « manifestation », which is not meant to be so
much a knowledge of the mystery of Christ as our
"immersion" and our absorption into it.

SEASON OF LENT

YOU ARE DUST

Never, perhaps, is the Word of God spoken so directly to us. Never is it addressed so directly to each one of us without exception:
"Remember that you are dust, and unto dust you shall return".

And each one also accepts these words. They are so evident! Their truth is confirmed with such exactness by the history of humanity. And by the experience of every man.

These words speak of death, which brings to an end the life of every man on earth. At the same time they recall each one of us to our « beginning ». They were spoken to the first Adam as a fruit of sin: « Of the tree of knowledge of good and evil you must not eat, because the day you eat of it, you will certainly die » (Gn 2:17).

Death as the fruit of the tree of knowledge of good and evil. The fruit of sin. God-Jahweh spoke these words.

God the Creator. He who called – and constantly calls – the world and man from nothing to existence. And he created man « from the dust of the earth » (Gn 2:7): he formed him with the same material with which he made the whole visible world.

When God says (and the Liturgy of Ashes repeats) « You are dust and unto dust you shall return » (Gn 3:19), these words utter a severe sentence.

And God, who pronounces them, is revealed in them as the Creator and as the Judge.

Yet these words are at the same time full of suffering. There is expressed in them a forecast of Good Friday. There is expressed in them the suffering of the Son of God, who says, « Abba, Father!... let this cup pass from me! » (Mk 14:36).

« PUT TO DEATH
WHATEVER IN YOUR NATURE
IS ROOTED IN EARTH »

« Put to death whatever in your nature is rooted in earth » (Col 3:5-10).

The Church with her maternally wise norms establishes « days of penance on which the faithful are in a special manner to devote themselves to prayer, to engage in works of piety and charity and to deny themselves, by fulfilling their obligations more faithfully and especially by observing fast and abstinence » (CCL, c. 1294).

During Lent, then, besides the « abstinence from meat or some other food as determined by the Episcopal Conference » of the particular place (c. 1251) every Friday, the Church, for our spiritual benefit, imposes « fast and abstinence on Ash Wednesday and on the Friday of the Passion and Death of our Lord Jesus Christ » (c. 1251). And these precepts deal with what should be considered the indispensable minimum: a whole style of penance should accompany the living out of a life of faith and be made concrete in precise acts, the fruit of generosity.

Urged on by God's intervention, the sinner has approached the sacrament of mercy and has received forgiveness for his sins. Before the absolution, however, he has received the assignment of "practical penances" which, with the Lord's grace, he will have to perform in his life.

This is not a question of a kind of « price » with which he « could pay for » the inestimable gift that God gives us with liberation from sins.

The « satisfaction » is rather "the expression of a renewed life" which, with a renewed help from God, sets out to be put into practice. Therefore, in

« Let the little children come to me...
for it is to such as these that the Kingdom of God belongs » (Mk 10:14)

its determined expressions, it should not be limited to only the area of prayer, but it should concern the various areas in which sin has devasted man.

JEALOUS LOVE

We do not understand the words of the liturgy, if we do not sense in them a great pain of God, if we do not feel in them the pain of love!

« May the Lord become jealous for his land and be moved to compassion for his people », the prophet Joel prays (Jl 2:18).

« Jealous love ». Human love is jealous because of the narrowness of the human heart and because of the smallness of man. But love can be « jealous » also because of the greatness of the Creator and Father: jealous because he has so loved the world..., and in this world has so loved man as to make him in his own image and likeness. It is the jealous love for the image and likeness of God that has been lost and erased in man by sin.

Jealous love means in this case readiness for everything to reconquer and rebuild the ruined good, the obscured beauty of the image and likeness of God. God has loved so much!

Man called to respond to the love of God: the jealous love for the lost good, for the disfigured work of God.

Man called to reconciliation with God in the death of Christ. Man called to penance.

And so he comes, he bows his head, receives ashes on his forehead and hears the words in which are concealed God's pain and his « jealous love ». « Remember that you are dust, and unto dust you shall return », and at the same time he hears the words, « Repent! » Do penance and believe in the Gospel!

METANOEITE

This special time of the liturgical year is marked by the biblical message that can be summed up in just one word: "metanoeite", that is, « repent ». This command is recalled to the mind of the faithful by the austere rite of the "imposition of blessed ashes". This rite, with the words « Turn away from sin and believe in the Good News » and the expression « Remember that you are dust, and unto dust you shall return », invites everyone to reflect on the obligation of conversion, recalling the inexorable transience and the ephemeral frailty of human life, subject to death.

The impressive ceremony of the ashes raises our mind to the eternal reality that never passes away, to God who is the beginning and the end, the Alpha and the Omega of our existence. Conversion, in fact, is nothing other than a turning to God, giving value to earthly realities in the unfailing light of his truth. It is an evaluation that brings us to an ever clearer awareness of the fact that we are in transit in the laborious vicissitudes of this life, and it urges and stimulates us to put forth every effort that the Kingdom of God be established within us and his justice triumph.

Synonymous with conversion is the word "penance". Lent calls us to exercise the spirit of penance, not in its negative meaning of sadness and frustration, but in its meaning of elevation of the spirit, liberation from evil, detachment from sin and from all the conditions that can obstruct our way toward the fulness of life. Penance as an expression of free and joyful commitment in the following of Christ, which implies accepting the demanding but fruitful words of the Master: « If anyone wishes to come after me, he must deny his very self, take up his cross, and begin to follow in my footsteps » (Mt 16:24).

THE WORK OF CONVERSION

Lent is the time for "entering" into oneself. It is the period of a particular intimacy with God in the secrecy of one's heart and conscience.

In such an "interior intimacy with God" the essential work of Lent takes place: the "work of conversion".

In such a secret interior and in the intimacy with God himself in all the truth of one's heart and conscience, there resound words like those of the psalm of today's liturgy: one of the most profound confessions that man has ever made to his God:

« Have mercy on me, o God, in your goodness; in the greatness of your compassion wipe out my offense.

Thoroughly wash me from my guilt and "of my sin cleanse me".

For I acknowledge my offense, and my sin is before me always: Against you only have I sinned, and done what is evil in your sight » (Ps 50 [51]:1-6).

These are purifying words, transforming words. They transform man interiorly, "and they are a proof of transformation".

Let us recite them often during Lent. And above all, let us try to renew "this spirit that makes them live"; that interior breath that has linked the power of conversion to these very words.

Lent, in fact, is essentially a call to conversion. The « works of piety » of which the Gospel speaks open the way to this. Let us perform them as much as possible.

But first of all, let us strive for an "interior encounter with God" in our whole life, in everything that makes up our life — and in view of this depth of conversion to him who shines forth from the penitential psalm of today's liturgy.

THE KINGDOM OF GOD IS AT HAND

With very concise words, Mark the evangelist alludes to that fast of Jesus of Nazareth, lasting forty days, which each year finds its reflection in the Lenten liturgy: « The Spirit drove him into the desert and he remained there forty days, tempted by Satan; he was with the wild beasts and the angels ministered to him » (Mk 1:12).

Then, after the arrest of John the Baptist, Jesus went into Galilee and began to teach. He said, « The time is fulfilled and the kingdom of God is at hand: repent and believe in the Gospel » (Mk 1:15). The forty-days fast of Jesus of Nazareth was an introduction to the announcement of the Kingdom of God. He mapped out in men's minds the route of faith, without which the Gospel of the Kingdom is like a seed thrown onto barren soil.

This beginning of the Gospel of the Kingdom, which comes to the Church through the forty days fast, is compared by the liturgy to the rainbow that was a sign of God's covenant with the descendents of Noah after the flood.

In the First Letter of St Peter the Apostle, the Church, in which Christ — after having accomplished the victory over death and sin — continually carries out the work of redemption, is compared to Noah's ark. However, Noah's ark was a closed space. The work of Christ is not limited in space and time. The Church serves this work as a sign and instrument.

« AWAY WITH YOU, SATAN! »

« ...Jesus was led into the desert by the Spirit "to be tempted..." » (Mt 4:1).

Every year at the beginning of Lent the Church recalls Christ's forty-days fast. At the end of this fast, which precedes the messianic activity of Jesus of Nazareth, the triple temptation by Satan takes place, whose description, according to the Gospel of Matthew, is read in the liturgy of today's Mass. The temptation ends with the defeat of the tempter: « Away with you, Satan! Scripture has it: "You shall do homage to the Lord your God; him alone shall you adore" » (Mt 4:10).

Through this revelation of his messianic power, Christ has touched the very beginning of man's sin. "The sin of man" in fact had its "beginning in the temptation of the first parents". "The temptation" takes place with regard to the tree, which the biblical text calls the tree of the knowledge of good and evil. The words which the tempter uses clearly indicate the reason for the act to which he leads the first parents: « God knows well that the moment you eat of it your eyes will be opened "and you will be like gods who know what is good and what is bad" » (Gn 3:5).

Temptation, which is at the beginning of the first sin of man, thus has to do with the very foundations of man's relationship with God, the creature with the Creator, the child with the Father. "Therefore, sin", which follows this temptation, "destroys this relationship at its very foundations". The grace of man's original innocence and justice is also destroyed along with it. The domination of sin begins in human history.

« I AM THE LIGHT OF THE WORLD »

« While I am in the world, I am the light of the world » (Jn 9:5).
Jesus Christ is in the world. He is in the midst of men, above all among the unfortunate. The entire Gospel confirms this.

At the centre of the Gospel and at the centre of the Liturgy we find "Jesus and a man blind from birth". Jesus restores his sight and he does it on the Sabbath.

In certain aspects, he performs this miracle in a « ritual » way. He first mixes the dirt of the ground with his saliva and smears it on the blind man's eyes.

Then he tells him to wash in the pool of Siloam. "After washing", the man born blind has his sight restored.

With this sign Jesus of Nazareth reveals himself as the light of the world, above all because "he makes sight possible" for the blind man: sight is the capacity of contact with the light of the outside world.

Then because he liberates this man from the blindness of the spirit. "He opens his soul's vision to God and to his mysteries". This opening of the soul is called faith, which means being in contact with the light of the inner world. The man blind from birth, after acquiring the ability to see, at the same time opens himself to the mystery of God in Christ. He confesses "faith in the Son of Man".

« Do you believe in the Son of Man? » Jesus asked (Jn 9:35).

« Who is he, sir, that I may believe in him? » answered the man who was cured (Jn 9:36).

« You have seen him: he is speaking to you now » (Jn 9:37).

« I do believe, Lord! », he said, and bowed down to worship him (Jn 9:38).

Indirectly this event also refers to Baptism, which is the first sacrament of faith: the sacrament which "opens eyes" through "rebirth" by water and the Holy Spirit, just as happened to the man born blind after he washed in the water of the pool of Siloam.

« LORD, IF YOU HAD BEEN HERE, MY BROTHER WOULD NEVER HAVE DIED »

« Lord, if you had been here, my brother would never have died » (Jn 11:21).
These words were said first by Martha and then by Mary, Lazarus' two sisters, and they were addressed to Jesus of Nazareth, who was a friend of theirs and their brother's.
« ...My brother would never have died ».
There resounds in these words "the voice of the human heart", the voice of a heart that loves and gives "witness to what death is". We continually hear death spoken of, and we read notices of the death of various people. There is systematic information on this subject. There are also statistics on death. We know that death is a common and unceasing phenomenon. If every day about 1,450,000 die on the face of the earth, we can say that people are dying at every moment. Death is a universal phenomenon and an ordinary fact. The universality and normality of the fact "confirm" the reality of death, but at the same time "obliterate", in a certain sense, the truth about death, its penetrating eloquence.
The language of statistic is not enough here. The voice of the human heart is necessary: the voice of a person who loves. "The reality of death can be expressed" in all its truth "with the language of love".
In fact, "love resists death and desires life..." Neither Lazarus' two sisters say « my brother is dead », but they both say, « Lord, if you had been here, my brother would never have died ».
The truth about death can be expressed only beginning "from a perspective of life", from a desire for life: that is, from the permanence of a person's loving communion.

THE ROOT OF DEATH

"The death of man", right from Adam, objects to love: it is set against the love of the Father, the God of life.

The root of death is sin, which also opposes the Father's love. In man's history, "death" is "joined" to "sin" and, like sin, it is opposed to love. Jesus Christ came into the world "in order to redeem man's sin", every sin that is rooted in man. For this reason "he placed himself in the face of the reality of death". Death, in fact, is joined to sin in man's history: it is the fruit of sin. Jesus Christ became man's "Redeemer through his death" on the cross, which was the sacrifice that has made reparation for every sin.

In his death, Jesus confirmed the witness of the Father's love. Love that resists death and desires life is expressed in the resurrection of Christ, who, in order to redeem the sins of the world, freely accepted death on the cross.

This event is called Easter: the Paschal Mystery. What happened in Bethany at the tomb of Lazarus was like the last "announcement of the Paschal Mystery".

Jesus of Nazareth stopped before the tomb of his friend Lazarus and said, « Lazarus, come out! » (Jn 11:43). With these words, full of power, Jesus raised him to life and had him come out of the tomb.

Before performing this miracle, Christ « looked upward and said, "Father, I thank you for having heard me.

I know that you always hear me but I have said this for the sake of the crowd, that they may believe that you sent me" » (Jn 11:41-42).

At the tomb of Lazarus there was a special "confrontation between death and Christ's redemptive mission". Christ was the witness of the Father's eternal love – that love which resists death and desires life.

THE SACRIFICE
AS THE MEANS OF THE LIBERATION

Jesus recognizes in the Father the one who has traced out the way of sacrifice as the way of salvation.

He does not wish to deny the responsibility of man in his condemnation to death. But in the drama which is being prepared he discerns the sovereign action of the Father who, while respecting human liberty, guides the events according to a higher design. At Gethsemane it is the will of the Father that he accepts, and at the moment of his arrest, by ordering Peter to put the sword back into its scabbard, he indicates the reason for his docility. Every explanation of the event of Calvary through merely historical causes would be insufficient. The redemptive sacrifice is not due to those who condemned Jesus but to the Father, who had taken the decision to procure the salvation of mankind in this way.

This mystery always surprises us, because those who hear the Good News cannot refrain from asking: why "did the Father choose the sacrifice as the means of the liberation of mankind?"

The reply of revelation is precise: far from being an act of cruelty or of rigorous severity, the Father's gesture in offering his Son in sacrifice "is the apex of love": « God so loved the world that he gave his only Son, that whoever believes in him should not perish but have eternal life ». St John who quotes these words in the Gospel (3:16) makes a comment on them in his first Letter: « In this is love, not that we love God but that he loved us and sent his Son to be the expiation for our sins » (4:10). The Father had willed a sacrifice of reparation for the sins of mankind, but he himself paid the price of this sacrifice by giving his Son. With this gift he showed in what measure he was the Saviour and to what extent he loved man. "His gesture is the definitive gesture of love".

THE SOLIDARITY OF SUFFERING

In itself human suffering constitutes as it were a specific « world » which exists together with man, which appears in him and passes, and sometimes does not pass, but which consolidates itself and becomes deeply rooted in him. This world of suffering, divided into many, very many subjects, exists "as it were « in dispersion »". Every individual, through personal suffering, constitutes not only a small part of that « world », but at the same time that « world » is present in him as a finite and unrepeatable entity. Parallel with this, however, is the interhuman and social dimension. The world of suffering possesses as it were its "own solidarity".

People who suffer become similar to one another through the analogy of their situation, the trial of their destiny, or through their need for understanding and care, and perhaps above all through the persistent question of the meaning of suffering. Thus, although the world of suffering exists « in dispersion », at the same time it contains within itself a singular challenge "to communion and solidarity".

We shall also try to follow this appeal in the present reflection.

THE WORLD OF SUFFERING

Considering the world of suffering in its personal and at the same time collective meaning, one cannot fail to notice the fact that this world, at some periods of time and in some eras of human existence, "as it were becomes particularly concentrated". This happens, for example, in cases of natural disasters, epidemics, catastrophes, upheavals and various social scourges: one thinks, for example, of a bad harvest and connected with it — or with various other causes — the scourge of famine.

One thinks, finally, of war. I speak of this in a particular way. I speak of the last two World Wars, the second of which brought with it a much greater harvest of death and a much heavier burden of human sufferings. The second half of our century, in its turn, brings with it — "as though in proportion to the mistakes and transgressions" of our contemporary civilization — such a horrible threat of nuclear war that we cannot think of this period except in terms of "an incomparable accumulation of sufferings", even to the possible self-destruction of humanity. In this way, that world of suffering which in brief has its subject in each human being, seems in our age to be transformed — perhaps more than at any other moment — into a special « world », the world which as never before has been transformed by progress through man's work and, at the same time, is as never before in danger because of man's mistakes and offences.

WHY DOES EVIL EXIST?

Within each form of suffering endured by man, and at the same time at the basis of the whole world of suffering, there inevitably arises the question:

"why?" It is a question about the cause, the reason, and equally about the purpose of suffering, and, in brief, a question about its meaning. Not only does it accompany human suffering, but it seems even to determine its human content, what makes suffering precisely human suffering.

It is obvious that pain, especially physical pain, is widespread in the animal world. But only the human being knows that he is suffering and wonders why; and he suffers in a humanly speaking still deeper way if he does not find a satisfactory answer.

This is "a difficult question", just as is a question closely akin to it, the question of evil. Why does evil exist? Why is there evil in the world? When we put the question in this way, we are always, at least to a certain extent, asking a question about suffering too.

Both questions are difficult, when an individual puts them to another individual, when people put them to other people, as also when man "puts them to God".

For man does not put this question to the world, even though it is from the world that suffering often comes to him, but he puts it to God as the Creator and Lord of the world.

And it is well known that concerning this question there not only arise many frustrations and conflicts in the relations of man with God, but it also happens that people reach the point of actually "denying God".

For, whereas the existence of the world opens as it were the eyes of the human soul to the existence of God, to his wisdom, power and greatness, evil and suffering seem to obscure this image, sometimes in a radical way, especially in the daily drama of so many faults without proper punishment.

THE MORAL JUSTICE OF THE EVIL

Man can put this question to God with all the emotion of his heart and with his mind full of dismay and anxiety; and God expects the question and listens to it, as we see in the Revelation of the Old Testament. In the Book of Job the question has found its most vivid expression.

The story of this just man, who without any fault of his own is tried by innumerable sufferings, is well known. He loses his possessions, his sons and daughters, and finally he himself is afflicted by a grave sickness. In this horrible situation three old acquaintances come to his house, and each one in his own way tries to convince him that since he has been struck down by such varied and terrible sufferings, "he must have done something seriously wrong". For suffering – they say – always strikes a man as punishment for a crime; it is sent by the absolutely just God and finds its reason in the order of justice. It can be said that Job's old friends wish not only to "convince him" of the moral justice of the evil, but in a certain sense they attempt to "justify" to themselves the moral meaning of suffering. In their eyes suffering can have a meaning only as a punishment for sin, therefore only on the level of God's justice, who repays good with good and evil with evil.

The point of reference in this case is the doctrine expressed in other Old Testament writings which show us suffering as punishment inflicted by God for human sins. The God of Revelation is the "Lawgiver and Judge" to a degree that no temporal authority can be. For the God of Revelation is first of all the Creator, from whom comes, together with existence, the essential good of creation. Therefore, the conscious and free violation of this good by man is not only a transgression of the law but at the same time an offence against the Creator, who is the first Lawgiver. Such a trangression has the character of sin, according to the exact meaning of this word, namely the biblical and theological one. "Corresponding to the moral evil of sin is punishment", which guarantees the moral order in the same transcendent sense in which this order is laid down by the will of the Creator and Supreme Lawgiver. From this there also derives one of the fundamental truths of religious faith, equally based upon Revelation, namely that God is a just judge, who rewards good and punishes evil: « For you are just in all you have done; all your deeds are faultless, all your ways right, and all your judgments proper » (Dn 3:27).

The opinion expressed by Job's friends manifests a conviction also found in the moral conscience of humanity: the objective moral order demands punishment for transgression, sin and crime. From this point of view, suffering appears as a « justified evil » (Jb 4:8).

THE SIN OF THE WORLD

When one says that Christ by his mission strikes at evil at its very roots, we have in mind not only evil and definitive, eschatological suffering (so that man « should not perish, but have eternal life »), but also — at least indirectly — "evil and suffering" in their "temporal and historical dimension". For evil remains bound to sin and death. And even if we must use great caution in judging man's suffering as a consequence of concrete sins (this is shown precisely by the example of the just man Job), nevertheless suffering cannot be divorced from the sin of the beginnings, from what Saint John calls « the sin of the world » (Jn 1:29), "from the sinful background" of the personal actions and social processes in human history. Though it is not licit to apply here the narrow criterion of direct dependence (as Job's three friends did), it is equally true that one cannot reject the criterion that, in the basis of human suffering, there is a complex involvement with sing.

It is the same when we deal with "death". It is often awaited even as a liberation from the suffering of this life. At the same time, it is not possible to ignore the fact that it constitutes as it were a definitive summing-up of the destructive work both in the bodily organism and in the psyche.

THE DOMINION OF SIN

Death primarily involves "the dissolution" of the entire psychophysical personality of man. The soul survives and subsists separated from the body, while the body is subjected to gradual decomposition according to the words of the Lord God, pronounced after the sin committed by man at the beginning of his earthly history: « You are dust and to dust you shall return » (Gn 3:19). Therefore, even if death is not a form of suffering in the temporal sense of the word, even if "in a certain way" it is "beyond all forms of suffering", at the same time the evil which the human being experiences in death has a definitive and total character. By his salvific work, the only-begotten Son liberates man from sin and death. First of all he "blots out" from human history "the dominion of sin", which took root under the influence of the evil Spirit, beginning with Original Sin, and then he gives man the possibility of living in Sanctifying Grace. In the wake of his victory over sin, he also takes away the dominion "of death", by his Resurrection beginning the process of the future resurrection of the body. Both are essential conditions of « eternal life », that is of man's definitive happiness in union with God; this means, for the saved, that in the eschatological perspective suffering is totally blotted out.

As a result of Christ's salvific work, man exists on earth "with the hope" of eternal life and holiness.

HE GAVE HIMSELF FOR ME

In his messianic activity in the midst of Israel, Christ drew increasingly closer "to the world of human suffering". « He went about doing good » (Acts, 10:38) and his actions concerned primarily those who were suffering and seeking help. He healed the sick, consoled the afflicted, fed the hungry, freed people from deafness, from blindness, from leprosy, from the devil and from various physical disabilities, three times he restored the dead to life. He was sensitive to every human suffering, whether of the body or of the soul. And at the same time he taught, and at the heart of his teaching there are "the eight beatitudes", which are addressed to people tried by various sufferings in their temporal life. These are « the poor in spirit » and « the afflicted » and « those who hunger and thirst for justice » and those who are « persecuted for justice sake », when they insult them, persecute them and speak falsely every kind of evil against them for the sake of Christ... (Mt 5:3-11).

At any rate, Christ drew close above all to the world of human suffering through the fact of having taken "this suffering upon his very self". During his public activity, he experienced not only fatigue, homelessness, misunderstanding even on

SEASON OF LENT

the part of those closest to him, but, more than anything, he became progressively more and more isolated and encircled by hostility and the preparations for putting him to death. Christ is aware of this, and often speaks to his disciples of the sufferings and death that await him: « Behold, we are going up to Jerusalem; and the Son of man "will be delivered" to the chief priests and the scribes, and they will condemn him to death and deliver him to the Gentiles; and they will mock him, and spit upon him, and scourge him, and kill him; and after three days he will rise » (Mk 10:33-34).

Christ goes toward his own suffering, aware of its saving power; he goes forward in obedience to the Father, but primarily he is "united to the Father in this love" with which he has loved the world and man in the world. And for this reason Saint Paul will write of Christ: « He loved me and gave himself for me » (Gal 2:20).

« LET THIS CUP PASS FROM ME »

Christ gives the answer to the question about suffering and the meaning of suffering not only by his teaching, that is by the Good News, but most of all by his own suffering, which is integrated with this teaching of the Good News in an organic and indissoluble way. And this is "the final", definitive word of this "teaching": « the word of the Cross », as Saint Paul one day will say (1 Cor 1:18). This « word of the Cross » completes with a definitive reality the image of the ancient prophecy. Many episodes, many discourses during Christ's public teaching bear witness to the way in which from the beginning he accepts this suffering which is the will of the Father for the salvation of the world. However, "the prayer in Gethsemane" becomes a definitive point here. The words: « My Father, if it be possible, let this cup pass from me; nevertheless, not as I will, but as you will », (Mt 26:39) and later: « My Father, if this cannot pass unless I drink it, your will be done », (Mt 26:42), have a manifold eloquence. They prove the truth of that love which the only-begotten Son gives to the Father in his obedience. At the same time, they attest to the truth of his suffering. The words of that prayer of Christ in Gethsemane prove "the truth of love through the truth of suffering". Christ's words confirm with all simplicity this human truth of suffering, to its very depths: suffering is the undergoing of evil before which man shudders. He says: « Let it pass from me », just as Christ says in Gethsemane.

His words also attest to this unique and incomparable depth and intensity of suffering which only the man who is the only-begotten Son could experience; they attest to "that depth and intensity" which the prophetic words quoted above in their own way help us to understand.

Gethsemane is the place where precisely this suffering, in all the truth expressed by the Prophet concerning the evil experienced in it, "is revealed as it were definitively before the eyes of Christ's soul".

« IT IS FINISHED »

After the words in Gethsemane come the words uttered on Golgotha, words which bear witness to this depth — unique in the history of the world — of the evil of the suffering experienced. When Christ says: « My God, My God, why have you abandoned me? », his words are not only an expression of that abandonment which many times found expression in the Old Testament, especially in the Psalms and in particular in that Psalm 22 from which come the words quoted (Ps 22 [21]:2). One can say that these words on abandonment are born at the level of that inseparable union of the Son with the Father, and are born because the Father « laid on him the iniquity of us all » (Is 53:6). They also foreshadow the words of Saint Paul: « For our sake he made him to be sin who knew no sin » (2 Cor 5:21). With this orrible weight, "encompassing the 'entire' evil of the turning away from God" which is contained in sin, Christ, through the divine depth of his filial union with the Father, perceives in a humanly inexpressible way "this suffering which is the separation", the rejection "by the Father", the estrangement from God. But precisely through this suffering he accomplished the Redemption, and can say as he breathes his last: « It is finished » (Jn 19:30).

One can also say that the Scripture has been fulfilled, that these words of the Song of the Suffering Servant have been definitively accomplished: « it was the will of the Lord to bruise him » (Is 53:10). Human suffering has reached its culmination in the Passion of Christ. And at the same time it has entered into a completely new dimension and a new order: "it has been linked to love", to that love which creates good, drawing it out by means of suffering, just as the supreme good of the Redemption of the world was drawn from the Cross of Christ, and from that Cross constantly takes its beginning. The Cross of Christ has become a source from which flow rivers of living water (Jn 7:37-38). In it we must also pose anew the question about the meaning of suffering, and read in it, to its very depths, the answer to this question.

SHARING IN THE CROSS

The Cross of Christ throws salvific light, in a most penetrating way, on man's life and in particular on his suffering. For through faith the Cross reaches man "together with the Resurrection": the mystery of the Passion is contained in the Paschal Mystery. The witnesses of Christ's Passion are at the same time witnesses of his Resurrection. Paul writes: « That I may know him (Christ) and the power of his Resurrection, and may share his sufferings, becoming like him in his death, that if possible I may attain the resurrection from the dead » (Phil 3:10-11). Truly, the Apostle first experienced the « power of the Resurrection » of Christ, on the road to Damascus, and only later, in this paschal light, reached that « sharing in his sufferings » of which he speaks, for example, in the Letter to the Galatians. The path of Paul is clearly paschal: "sharing in the Cross" of Christ comes about "through the experience of the Risen One", therefore through a special sharing in the Resurrection. Thus, even in the Apostle's expression on the subject of suffering there so often appears the motif of glory, which finds its beginning in Christ's Cross.

WORTHY OF THE KINGDOM OF GOD

The witnesses of the Cross and Resurrection were convinced that « through many tribulations we must enter the Kingdom of God » (Acts 14:22). And Paul, writing to the Thessalonians, says this: « We ourselves boast of you... for your steadfastness and faith in all your persecutions and in the afflictions which you are enduring. This is evidence of the righteous judgment of God, that you may be

SEASON OF LENT

made "worthy of the Kingdom of God", for which you are suffering » (2 Thes 1:4-5). Thus to share in the sufferings of Christ is, at the same time, to suffer for the Kingdom of God. In the eyes of the just God, before his judgment, those who share in the suffering of Christ become worthy of this Kingdom. Through their sufferings, in a certain sense they repay the infinite price of the Passion and death of Christ, which became the price of our Redemption: at this price the Kingdom of God has been consolidated anew in human history, becoming the definitive prospect of man's earthly existence. Christ has led us into this Kingdom through his suffering. And also through suffering those surrounded by the mystery of Christ's Redemption "become mature" enough to enter this Kingdom.

« FELLOW HEIRS WITH CHRIST »

To the prospect of the Kingdom of God is linked hope in that glory which has its beginning in the Cross of Christ. The Resurrection revealed this glory – eschatological glory – which in the Cross of Christ was completeley obscured by the immensity of suffering. Those who share in the sufferings of Christ are also called, through their own sufferings, to share "in glory". Paul expresses this in various places. To the Romans he writes: « We are... fellow heirs with Christ, provided we suffer with him in order that we may also be glorified with him. I consider that the sufferings of this present time are not worth comparing with the glory that is to be revealed in us » (Rom 8:17-18). In the Second Letter to the Corinthians we read: « For this slight momentary affliction is preparing for us an eternal weight of glory beyond all comparison, because we look not to the things that are seen but to things that are unseen » (2 Cor 4:17-18). The Apostle Peter will express this truth in the following words of his First Letter: « But rejoice in so far as you share Christ's sufferings, that you may also rejoice and be glad when his glory is revealed » (1 Pt 4:13).

The motif of "suffering and glory" has a strictly evangelical characteristic, which becomes clear by reference to the Cross and the Resurrection. The Resurrection became, first of all, the manifestation of glory, which corresponds to Christ's being lifted up through the Cross.

« FATHER, FORGIVE THEM... »

If, in fact, the Cross was to human eyes Christ's "emptying of himself", at the same time it was in the eyes of God "his being lifted up". On the Cross, Christ attained and fully accomplished his mission: by fulfilling the will of the Father, he at the same time fully realized himself. In weakness he manifested his "power", and in humiliation he manifested all "his messianic greatness". Are not all the words he uttered during his agony on Golgotha a proof of this greatness and especially his words concerning the perpetrators of his crucifixion: « Father, forgive them for they know not what they do »? (Lk 23:34). To those in Christ's sufferings these words present themselves with the power of a supreme example. Suffering is also an invitation to manifest the moral greatness of man, his "spiritual maturity". Proof of this has been given, down through the generations, by the martyrs and confessors of Christ, faithful to the words: « And do not fear those who kill the body, but cannot kill the soul » (Mt 10:28).

Christ's Resurrection has revealed « the glory of the future age » and, at the same time, has confirmed « the boast of the Cross »: the "glory that is hidden in the very suffering of Christ" and which has been and is often mirrored in human suffering, as an expression of man's spiritual greatness. This glory must be acknowledged not only in the martyrs for the faith but in many others also who, at times, even without belief in Christ, suffer and give their lives for the truth and for a just cause. In the sufferings of all of these people the great dignity of man is strikingly confirmed.

THE SALVIFIC POWER OF GOD

In the Second Letter to Timothy we read: « And therefore I suffer as I do. But I am not ashamed, for I know whom I have believed » (2 Tim 1:12). And in the Letter to the Philippians he will even say: « I can do all things in him who strengthens me » (Phil 4:13).

Those who share in Christ's sufferings have before their eyes the Paschal Mystery of the Cross and Resurrection, in which Christ descends, in a first phase, to the ultimate limits of human weakness and impotence: indeed, he dies nailed to the Cross. But if at the same time in this "weakness" there is accomplished his "lifting up", confirmed by the power of the Resurrection, then this means that the weaknesses of all human sufferings are capable of being infused with the same power of God manifested in Christ's Cross. In such a concept, to "suffer" means to become particularly "susceptible", particularly "open to the working of the salvific power of God", offered to humanity in Christ. In him God has confirmed his desire to act especially through suffering, which is man's weakness and emptying of self, and he wishes to make his power known precisely in this weakness and emptying of self. This also explains the exhortation in the First Letter of Peter: « Yet if one suffers as a Christian, let him not be ashamed, but under that name let him glorify God » (1 Pt 4:16).

CALL TO THE VIRTUE

In the Letter to the Romans, the Apostle Paul deals fully with the theme of this « birth of power in weakness », this "spiritual tempering" of man in the midst of trials and tribulations, which is the particular vocation of those who share in Christ's sufferings. « More than that, we rejoice in our sufferings, knowing that suffering produces endurance, and endurance produces character, and character produces hope, and hope does not disappoint us, because God's love has been poured into our hearts through the Holy Spirit which has been given to us » (Rom 5:3-5). Suffering as it were contains a special "call to the virtue" which man must exercise on his own part. And this is the virtue of perseverance in bearing whatever disturbs and causes harm. In doing this, the individual unleashes hope, which maintains in him the conviction that suffering will not get the better of him, that it will not deprive him of his dignity as a human being, a dignity linked to awareness of the meaning of life. And indeed this meaning makes itself known together with "the working of God's love", which is the supreme gift of the Holy Spirit. The more he shares in this love, man rediscovers himself more and more fully in suffering: he rediscovers the « soul » which he thought he had « lost » (Mk 8:35) because of suffering.

SEASON OF LENT

THE CREATIVE CHARACTER
OF SUFFERING

In the Paschal Mystery Christ began "the union with man in the community of the Church". The mystery of the Church is expressed in this: that already in the act of Baptism, which brings about a configuration with Christ, and then through his Sacrifice — sacramentally through the Eucharist — the Church is continually being built up spiritually as the Body of Christ. In this Body, Christ wishes to be united with every individual, and in a special way he is united with those who suffer.

The words quoted above from the Letter to the Colossians bear witness to the exceptional nature of this union. For, "whoever suffers in union with Christ" — just as the Apostle Paul bears his « tribulations » in union with Christ — not only receives from Christ that strength already referred to but also « completes » by his suffering « what is lacking in Christ's afflictions ». This evangelical outlook especially highlights the truth "concerning the creative character of suffering". The sufferings of Christ created the good of the world's redemption. This good in itself is inexhaustible and infinite. No man can add anything to it. But at the same time, in the mystery of the Church as his Body, Christ has in a sense opened his own redemptive suffering to all human suffering. In so far as man becomes a sharer in Christ's sufferings — in any part of the world and at any time in history — to that extent "he in his own way completes" the suffering through which Christ accomplished the Redemption of the world.

Does this mean that the Redemption achieved by Christ is not complete? No. It only means that the Redemption, accomplished through satisfactory love, "remains always open to all love" expressed "in human suffering". In this dimension – the dimension of love – the Redemption which has already been completely accomplished is, in a certain sense, constantly being accomplished.

CHRIST'S REDEMPTIVE SUFFERING

Christ achieved the Redemption completely and to the very limit; but at the same time he did not bring it to a close. In this redemptive suffering, through which the Redemption of the world was accomplished, Christ opened himself from the beginning to every human suffering and constantly does so. Yes, it seems to be part "of the very essence of Christ's redemptive suffering" that this suffering requires to be unceasingly completed.

Thus, with this openness to every human suffering, Christ has accomplished the world's Redemption through his own suffering. For, at the same time, this Redemption, even though it was completely achieved by Christ's suffering, lives on and in its own special way develops in the history of man. It lives and develops as the body of Christ, the Church, and in this dimension every human suffering, by reason of the loving union with Christ, completes the suffering of Christ. It completes that suffering "just as the Church completes the redemptive work of Christ". The mystery of the Church – that body which completes in itself also Christ's crucified and risen body – indicates at the same time the space or context in which human sufferings complete the sufferings of Christ. Only within this radius and dimension of the Church as the Body of Christ, which continually develops in space and time, can one think and speak of « what is lacking » in the sufferings of Christ.

MARY'S SUFFERING

It is especially consoling to note — and also accurate in accordance with the Gospel and history — that at the side of Christ, in the first and most exalted place, there is always his Mother through the exemplary testimony that she bears "by her whole life" to this particular Gospel of suffering. In her, the many and intense sufferings were amassed in such an interconnected way that they were not only a proof of her unshakeable faith but also a contribution to the redemption of all. In reality, from the time of her secret conversation with the angel, she began to see in her mission as a mother her « destiny » to share, in a singular and unrepeatable way, in the very mission of her Son. And she very soon received a confirmation of this in the events that accompanied the birth of Jesus in Bethlehem, and in the solemn words of the aged Simeon, when he spoke of a sharp sword that would pierce her heart. Yet a further confirmation was in the anxieties and privations of the hurried flight into Egypt, caused by the cruel decision of Herod.

And again, after the events of her Son's hidden and public life, events which she must have shared with acute sensitivity, it was on Calvary that Mary's suffering, beside the suffering of Jesus, reached an intensity which can hardly be imagined from a human point of view but which was mysterious and supernaturally fruitful for the redemption of the world. Her ascent of Calvary and her standing at the foot of the Cross together with the Beloved Disciple were a special sort of sharing in the redeeming death of her Son. And the words she heard from his lips were a kind of solemn handing-over of this Gospel of suffering so that it could be proclaimed to the whole community of believers.

As a witness to her Son's Passion by her "presence", and as a sharer in it by her "compassion", Mary offered a unique contribution to the Gospel of suffering, by embodying in anticipation the expression of Saint Paul. She truly has a special title to be able to claim that she « completes in her flesh » — as already in her heart — « what is lacking in Christ's afflictions ».

« LET HIM TAKE UP HIS CROSS »

In the light of the unmatchable example of Christ, reflected with singular clarity in the life of his Mother, the Gospel of suffering, through the experience and words of the Apostles, becomes "an inexhaustible source for the ever new generations" that succeed one another in the history of the Church. The Gospel of suffering signifies not only the presence of suffering in the Gospel, as one of the themes of the Good News, but also the revelation "of the salvific power and salvific significance" of suffering in Christ's messianic mission and, subsequently, in the mission and vocation of the Church.

Christ "did not conceal" from his listeners "the need for suffering". He said very clearly: « Whoever wishes to be my follower... must take up his cross daily » (Lk 9:23), and before his disciples he placed demands of a moral nature that can only be fulfilled on condition that they should « deny themselves » (Lk 9:23). The way that leads to the Kingdom of heaven is « hard and narrow », and Christ contrasts it to the « wide and easy » way that « leads to destruction » (Mt 7:13-14). On various occasions Christ also said that his disciples and confessors would "meet with much persecution", something which — as we know — happened not only in the first centuries of the Church's life under the Roman Empire, but also came true in various historical periods and in other parts of the world, and still does even in our own time.

Here are some of Christ's statements on this subject: « They will lay their hands on you and persecute you, delivering you up to the synagogues and prisons, and you will be brought before kings and governors for my name's sake. This will be a time for you "to bear testimony". Settle it therefore in your minds, not to meditate beforehand how to answer; for I will give you a mouth and wisdom, which none of your adversaries will be able to withstand or contradict. You will be delivered up even by parents, brothers, kinsmen and friends, and some of you they will put to death; you will be hated by all "for my name's sake". But not a hair of your head will perish. By your endurance you will gain your lives » (Lk 21:12-19).

« FOR CHRIST » AND « FOR THE SAKE OF CHRIST »

The Gospel of suffering speaks first in various places of suffering « for Christ », « for the sake of Christ », and it does so with the words of Jesus himself or the words of his Apostles. The Master does not conceal the prospect of suffering from his disciples and followers. On the contrary, he reveals it with all frankness, indicating at the same time the supernatural assistance that will accompany them in the midst of persecutions and tribulations « for his name's sake ». These persecutions and tribulations will also be, as it were, "a particular proof" of likeness to Christ and union with him. « If the world hates you, know that it has hated me before it hated you...; but because you are not of the world, but I chose you out of the world, therefore the world hates you... A servant is not greater than his master. If they persecuted me they will persecute you... But all this they will do to you on my account, because they do not know him who sent me » (Jn 15: 18-21) « I have said this to you, that in me you may have peace. In the world you have tribulation; but take courage! I have overcome the world » (Jn 16:33).

This first chapter of the Gospel of suffering, which speaks of persecutions, namely of tribulations experienced because of Christ, contains in itself "a special call to courage and fortitude", sustained by the eloquence of the Resurrection. Christ has overcome the world definitively by his Resurrection. Yet, because of the relationship between the Resurrection and his Passion and death, he has at the same time overcome the world by his suffering. Yes, suffering has been singularly present in that victory over the world which was manifested in the Resurrection.

THE GOSPEL OF SUFFERING

Christ retains in his risen body the marks of the wounds of the Cross in his hands, feet and side. Through the Resurrection, he manifests "the victorious power of suffering", and he wishes to imbue with the conviction of this power the hearts of those whom he chose as Apostles and those whom he continually chooses and sends forth. The Apostle Paul will say: « All who desire to live a godly life in Christ Jesus will be persecuted » (2 Tim 3:12).

While the first great chapter of the Gospel of suffering is written down, as the generations pass, by those who suffer persecutions for Christ's sake, simultaneously another great chapter of this Gospel unfolds through the course of history. This chapter is written by all those "who suffer together with Christ", uniting their human sufferings to his salvific suffering. In these people there is fulfilled what the first witnesses of the Passion and Resurrection said and wrote about sharing in the sufferings of Christ.

Therefore in those people there is fulfilled the Gospel of suffering, and, at the same time, each of them continues in a certain sense to write it: they write it and proclaim it to the world, they announce it to the world in which they live and to the people of their time.

THE POWER OF SUFFERING

Down through the centuries and generations it has been seen that "in suffering there is concealed" a particular "power that draws a person interiorly close to Christ", a special grace. To this grace many saints, such as Saint Francis of Assisi, Saint Ignatius of Loyola and others, owe their profound conversion. A result of such a conversion is not only that the individual discovers the salvific meaning of suffering but above all that he becomes a completely new person. He discovers a new dimension, as it were, of "his entire life and vocation". This discovery is a particular confirmation of the spiritual greatness which in man surpasses the body in a way that is completely beyond compare. When this body is gravely ill, totally incapacitated, and the person is almost incapable of living and acting, all the more do interior "maturity and spiritual greatness" become evident, constituting a touching lesson to those who are healthy and normal.

This interior maturity and spiritual greatness in suffering are certainly the "result" of a particular "conversion" and cooperation with the grace of the Crucified Redeemer. It is he himself who acts at the heart of human sufferings through his Spirit of truth, through the consoling Spirit. It is he who transforms, in a certain sense, the very substance of the spiritual life, indicating for the person who suffers a place close to himself. "It is he" – as the interior Master and Guide – "who reveals" to the suffering brother and sister this "wonderful interchange", situated at the very heart of the mystery of the Redemption.

A NEW KIND OF MOTHERHOOD

Suffering is, in itself, an experience of evil. But Christ has made suffering the firmest basis of the definitive good, namely the good of eternal salvation. By his suffering on the Cross, Christ reached the very roots of evil, of sin and death. He conquered the author of evil, Satan, and his permanent rebellion against the Creator. To the suffering brother or sister Christ "discloses" and gradually reveals "the horizons of the Kingdom of God": the horizons of a world converted to the Creator, of a world free from sin, a world being built on the saving power of love. And slowly but effectively, Christ leads into this world, into this Kingdom of the Father, suffering man, in a certain sense through the very heart of his suffering. For suffering cannot be "transformed" and changed by a grace from outside, but "from within". And Christ through his own salvific suffering is very much present in every human suffering, and can act from within that suffering by the power of his Spirit of truth, his consoling Spirit.

This is not all: the Divine Redeemer wishes to penetrate the soul of every sufferer through the heart of his holy Mother, the first and the most exalted of all the redeemed. As though by a continuation of that motherhood which by the power of the Holy Spirit had given him life, the dying Christ conferred upon the ever Virgin Mary a "new kind of motherhood" – spiritual and universal – towards all human beings, so that every individual, during the pilgrimage of faith, might remain, together with her, closely united to him unto the Cross, and so that every form of suffering, given fresh life by the power of this Cross, should become no longer the weakness of man but the power of God.

THE MEANING OF SUFFERING

Almost always the individual enters suffering with a "typically human protest" and with the question « why ». He asks the meaning of his suffering and seeks an answer to this question on the human level. Certainly he often puts this question to God, and to Christ. Christ does not answer directly and he does not answer in the abstract this human questioning about the meaning of suffering. Man hears Christ's saving answer as he himself gradually becomes a sharer in the sufferings of Christ. Christ does not explain in the abstract the reasons for suffering, but before all he says: « Follow me! ». Come! Take part through your suffering in this work of saving the world, a salvation achieved through my suffering! Through my Cross. Gradually, "as the individual takes up his cross", spiritually uniting himself to the Cross of Christ, the salvific meaning of suffering is revealed before him. He does not discover this meaning at his own human level, but at the level of the suffering of Christ. At the same time, however, from this level of Christ the salvific meaning of suffering "descends to man's level" and becomes, in a sense, the individual's personal response. It is then that man finds in his suffering interior peace and even spiritual joy.

Saint Paul speaks of such joy in the Letter to the Colossians: « I rejoice in my sufferings for your sake » (Col 1:24). A source of joy is found in the "overcoming of the sense of the uselessness of suffering", a feeling that is sometimes very strongly rooted in human suffering. This feeling not only consumes the person interiorly, but seems to make him a burden to others. The person feels condemned to receive help and assistance from others, and at the same time seems useless to himself. The discovery of the salvific meaning of suffering in union with Christ "transforms" this depressing "feeling".

Faith in sharing in the suffering of Christ brings with it the interior certainty that the suffering person « completes what is lacking in Christ's afflictions »; the certainty that in the spiritual dimension of the work of Redemption "he is serving", like Christ, "the salvation of his brothers and sisters".

THE REAL NEIGHBOUR

To the Gospel of suffering there belongs the parable of the Good Samaritan. Through this parable Christ wished to give an answer to the question: « Who is my neighbour? » (Lk 10:29).

For of the three travellers along the road from Jerusalem to Jericho, on which there lay half-dead a man who had been stripped and beaten by robbers, it was precisely the Samaritan who showed himself to be the real « neighbour » of the victim: « neighbour » means also the person who carried out the commandment of love of neighbour. The parable of the Good Samaritan belongs to the Gospel of suffering. For it indicates what the relationship of each of us must be towards our suffering neighbour. We are not allowed to « pass by on the other side » indifferently; we must « stop » beside him. Everyone who stops beside the suffering of another person, whatever form it may take, is a Good Samaritan. This stopping does not mean curiosity but availability. It is like the opening of a certain interior disposition of the heart, which also has an emotional expression of its own. The name « Good Samaritan » fits every individual who is sensitive to the sufferings of others, who « is moved » by the misfortune of another. If Christ, who knows the interior of man, emphasizes this compassion, this means that it is important for our whole attitude to others' suffering.

Therefore one must cultivate this sensitivity of heart, which bears witness to "compassion" towards a suffering person. Sometimes this compassion remains the only or principal expression of our love for and solidarity with the sufferer.

Nevertheless, the Good Samaritan of Christ's parable does not stop at sympathy and compassion alone. A Good Samaritan is "one who brings help in suffering", whatever its nature may be. Help which is, as far as possible, effective. He puts his whole heart into it, nor does he spare material means. We can say that he gives himself, his very « I », opening this « I » to the other person. Here we touch upon one of the key-points of all

Christian anthropology. Man cannot « fully find himself except through a sincere gift of himself » (GS, 24). A Good Samaritan is the person capable of exactly such a gift of self.

THE APOSTOLATE OF « THE GOOD SAMARITAN »

The world of human suffering unceasingly calls for, so to speak, another world: the world of human love; and in a certain sense man owes to suffering that unselfish love which stirs in his heart and actions.

The person who is a « neighbour » cannot indifferently pass by the suffering of another: this in the name of fundamental human solidarity, still more in the name of love of neighbour. He must « stop », « sympathize », just like the Samaritan of the Gospel parable. The parable in itself expresses "a deeply Christian truth", but one that at the same time is very universally human. It is not without reason that, also in ordinary speech, any activity on behalf of the suffering and needy is called « Good Samaritan » work.

In the course of the centuries, this "activity" assumes organized "institutional forms" and constitutes a field of work in the respective "professions".

How much there is of « the Good Samaritan » in the profession of the doctor, or the nurse, or others similar!

Considering its « evangelical » content, we are inclined to think here of a vocation rather than simply a profession. And the institutions which from generation to generation have performed « Good Samaritan » service have developed and specialized even further in our times. This undoubtedly proves that people today pay ever greater and closer attention to the sufferings of their neighbour, seek to understand those sufferings and deal with them with ever greater skill. In view of all this, we can say that the parable of the Samaritan of the Gospel has become "one of the essential elements of moral culture and universally human civilization".

These words are directed to all those who are of service to their suffering neighbour in an unselfish way, freely undertaking to provide « Good Samaritan » help, and devoting to this cause all the time and energy at their disposal outside their professional work. This kind of voluntary « Good Samaritan » or charitable activity can be called social work; it can also be called an "apostolate", when it is undertaken for clearly evangelical motives, especially if this is in connection with the Church or another Christian Communion.

« THE SPIRIT OF THE LORD IS UPON ME »

The parable of the Good Samaritan witnesses to the fact that Christ's revelation of the salvific meaning of suffering "is in no way identified with an attitude of passivity". Completely the reverse is true. The Gospel is the opposite of passivity in the face of suffering. Christ himself is especially active in this field. In this way he accomplishes the messianic programme of his mission, according to the words of the prophet: « The Spirit of the Lord is upon me, because he has anointed me to preach good news to the poor. He has sent me to proclaim release to the captives and recovering of sight to the blind, to set at liberty those who are oppressed, to proclaim the acceptable year of the Lord » (Lk 4:18-19). In a superabundant way Christ carries out this "messianic programme" of his mission: he goes about « doing good » (Acts 10:38) and the good of his works became especially evident in the face of human suffering. The parable of the Good Samaritan is in profound harmony with the conduct of Christ himself.

Finally, this parable, through its essential content, will enter into those disturbing words of the Final Judgment, noted by Matthew in his Gospel: « Come, O blessed of my Father, inherit the Kingdom prepared for you from the foundation of the world; for I was hungry and you gave me food, I was thirsty and you gave me drink, I was a stranger and you welcomed me, I was in prison and you came to me » (Mt 25:34-36). To the just, who ask when they did all this to him, the Son of Man will respond: « Truly, I say to you, as you did it to one of the least of these my brethren, you did it to me » (Mt 25:40).

The opposite sentence will be imposed on those who have behaved differently: « As you did it not to one of the least of these, you did it not to me » (Mt 25:45).

A « CIVILIZATION OF LOVE »

One could certainly extend the list of the forms of suffering that have encountered human sensitivity, compassion and help, or that have failed to do so.

The first and second parts of Christ's words about the Final Judgment unambiguously show how essential it is, for the eternal life of every individual, to « stop », as the Good Samaritan did, at the suffering of one's neighbour, to have « compassion » for that suffering, and to give some help. In the messianic programme of Christ, which is at the same time the programme "of the Kingdom of God", suffering is present in the world in order to release love, in order to give birth to works of love towards neighbour, in order to transform the whole of human civilization into a « civilization of love ». In this love the salvific meaning of suffering is completely accomplished and reaches its definitive dimension. Christ's words about the Final Judgment enable us to understand this in all the simplicity and clarity of the Gospel.

These words about love, about actions of love, acts linked with human suffering, enable us once more to discover, at the basis of all human sufferings, the same redemptive suffering of Christ.

THE MESSIAH'S EXALTATION

The Palm Sunday liturgy is wonderful, as wonderful as the events of the day to which it refers. Over the enthusiasm of the messianic « Hosanna » hangs a dark shadow. It is the shadow of the passion that is drawing near. How meaningful are the words of the prophet which are fulfilled on this day: « Fear not, daughter of Zion! Behold, your king is coming, sitting on a donkey's colt! » (Jn 12:15; Zec 9:9).

On the day of the people's general enthusiasm for the coming of the Messiah, can the daughter of Zion have reason to fear?

Indeed yes. The time is now close at hand when the words of the psalmist will be fulfilled on the lips of Jesus of Nazareth: « My God, my God, why have you abandoned me? » (Ps 21 [22]:2). He himself will say these words from the height of the cross.

Then instead of the enthusiasm of the people singing « Hosanna », we will be witnesses of the sneers in Pilate's courtyard, on Golgotha, just as the psalmist proclaims:
« All who see me mock at me, they sneer at me, they wag their heads: "He committed his cause to the Lord; let him deliver him; let him rescue him, for he delights in him" » (Ps 21 [22]:8-9).
The liturgy of Palm Sunday, in allowing us to pause on Christ's triumphal entry into Jerusalem, at the same time leads us to the moment of the passion. As though the psalmist already saw with his own eyes the unfolding of the events of Good Friday. Truly, on that day, now near, Christ will be made obedient unto death, and this will be the death on the cross (Phil 2:8).
And precisely here, at the moment of the passion, the mystery of the Messiah's exaltation has its beginning. This exaltation is different from the « historical » exaltation before men on the day of the joyous « Hosanna ». This exaltation is in God himself.
The humiliation of Christ and his utter stripping through the cross became the immediate introduction to this exaltation in God.

THE BEGINNING
OF THE EXALTATION

« (Jesus Christ), though he was in the form of God, did not count equality with God a thing to be grasped, but emptied himself, taking the form of a servant... » (Phil 2:6-7).
These words from the Letter to the Philippians do not refer only to the passion. In a certain sense they constitute the summary of Christ's whole life. They constitute the gauge of the whole mystery of the

Incarnation. Indeed, it clearly follows from these words that he « stripped himself » through the very fact that, « though he was in the form of God », he accepted the human condition, human nature: he took « the form of a servant ». Being able at every step « to take advantage of being equal to God », he knowingly chose everything that put him « on a par » with man: « being found in human form ». And so we approach the moment of this levelling. We will arrive at it then when Christ « will humble himself, becoming obedient unto death, death on a cross ».

This very moment, however, signifies the beginning of the exaltation. The exaltation of Christ is contained in the stripping of Christ. Glory has its beginning and its source in the cross.

In his Letter to the Philippians, St. Paul clearly emphasizes this when he has the following sentence of his magnificent text begin with the words « because of this ».

« Because of this, God exalted him and gave him the name that is above every other name » (Phil 2:9). The Apostle sees this exaltation extending through the visible and the invisible world. He therefore writes, « and he bestowed on him the name which is above every name, that at the name of Jesus every knee should bend, in heaven and on earth and under the earth, and every tongue confess that Jesus Christ is Lord, to the glory of God the Father » (Phil 2:9-11).

Such is the extent of Christ's exaltation in God.

SACRAMENT OF LOVE

Jesus « rose from the meal and took off his cloak... and began to wash his disciples' feet », like a servant (Jn 13:4-5).

With this service of Holy Thursday the Sacrifice of the Cross begins to be fulfilled. In the Sacrifice of the Cross, the mystery of the Lamb of God must be fulfilled to the very end: it must be fulfilled with the entire content of the mystery of the Redemption.

The Passover Lamb was its herald.

The mystery of the Redemption fulfilled in the reality of the Lamb of God must remain as a "sacrament of the Church": the sacrament of love.

This is the sacrament linked to the rite of the meal, the Passover banquet. The liberation from the power of evil, from the slavery of sin and death, must be accomplished at the price of the death of the Lamb of God. This liberation in "the mystery of the Redemption is joined anew to the Passover banquet".

The Lord Jesus takes the bread « and after he had given thanks », breaks it and says: « This is my body, which is for you. Do this in remembrance of me » (1 Cor 11:24).

Then he takes the cup of wine and says: « This cup is the new covenant in my blood. Do this, whenever you drink it, in remembrance of me » (1 Cor 11:25).

« Every time, then, you eat this bread and drink this cup, you proclaim the death of the Lord until he comes! » (1 Cor 11:26).

In this way the sacrament of bread and wine "embraced" once and for ever "the reality" of the Lamb of God.

Or, rather, "the reality of the Lamb of God", accomplishing the Redemption of the world in Christ's death, embraces for all times the sacrament of bread and wine instituted during the Last Supper: the Passover banquet.

THE LAMB OF GOD

During the Passover supper, through Christ's choice, through his perfect freedom and his perfect love, the figure of the paschal lamb had reached the height of its meaning.

This reading from the Book of Exodus speaks of its institution: « In this manner you shall eat it: your loins girded, your sandals on your feet, and your staff in your hand; and you shall eat it in haste. It is the passover of the Lord ».

« Your lamb shall be without blemish... and you shall keep it until the fourteenth day of this month, when the whole assembly of the congregation of Israel shall kill their lambs in the evening. Then they shall take some of the blood, and put it on the two doorposts and the lintel of the houses... ».

« For I will pass through the land of Egypt that night... and when I see the blood, I will pass over you, and no plague shall fall upon you to destroy you, when I strike the land of Egypt » (Ex 12:11; 5-7; 12:13).

This is the Passover of the Old Covenant.

The memory of the passage of the punishing hand of the Lord through Egypt.

The memory of salvation through the blood of the innocent lamb.

The memory of the release from slavery.

Each year, on the fourteenth day of Nisan, Israel celebrates the Passover once again. Christ for his part celebrates the Last Supper with his Apostles. They meditate on the release from slavery through the blood of the innocent lamb.

And here Christ says over the bread: « Take, eat; this is my body which is given for you ». Then he says over the wine: « Take, drink. This is the cup of my blood which is poured out for you. For you and for many » (Mt 26:26-28; Lk 22:19-20).

THE SIGN
OF THE UNIVERSAL REDEMPTION

On the Cross Christ "showed that he was Lord": he accepted death and gave life.

He did not simply « die »; he « gave life ». « Greater love has no man than this, that a man lay down his life for his friends » (Jn 15:13).

He gave life! He accepted death and gave life. His last words on the Cross: « Father into your hands I commend! ...I commend my spirit » (Lk 23:46). He gave his life for us. For "everyone". « We » are only a small part of all those for whom Christ gave his life.

There is not a single human being, "from the beginning until the end of the world", for whom he did not give his life.

He gave his life for all. The Cross is the sign of the "universal redemption".

The Cross is the gate through which God entered definitively into man's history. And he remains in it.

The Cross is the gate through which God unceasingly enters into our lives. Precisely for this reason "we make the sign of the Cross" and say at the same time « In the name of the Father, and of the Son, and of the Holy Spirit ».

And as we trace the sign of the Cross on our forehead, heart and shoulders, we also say the words.

These words are "an invitation to God, an invitation to come". And we unite them to the sign of the Cross in order that God may enter man's heart through the Cross.

And thus he enters into every deed, thought and word: "into the whole life of man and the world".

The Cross opens us to God. The Cross opens the world to God. And in the sign of the Cross a blessing is given as well.

This is what is done by bishops and priests. This is what is done by parents to their children. Through the Cross of Christ we await the definitive good from God himself, and all the good things which bring us close to him.

THE CROSS,
A GUARANTEE OF LIFE

"The Cross with Christ" is the great revelation of the meaning of suffering and of the value which it has in life and in history. He who understands the Cross, who embraces it, begins a journey very different from that of the process of contestation against God: in it there is found rather the motive of a new ascent to him on the way of Christ, which is, in fact, "the way of the Cross".

The Cross is the proof of an infinite Love which precisely in that victim of expiation and of peacemaking has placed the beginning of the universal restoration and especially of human redemption: redemption from sin and, at least in root, from evil, from suffering and from death.

But the Cross invites us "to respond to love with love". To God who loved us first we can give in our turn the sign of our intimate participation in his plan of salvation. We do not always succeed in discovering in this design the explanation of the sufferings which mark the pathway of our life. Supported by faith we can however reach the certainty that it is a design of love in which the whole immense gamut of crosses, great and small, tends to be fused into the one Cross.

The Cross is therefore for us a guarantee of life, of

resurrection and salvation because it contains in itself and shares with believers the renewing power of Christ's redemption. In it, according to St. Paul, there is a reality already acquired and the future resurrection and heavenly glorification which will be in eternity the glorious manifestation of the victory achieved in Christ by his Passion and Death. We, with the experience of our daily suffering, are called to participate in this mystery which is, indeed, one of suffering but also of glory.

IN THE CROSS OF CHRIST, THE FOUNDATION OF OUR HOPE

The Cross is Christ's standard which we venerate and of which we sing. In fact, to adore the Cross, is to adore Christ himself: « We adore thee, o Christ, and praise thee, because by thy Holy Cross thou hast redeemed the world! ».

In reality the cross belongs to our "existential condition", as is proved by our everyday experience. Rather it might be said that it has its root in the very "essence" of created things.

Man is aware of values, but also of limits. Hence, the problem of evil, which in determinate conditions of physical, psychological, spiritual disorder, is pain, suffering, or even sin. Why evil, why pain, why this human cross which seems coessential to our nature, and yet, in so many cases, so absurd. They are questions which have always tormented the heart and mind of man and to which perhaps there can be given partial answers of a theoretical order, but which continue to crop up again in the reality of life, sometimes in a dramatic way, especially when it is a case of the suffering of the innocent, of children, and also of groups and entire peoples subjected to overbearing forces which seem to indicate in the world the triumph of evil. Which of us does not feel pierced to the heart in the presence of so many painful facts, so many crosses? It is true that universal experience teaches also the beneficial effects that pain has for so many people as the source of maturity, wisdom, goodness, understanding, solidarity, so that one can speak of the fruitfulness of pain. But this observation leaves the basic problem unresolved and does not eliminate Job's temptation which confronts also the spirit of the Christian when he feels impelled to ask of God: "why"?

SEASON OF EASTER

« PEACE BE WITH YOU »

« Jesus came and stood among them and said to them, "Peace be with you" » (Jn 20:19).
The experience that the Apostles lived « on the evening of that day, the first day of the week » (Jn 20:19), was repeated a week later in the same Upper Room.
The Upper Room in Jerusalem is the first place of the Church on earth. And it is, in a way, the prototype of the Church in every place and in every age. Christ, who came to the Apostles on the first evening after his Resurrection, always comes to us again to repeat continually the words: « Peace be with you. As the Father has sent me, even so I send you... Receive the Holy Spirit. If you forgive the sins of any, they are forgiven; if you retain the sins of any, they are retained... » (Jn 20:21-23).
Did not the truth contained precisely in these words become the guiding idea of the Second Vatican Council? Of the Council which dedicated its work to the mystery of the Church and the mission of the People of God, received from Christ through the Apostles? The mission of bishops, priests, religious and laymen?... « As the Father has sent me, even so I send you » (Jn 20:21).

THE EMPTY TOMB

Beginning on the next day — the day after the sabbath — Christ's disciples began to become familiar with this new reality: the empty tomb. They began to call it by name.
Little by little they also came to understand that in the "Resurrection" of the Lord everything that he had done and everything that he had taught found its fulfilment.

The Apostle Paul, in the Letter to the Romans, about the year 57, that is, some 25 years after the Easter events, writes:

« Do you not know that all of us who have been baptized into Christ Jesus were baptized into his death? We were buried therefore with him by baptism into death, so that as Christ was raised from the dead by the glory of the Father, we too might walk in newness of life » (Rom 6:3-4). For them, then: for the first apostolic generation of the confessors of Christ – and also for us: "at the heart of the Easter Vigil" stands first "the old man", the man of sin, who must die with Christ, and be buried together with him – so that in the redemptive death of Christ sin may die – and so that at the dawn of Easter Sunday « the new man » may be born. The man who comes back to life again through Christ.

This is the pauline "analogy" of "the empty tomb".

« The empty tomb » stands not only for the Resurrection of Christ. It stands also for a new life – the life of grace. It signifies the « new man ».

« I AM THE RESURRECTION AND THE LIFE »

We are in the atmosphere of the Easter solemnity, in which an ineffable spiritual experience has let us taste the profound truth of our faith in the Risen Christ, « our Passover » (1 Cor 5:7), who was immolated for us but was not defeated by death, who did not exhaust his mystery and his mission when, hanging on the cross, he uttered these words: « Now it is finished » (Jn 19:30). In fact, at that very moment the fulfilment of God's salvific plan opened a new phase in human history, which

Christ himself would consecrate with his resurrection from the dead: the new "Kairos" of the certainty of life, founded on that manifestation of divine omnipotence. Christ is risen, as he had promised, because the depth of his being is identified with the eternal principle of life, God, so much so that he could say of himself: « I am the life » (Jn 14:6), as on another occasion he had proclaimed: « I am the resurrection and the life » (Jn 11:25). With him, therefore, the omnipotent power of life entered the world and, after the sacrifice of justice and love was offered on the cross, it burst into humanity and, through humanity, into the human race and in some way into the entire universe. From that moment creation contains the secret of an ever new youth and we are no longer slaves of the « fear of death » (Heb 2:15). Christ has liberated us for ever!

PASSOVER: THE PASSAGE FROM DEATH TO LIFE

For us, the Easter Vigil "means awaiting what will certainly take place". It will take place – "because it has already taken place".
Mary Magdalene, Mary the Mother of James, and Salome arrive at the tomb. And here, suddenly, "the perspective of death changes". Above all, they see that that stone, which constituted the main object of their worries and fears, has been rolled away and no longer blocks the entrance. Then they enter, "and they do not find Jesus' body", but in the tomb they meet an angel clothed in white. Instead of waiting for their questions, the angel is the first to speak. Here are his words: « Do not be frightened. I know you are looking for Jesus the

crucified, but he is not here. "He has been raised, exactly as he promised" » (Mt 28:5-6).

In the light of these words, the perspective of death changes. If Jesus of Nazareth "has been raised, it means that he lives". It is difficult to comprehend this, but the tomb is truly empty. Almost as a confirmation, the angel adds: « Come and see the place where he was laid » (Mt 28:6). Thus, therefore, "the perspective of death gives way before the proclamation of life!".

Mary Magdalene, Mary the mother of James, and Salome by themselves would not have dared to say it. The truth about Jesus' Resurrection "is expressed by the angel's words". Just as years earlier the truth about the birth of the Son of God in Bethlehem was announced by angels.

And therefore the perspective has changed: "death has given way to life". The Sabbath day which came after the Crucifixion and the entombment is revealed to be truly "the day of expectation. The Easter Vigil".

EASTER JOY
MUST BE STEEPED IN THANKSGIVING

Easter joy must be "steeped in thanksgiving". The Church invites us to look with the eyes of faith, in the light of the Resurrection of Christ, at all of God's gifts from the beginning.

« Know that the Lord is God; "he made us, his we are"; his people, the flock he tends » (Ps 99 [100]:3).

Here is the first reason for joy which is expressed in thanksgiving. We rejoice with Easter joy for the fact that "God is"; because the world is not a wilderness abandoned and without a master. We rejoice with Easter joy for the fact that "God created the world"; he created us; he created man in the visible world. We rejoice and give thanks because this man — although he has much in common with the world in which he lives on earth — at the same time bears the signs of a superior being: "that is, the signs of his likeness to God himself". We rejoice and give thanks because, through this singular resemblance to the divine likeness, man "belongs to God". Because he is his special property. Christ's Resurrection reconfirms this sacred ownership with the greatest efficacy. If man did not belong to God, as Christ attests, he would be condemned to a definitive "submission to the world". His whole life would be directed exclusively towards death. Through death, the material world would take total possession of the marvellous human being, making him « dust of the earth ».

Without faith in Christ, all that would remain to human existence is these prospects.

Christ's Resurrection allows man to break away from such prospects dominated by death.

THE THIRD DAY HE ROSE
FROM THE DEAD

"The third day he rose from the dead".

Saint Peter says: « You must have heard about the recent happenings... about Jesus of Nazareth and how... God had anointed him with the Holy Spirit and with power » (Acts 10:37-38).

With this same power, he who « was crucified, died and was buried » rose from the dead on the third day.

"Victimæ paschali laudes immolent christiani"! We glorify Christ — the Paschal Victim — as the "Conqueror of death". We glorify that Power which has brought victory over death and has brought to completion, by means of the definitive testimony of life, the Gospel of the work and words of Christ.

"We glorify the Holy Spirit", in virtue of whom Christ was conceived in the womb of the Virgin, with the power of whose anointing he went through his passion, death and descent among the dead, and "with whose strength he lives"! For « death has no more power over him » (Rom 6:9). We glorify the Holy Spirit « who is the Lord and giver of life ». We profess our faith in the Holy Spirit, who « with the Father and the Son is adored and glorified ».

We glorify the power of this Spirit « who is the Lord and giver of life », the power manifested in the fullest way in the Resurrection of Christ. The risen Christ will pass through the closed doors of the Upper Room, in which the Apostles were gathered; he will stop in their midst and say « "Peace be with you!"... Receive the Holy Spirit ».

« I AM WITH YOU ALWAYS,
TO THE CLOSE OF THE AGE »

« I have set you to be a light for the Gentiles, that you may bring salvation to the uttermost parts of the earth » (Acts 13:47).

« My sheep hear my voice and I know them, and they follow me » (Jn 10:27).

The word of God reveals to us a mystery which has been manifested in the life of humanity. A decisive event has taken place: the Lord Jesus, the Lamb of God, has offered himself for the salvation of the world. From that moment a new history has begun, and the Church of Jesus, by the power of the Holy

Spirit, is called to bring this proclamation of salvation to all peoples, to the uttermost parts of the earth. It is a demanding mission, entrusted to the humble persons of the Apostles, their successors and fellow workers, taken from every nation, century after century, with the promise that no earthly power will ever be able to interrupt it. The mystery of this invincible continuity is illumined by the presence of the Lord Yesus, who, though living in his immortal glory, is ever near us: « So, I am with you always, to the close of the age » (Mt 28:20). He is with us, he knows us, he lets us hear his voice, he calls us, he guides us, not just in order to offer his salvation to each one of us, but also in order to save others through us.

Among his many calls we can distinguish those calls to a more immediate collaboration in his own mission: the ordained ministries, the consecrated life, the missionary life. These are a privilege which, in reality, corresponds to a limitless measure of love and sacrifice in the total dedication of self to God and the Church.

« I CAME THAT THEY MAY HAVE LIFE! »

« I came "that they may have life, and have it abundantly" » (Jn 10:10).
It is Christ the Good Shepherd who speaks these words. It is Christ, who calls himself « the sheepgate » (Jn 10:7).
I wish to refer these words about the abundance of life first of all to the gift of grace, which Christ brought us by his Cross and Resurrection. I wish to refer them in the first place to the Holy Spirit, « who is the Lord and gives life », and we confess faith in him with the words that, sixteen centuries

ago, the First Council of Constantinople set on the lips of the Church.

The Holy Spirit is the author of our sanctification: he transforms man deep down, divinizes him, makes him a participant in divine nature (2 Pt 1:4), just as fire makes metal incandescent, just as spring water quenches thirst: « fons vivus, ignis, caritas ». Grace is communicated by the Holy Spirit through the sacraments, which accompany man during the whole span of his existence. By means of grace, he becomes the sweet guest of the soul: « dulcis hospes animae »: he dwells in our heart; he is the animator of secret energies, of courageous choices, of unshakable faithfulness. He makes us live in abundance of life: divine life itself.

Precisely through this solicitude about the abundance of life "Christ reveals himself as the Good Shepherd of human souls": the Shepherd who foresees the definitive future of man in God; the Shepherd who knows his sheep (Jn 10:14) to the very depths of the inner truth of man, who can speak of himself with the words of St. Augustine: « My heart is restless until it rests in Thee » (Conf. I, 1). « I came that they may have life ». In order that these human beings, the smallest, the weakest and the most helpless, may have life; in order that this life may never be taken from them before they are born; this is precisely the purpose we serve and will serve, in union with the Good Shepherd, because this is a holy cause. Serving this cause, we serve man and we serve society; we serve our country.

THE INNER LIFE OF MAN

Service for man is manifested not only in the fact that we defend the life of an unborn child. It is manifested at the same time in the fact that "we defend human consciences". We defend the rectitude of human conscience, so that it will call good good and evil evil, so that it will live in truth. So that man will live in truth, so that society will live in truth.

When Christ says: « I came that they may have life... », he is also thinking, in fact he is thinking especially, of that "inner life of man" which is manifested in the voice of a correct conscience. The Church has always considered her service of conscience as being her essential service: the service rendered to the consciences of all her sons and daughters — but also to the conscience of every man. Since man lives a "life worthy of man" when he follows the voice of a correct conscience — and when he does not allow this conscience to be deafened in himself and to become insensitive.

JOSEPH, A JUST MAN

The mystery of the Church, that is, the reality of the Church, is already born in some way from the promise that God made to Abraham, and at the same time from that faith with which Abraham responded to God's call. Rightly, in St. Joseph's day, we read the following sentences from the Letter to the Romans: « The promise to Abraham and his descendants, that they should inherit the world, did not come through the law, but through the righteousness of faith. That is why it depends on faith, in order that the promise may rest on grace and be guaranteed to all his descendants, not only to the adherents of the law, but also to those who share the faith of Abraham » (Rom 4:13, 16). And further on, the Apostle writes of the same Abraham: he « is the father of us all, as it is written: "I have made you the father of many nations"; he is our father in the presence of God in whom he believed, who gives life to the dead and calls into existence the things that do not exist » (Rom 4:16-17).

Hand in hand with faith there is hope. Abraham is « father » of our faith and of our hope. « In hope he believed against hope, that he should become the father of many nations » (Rom 4:18).

And St. Paul continues: « That is why his faith was reckoned to him as righteousness » (Rom 4:22). It is fitting that we re-read these words of the liturgy. We re-read them thinking of St. Joseph of Nazareth, who was a « Just man », to whom was accredited « as justice » the fact that he believed in the God who « gives life to the dead and calls into existence the things that do not exist ».

HOPING AGAINST EVERY HOPE

These words, written about Abraham, we re-read today thinking of St. Joseph of Nazareth, who « had faith, hoping against every hope ». That happened at the decisive moment for the history of salvation when God, the Eternal Father, fulfilling the promise made to Abraham, « sent his Son into the world ». It is precisely then that the faith of Joseph of Nazareth is manifested, and it is manifested in the measure of Abraham's faith. It is manifested more greatly when the Word of the Living God was madeflesh in Mary, Joseph's spouse, who at the announcement of the angel « was found to be with child through the work of the Holy Spirit ». And this occurred, as Matthew the Evangelist writes, after Mary's marriage to Joseph, but « before they came to live together ».

So then St. Joseph's faith was to be manifested in

the presence of the mystery of the Incarnation of the Son of God.

At that precise time Joseph of Nazareth passed the great test of his faith, as Abraham had passed it. It is then that Joseph the « just man » believed in God as the one who « calls into existence the things that do not exist ».

WITNESS OF THE DIVINE MYSTERY

What emanates from his whole figure is faith, the true heritage of Abraham's faith. His faith is the closest likeness and comparison with the faith of Mary of Nazareth. Both Mary and Joseph are united by this marvellous bond. Before men, the bond was one of marriage. Before God and the Church, it is the marriage of the Holy Spirit. Through this marriage in faith, both of them, Mary and Joseph beside her, became witnesses and dispensers of the mystery through which the created world, and especially human hearts, become again the dwelling of the Living God.

Joseph of Nazareth is a « just man » because he totally « lives by faith ». He is holy because his faith is truly heroic.

Sacred Scripture says little of him. It does not record even one word spoken by Joseph, the carpenter of Nazareth. And yet, even without words, he shows the depth of his faith, his greatness.

St. Joseph is a man of great spirit. He is great in faith, not because he speaks his own words, but above all because he listens to the words of the Living God. He listens in silence. And his heart ceaselessly perseveres in readiness to accept the Truth contained in the word of the Living God. In order to receive it and fulfill it with love.

Therefore Joseph of Nazareth becomes truly a marvellous witness of the Divine Mystery. He becomes a provider for the Tabernacle that God has chosen for himself on earth to carry out the work of salvation.

We see how the word of the Living God penetrates deeply into the soul of that man — that just man. And we, do we know how to listen to the word of God? Do we know how to absorb it into the depths of our human « I »? Do we open our conscience in the presence of this word?

« KEKARITOMÉNE »

Mary gives her consent to the announcing Angel. The page of Luke, even in its scant terseness, is very rich in Old Testament biblical contents, and in the unprecedented novelty of Christian revelation. Its protagonist is a woman, Woman par excellence (Jn 2:4; 19:26), chosen from all eternity to be the first indispensable collaborator of the divine plan of salvation. She is the "almah" prophesied by Isaiah (7:14), the girl of royal race whose name is Miriam, Mary of Nazareth, a very humble and secluded town of Galilee (Jn 1:46). The real Christian "novitas", which put woman in an incomparable lofty dignity, unconceivable to the Jewish mentality of the time as in Graeco-Roman civilization, begins with announcement addressed to Mary by Gabriel in the very name of God. She is greeted with such lofty words, which fill her with awe: « Kaire, Ave, rejoice »! Messianic joy rings out for the first time on earth. « "Kekaritoméne, gratia plena", full of grace »! Mary Immaculate is here, carved in her mysterious fullness of divine election, of eternal predestination, of shining clarity. « Dominus tecum », « the Lord is with you »!

God is with Mary, the chosen member of the human family who is to be the mother of Emmanuel, of him who is « God-with-us »: God will be from now on, always, without regrets and without retractions, together with mankind, made one with it in order to save it and give it his Son, the Redeemer: and Mary is the living, concrete guarantee of this salvific presence of God.

THE SON OF GOD

From the conversation between the elect Creature and the Angel of God, fundamental truths continue to flow for us: « And behold, you will conceive in your womb and bear a son, and you shall call his name Jesus.
He will be great, and will be called the Son of the Most High; and the Lord God will give to him the throne of his father David... The Holy Spirit will come upon you, and the power of the Most High will overshadow you; therefore the child to be born will be called holy, the Son of God » (Lk 1:31 f., 35).
He, who from the line of Adam enters the genealogies of Abraham and David, is coming (Mt 1:1-17; Lk 3:23-38): he is in the line of the divine promises, but he comes into the world without needing the intervention of human fatherhood, in fact he goes beyond it in the line of immaculate faith.
The whole Trinity is committed in this work, as the Angel announces: Jesus, the Saviour, is the « Son of the Most High », the « Son of God »; the Father is present, overshadowing Mary, the Holy Spirit is present to come upon her, to make her

intact womb fruitful with his power. As St. Ambrose subtly commented in his exposition on this passage of Luke's Gospel, the revelation of the Holy Spirit was heard for the first time that day, and is at once believed: "et auditur et creditur" (Exp. Ev. sec. Lucam, II, 15).

PROTOTYPE AND MODEL
OF THE CHURCH

The Angel asks for Mary's consent for the Word's entrance into the world.
The expectation of past centuries is concentrated on this point; the salvation of man depends on it.
St. Bernard, commenting on the Annunciation, expresses this unique moment in a stupendous way, when he says, addressing Our Lady: « The whole world waits, prostrate at your feet; not without reason, for on your mouth depends the consolation of the afflicted, the release of prisoners, the liberation of the condemned, the salvation, in a word, of all the children of Adam, your whole race. Make haste, Virgin, to reply » (In laudibus Virginis Matris Homilia IV, 8; in "Sermones", I).
And Mary's assent is the assent of faith. It is along the line of faith.
Rightly, therefore, the Second Vatican Council, reflecting on Mary as the prototype and model of the Church, has proposed her example of active faith precisely at the moment of her "fiat": « The Fathers see Mary not merely as passively engaged by God, but as freely cooperating in the work of man's salvation through faith and obedience » (LG, 56).

« And may the peace of Christ reign in your hearts » (Col 3:15).
In Hiroshima.

« BEHOLD »

Mary's answer was the perfect echo of the Word's reply to the Father. Her « Behold » is possible, since it was preceded and sustained by the « Behold » of the Son of God, who, at the moment of Mary's consent, becomes the Son of Man. The Letter to the Hebrews enables us to penetrate, as it were, into the unfathomable abysses of this abasement of the Word, this humiliation of himself for the sake of men even to death on the cross: « When Christ came into the world, he said, "Sacrifices and offerings you did not desire, but a body you have prepared for me; in burnt offerings and sin offerings you have taken no pleasure ». Then I said, 'Behold, I have come to do your will, O God, as it is written of me in the roll of the book' » (Heb 10:5 ff.).

A body you have prepared for me: certainly refers us to the date of Christmas, in nine months' time; but, with a mystically deep thought which, as I said, was grasped by our brothers and sisters of the Church of the first centuries, it refers us above all to the approaching passion, death and resurrection of Jesus. The fact that the Annunciation of the Lord falls within and against the background of the Lenten season, makes us understand its redemptive significance: the Incarnation is closely connected with the Redemption, which Jesus carried out by shedding his blood for us on the Cross.

I HAVE COME TO DO YOUR WILL

"Behold, I have come to do your will, O God". Why this obedience, why this humiliation, why this suffering? The Creed answers us: « "Propter nos homines et propter nostram salutem": for us men and for our salvation ». Jesus come down from Heaven in order to enable man to have the full right to go up there, and making him a son in the Son, to restore him to the dignity lost by sin. He came to complete the original plan of the Covenant. The Incarnation confers on man forever his extraordinary, unique and ineffable dignity. And the way that the Church goes takes its origin from here. « Christ the Lord indicated this way especially when, as the Council teaches, "by his Incarnation, he, the Son of God, in a certain way united himself with each man" (GS, 22). The Church therefore sees its fundamental task in enabling that union to be brought about and renewed continually. The Church wishes to serve this single purpose: that each person may be able to find Christ, in order that Christ may walk with each person the path of life, with the power of the truth about man and the world that is contained in the mystery of the Incarnation and the Redemption » (RH, 13).

HE DWELT AMONG US

The Church does not forget – and how could she? – that the Word offers himself to the Father for the salvation of man, for the dignity of man. In that act of the offering of himself, the whole salvific value of his Messianic mission is already contained; everything is already contained in a nutshell here, in this mysterious entrance of the « Sun of justice » (Mt 4:2) into the darkness of this world, which did not accept him (Jn 1:5). Yet, as John the Evangelist testifies for us, « But to all who received him, who believed in his name, he gave power to become children of God; who were born... of God. And the Word became flesh and dwelt among us, full of grace and truth; we have beheld his glory, glory as of the only Son from the Father » (Jn 1:12 ff.).

« The Word became flesh and dwelt among us ». Let us welcome him. Let us, too, say: Behold, I have come to do your will. Let us be available for the action of the Word, who wishes to save the world also through the collaboration of those who have believed in him. Let us welcome him. And, with him, let us welcome every man. The darkness still seems always to want to prevail: wicked riches, selfish indifference to the sufferings of others, mutual mistrust, hostility between peoples, the hedonism that obscures reason and perverts human dignity, all the sins that offend God and go against love of our neighbour. We must bear witness to faithfulness, though in the midst of so many counter-testimonies; we must be, although among so many non-values, the value of good which overcomes evil with its intrinsic power.

ONLY HOPE

Rightly, with the Church's Liturgy, we can hail the cross as our « only hope » and font of « grace » and « pardon » not only "in hoc Passionis tempore" (in this season of the Passion), as we did on Good Friday, but also in "hac triumphi gloria" (in this glory of triumph), as we will sing on the feast of its Exaltation almost as an echo of the Easter "Alleluia". Of this mystery of sparkling glory in the cross ("fulget Crucis mysterium") (the mystery of the Cross shines) St. Peter speaks to us in his first letter to the Christian communities of Asia Minor. « Praised be the God and Father of our Lord Jesus Christ, he who in his great mercy gave us new birth; a birth unto hope which draws its life from the resurrection of Jesus Christ from the dead; a birth to an imperishable inheritance, incapable of fading or defilement » (1 Pt 1:3, 4).

The Risen Christ therefore dominates the scene of history and gives a generating power of eternal hope to Christian life, in this "Kairos", in this eschatological age that has already begun with the victory over death on the part of him who was « chosen before the world's foundation and revealed for your sake in these last days » (1 Pt 1:20). This was the certainty needed by the world in which the Apostles preached the Gospel of Christ; this is the hope needed by mankind in our times: Christ has risen, and by rising he has interrupted what seemed and still seems to many a bottomless whirlpool of decadence, degradation and corruption in history. The Risen Christ gives us the guarantee of a life that does not pass away, of an « incorruptible inheritance », of a « protection » on the part of God for the just who, liberated and renewed by the Redeemer, now belong in faith and hope to the kingdom of eternal life.

REDEMPTION COMES FROM THE CROSS

Redemption comes from the Cross and is fulfilled in the Resurrection.
« The Lamb has redeemed the sheep.
The innocent Christ has reconciled sinners to the Father ».
Behold, man has "been snatched from death" and restored to life.
Behold, man is "snatched from sin" and restored to Love.
All of you, everywhere, who enter the darkness of death, listen: Christ "is risen"!

All of you who live under the burden of sins, listen: Christ has conquered sin by his Cross and Resurrection: "Submit yourselves to his power"! World of today! Submit yourself to his power! The more you find in yourself the old structure of sin, the more you notice the horror of death on the horizon of your history, "submit yourself" all the more fully "to his power"!

INTELLECTUAL AND MORAL FORMATION

The power of love manifested in Christ's death and resurrection become the exclusive inspiration and only power in whose name the Apostles spoke: « in the name of Jesus Christ the Nazorean, whom you crucified and whom God has raised from the dead » (Acts 4:10).

In Christ's name they also performed signs, restoring health to people who where sick and condemned to suffering.

And with that certitude that comes from the light and the power of the Holy Spirit himself, the Apostles announced salvation in Jesus Christ, in him alone:

« There is no salvation in any other; there is in fact no other name under heaven given to men by which we can be saved » (Acts 4:12).

« To save » really means to give love, that love which the Father gave us in making us his children in his only-begotten Son; that love which the Son as the Good Shepherd has revealed, giving his own life on the cross for his sheep, and recovering this life for everyone in the resurrection; that love which overcomes evil in souls and in the history of man with the power of the Crucified and Risen One.

CHRIST IS THE CORNERSTONE

Good Shepherd is the cornerstone: « He is the stone rejected by the builders, which has become the cornerstone » (Acts 4:11).
Was not this stone rejected by those who did not accept the testimony of the Good News and who sentenced Christ to death on the cross? And is he not always rejected anew by men who want to give order to the world and to human life in the world apart from him and against him? And yet this rejected stone — rejected so many times! — Jesus Christ, is the cornerstone. The building of human salvation can rest only on him. The building of order in man and among men can find a sure foundation only in him. Man can grow spiritually renewed, and grow in the measure of his eternal destiny, only in him.
And only through him can the human world become more human.

THE TRUE CHRISTIAN
IS A « LIVING GOSPEL »

Every Christian, drawing upon historical tradition and above all the certainties of faith, experiences that Christ is the Risen One and, therefore, the eternally Living One. It is a profound and complete experience which cannot stay locked in the exclusively personal sphere but necessarily demands to be poured out: like the light that irradiates; like the leaven that makes the mass of dough rise.
The true Christian is constitutionally a « living Gospel ». Not, therefore, the latter disciple of a doctrine far off in time and foreign to lived-out reality; not the mediocre repeater of empty formulas, but the convinced and persistent assertor that

Christ is contemporary and the novelty of the Gospel is ceaseless, and he is always ready, before any one and at any time, to give reason for the hope that he nourishes in his heart (1 Pt 3:15).

WITNESS IS AN ESSENTIAL ELEMENT

Witness, as Paul VI stressed, « is an essential element of evangelization, and generally the first » (*Evangelii Nuntiandi,* n. 21). It is particularly urgent in our era, in the confusion of minds and in the eclipse of values that are shaping a crisis which is revealed ever more clearly as a total crisis of civilization.

Modern man, drunk with material conquests and nonetheless worried by the destructive consequences that threaten to spring from them, needs absolute certainties, horizons capable of resisting the corrosion of time.

Unsatisfied or disappointed by his wandering among the mazes of ideological systems that distance him from his deepest aspirations, he is searching for truth, he is searching for light. Often, perhaps without fully realizing it, he is searching for Christ. With the bitterness of one who has fruitlessly traveled the paths of varied cultural formulas, the man of our time, according to Paul VI's keen observation, « more willingly listens to witnesses than to teachers, or if he listens to teachers, it is because they are witnesses » (AAS 66; 1974, p. 568).

WE ARE WITNESSES

When, after receiving the Holy Spirit, these men, these apostles and disciples of the Lord, began to speak publicly about Christ, when they began to announce him to men, before anything else they recalled the facts that were commonly known. « You delivered him up and denied him in the presence of Pilate, when he had decided to release him », Peter said to the inhabitants of Jerusalem.

« You denied the Holy and Just One, and asked for a murderer to be released to you »! (that is, Barabbas) (Acts 3:13-14).

From the events surrounding Christ's death, the speaker passes to the resurrection: « ...you killed the Author of life.

But God has raised him from the dead, and of this we are witnesses » (Acts 3:15).

Peter alone does the speaking, but at the same time he speaks in the name of the whole apostolic college: « We are witnesses ». And he adds: « Now, brethren, I know that you acted in ignorance, as did also your rulers » (Acts 3:17).

From the description of the events, from the witness of the resurrection, the apostle passes on to prophetic exegesis. His disciples had been prepared for this exegesis of his death and resurrection by Christ himself. We have proof of this in the meeting described by the Gospel (according to Luke).

The Risen Christ says to his disciples, « These are the words which I spoke to you when I was still with you: that everything written about me in the law of Moses and the prophets and the psalms must be fulfilled » (Lk 24:44).

« ...And he said, "thus it is written that the Christ should suffer and on the third day rise from the dead, and that repentance and forgiveness of sins should be preached in his name to all nations, beginning from Jerusalem. You are witnesses of these things" » (Lk 24:46-48).

TO WITNESS MEANS TO ATTEST

I would like to call upon you to reflect on a sentence from the Acts of the Apostles: « This is the Jesus God has raised up, and we are his witnesses » (Acts 2:32). This strong proclamation of Peter's at the dawning of apostolic preaching acquires a special significance in the climate of the Easter Alleluia, whose festive rhythms the Liturgy stresses for fifty days. Christ, who truly died, is truly risen! For twenty centuries the Church has continued to render this overwhelming testimony before the world. She has done so in every cultural and social context, under every single sky, with the voice of her pastors, with the sacrifice of her martyrs, with the dedication of the numberless band of her saints.

Witness to the Risen One is a commitment that concretely binds all the members of the People of God. The Council made this the object of an explicit reminder for the lay faithful, summing up the mission that is proper to them in virtue of their incorporation into Christ through Baptism, with these compelling words: « Each individual layman must stand before the world as a witness to the resurrection and life of the Lord Jesus » (LG, 38).

To witness means essentially to attest to a fact on the basis of a certainty which in some way is the fruit of personal experience. The pious women were the first witnesses of the Lord's return to life (Mt 28:5-8). They did not at that time see Jesus, but they acquired the certainty of his resurrection on the basis of the discovery of the empty tomb and the explanation of the astonishing event given them by the angel. This was the first experience of the mystery that they had, which was subsequently strengthened by the appearances of the Risen One.

THE SIGN OF JUDGMENT

The cross is the sign of judgment. What do these words mean: « He who does not believe is condemned "already" »? Apparently, this happens not only « after... as a result... ». The Gospel says « already ». Can man be already condemned while in this life? Let us listen as Christ, answering Nicodemus, who is a « teacher of Israel », explains in what this judgment, of which the cross is also the sign, consists. « And this is the judgment, that the light has come into the world, and men loved darkness rather than light, because their deeds were evil. For every one who does evil hates the light, lest his deeds should be exposed. But he who does what is true comes to the light, that it may be clearly seen that his deeds have been wrought in God » (Jn 3:19-21).

Yes. The cross is a sign of judgment. And the judgment has a twofold purpose: to distinguish good from evil and to pass a sentence.

According to Christ's words to Nicodemus, the one who passes sentence, however, is first of all the man himself. Man through his deeds – good or bad. The sentence is passed first of all in conscience.

The cross of Christ is a witness of that judgment and of that sentence. A mute witness? No! An eloquent witness. He gives witness whom the Father has « sent into the world, that the world might be saved through him »: Witness and Saviour.

And we, in our turn, are « created in Christ Jesus for good works ».

If, therefore, we are no saved, if we are condemned for evil deeds, it is because « we have not come to the light »: to this light which is precisely the cross of Christ.

136   *SEASON OF EASTER*

« THAT THE WORLD MIGHT BE SAVED THROUGH HIM »

« There is no salvation in anyone else, for there is no other name in the whole world given to men by which we are to be saved » (Acts 4:12).

With these words, Peter declared before the Sanhedrin what today the Church repeats to modern society, fulfilling its sublime duty to penetrate and perfect the world, to be the « sacrament of salvation »: that salvation which is wrought by him who came to give life and to give it to the full, drawing it from his own inexhaustible fullness, since everything has been created precisely through him, everything subsists in him, while he affirms over everything a primacy which makes him the Mediator "par excellence", Herald of peace, the only King, and Lord, Shepherd and Teacher, The Resurrection and the Life.

The salvation which he offers is therefore a respect and defence, a salvage and strengthening of all the values which in the human person transcend every limit of visible creation, and which in Christ share in the infinite dignity of the Word in the most sublime « return » of all creation to the « bosom of Father ».

Obviously "salvation", in the Christian mystery, presumes a fall — original sin — which had the gravity of being « sin » understood as a refusal of what God gave man in making him the lord of creation, a friend of the angels and destined for eternal bliss.

Now in Christ God the Father has given himself and in him he has redeemed everything: « God did not send the Son into the world to condemn the world, but that the world might be saved through him » (Jn 3:17).

RADICALLY A GIFT

The word of the Gospel makes clear this Church's « being sent » in his Apostles on the part of Christ for the remission of sins. « As the Father has sent me, so I send you », says the risen Lord Jesus. And after saying this, breathing on them he adds: « Receive the Holy Spirit; if you forgive men's sins, they are forgiven them; if you hold them bound, they are held bound » (Jn 20:22-23).

We can never sufficiently insist on emphasizing « the gratuity of this intervention of God » to ransom us from our misery and our despair. Absolution is certainly not a « right » that the sinner can claim before God: « it is radically a gift » for which gratitude must be expressed by one's words and by one's life. And so also: we can never sufficiently insist on emphasizing the "concrete" and "personal" character of the pardon offered by the Church to the "individual" sinner. It is not enough for man in some way or other to refer to a far-off and abstract « God ». It is a human requirement that coincides with the historic plan carried out by God in Christ and continuing in the Church, the plan of enabling us to meet with a man in the concrete like ourselves, a man who, sustained by the prayers and good works of his brothers and sisters and acting "in persona Christi", assures us of the mercy that is granted us. With regard, then, to the personal character of forgiveness, following the constant tradition of the Church. I have insisted not only on the "duty" of personal absolution, but also on the "right" that the individual sinner has to be received and reached in his irreplaceable and unrepeatable originality. "Nothing is so personal and inescapable as the responsibility for guilt". And nothing is so personal and inescapable as repentance and the hope and prayer for God's mercy.

« IF YOU FORGIVE MEN'S SINS »

« If you forgive men's sins, they are forgiven them; if you hold them bound, they are held bound » (Jn 20:23). The risen Jesus passes on to the Apostles the power to forgive in his name.

In the effort to grasp the significance of the acts we are called upon to perform when we approach the Sacrament of Penance, we considered the meaning and the value of the confession of sins as the moment that "identifies the sinner to himself" before the God of Jesus Christ who forgives. "The absolution" is, precisely, God's "response" to the individual who acknowledges and declares his sin, expresses sorrow for it, and disposes himself to the change of life arising from the mercy he has received.

On the part of the priest, in fact, who acts in the heart of the Church, the absolution expresses the "judgment of God on the bad action of man". And the penitent, who is accusing himself before God as guilty, acknowledges the Creator as his Lord and accepts his « judgment » as the judgment of a Father who does not want the sinner to die but to turn to him and live (Ez 33:11).

This « judgment » is manifested in the death and resurrection of Christ: though he knew no sin « for our sakes God made him to be sin, so that in him we might become the very holiness of God » (2 Cor 5:21). The Lord Jesus thus became « our reconciliation » (Rom 5:11) and our « peace » (Eph 2:14). The Church, therefore, through the priest, in a singular way, does not act as an autonomous reality: she is structurally dependent on the Lord Jesus who founded her, dwells and acts in her, so as to make present in the various times and in the various environments, the mystery of the Redemption.

« BLESSED ARE THOSE WHO HAVE NOT SEEN AND YET BELIEVE! »

John was witness to the first coming of the Risen One in the Upper Room « the evening of the same day, the first after the Sabbath ». He was also witness to Thomas's disbelief. Thomas was not with the Apostles in the Upper Room that first evening. When the others told him: « We have seen the Lord! » (Jn 20:25), he reacted in a very significant way. Here are his well-known words: « Unless I see in his hands the print of the nails, and place my finger in the mark of the nails, and place my hand in his side, I will not believe » (Jn 20:25).

Eight days later, John was witness to the event which has been described by him in great detail. Christ came again to the Upper Room, behind closed doors and, after having greeted the Apostles, addressed Thomas directly.

He turned to him as if he had known of his reaction of a week earlier and had heard the words Thomas had said then. « Put your finger here », said Jesus, « and see my hands; and put out your hand and place it in my side; do not be faithless, but believing! » (Jn 20:27).

John saw all that with his own eyes. And he also heard with his own ears Thomas's reply: « My Lord and my God! » (Jn 20:28), a profession of faith in the divinity of Christ that is perhaps even more resolute and spontaneous than that of Peter at Caesarea Philippi!

And, finally, the words of the Lord: « Because you have seen me, you have believed: blessed are those who have not seen and yet believe! » (Jn 20:29).

140   *SEASON OF EASTER*

« SEE MY HANDS AND MY FEET... »

When we pray, « shine upon us, O Lord, the light of your countenance » (Ps 4:7), we are asking that through Christ's resurrection there may be renewed in us the faith that enlightens the ways of our life and directs them toward the living God.

At the same time, the liturgy points out to us how this faith was built up, and continues to be built up. This faith, being truly a gift of God, at the same time has its human dimension and shape. The resurrection of Jesus of Nazareth is the principal source of irradiation for this light, by which there is developed in us the knowledge of the truth revealed by God. The knowledge and acceptance of it as divine truth. In order to shape the human dimension of faith, Christ himself chose witnesses of the resurrection from among men. These witnesses were to be those who from the very beginning were connected with him as disciples, from whom he alone chose twelve, making them his apostles. And to them who were witnesses of his death on the cross, Jesus of Nazareth appeared alive after the resurrection. He spoke with them, and in various ways convinced them of his personal identity, of the reality of his human body.

« Why are you troubled, and why do doubts arise in your heart? See my hands and my feet: it is really I! Touch me and see; a spirit does not have flesh and bones as you see that I have » (Lk 24:38-39). This is how he spoke to them when they « startled and frightened, thinking they were seeing a spirit » (Lk 24:37).

« But while they still disbelieved for joy, and wondered, he said to them, "Have you anything here to eat?" They gave him a piece of broiled fish, and he took it and ate before them » (Lk 24:41-43). And so was formed the group of witnesses of the resurrection. They were men who knew Christ personally, listened to his words, saw his works, experiences his death on the cross, and subsequently saw him alive and kept company with him as with a live person after the resurrection.

MOTHER OF THE CHURCH

The words addressed by the crucified Christ to his mother and to the beloved disciple brought a new dimension to man's religious condition. The presence of a mother in the life of grace is a source of comfort and joy. On Mary's motherly face Christian recognize a most particular expression of the merciful love of God, who with the mediation of a maternal presence has us better understand the Father's own care and goodness. Mary appears as the one who attracts sinners and reveals to them, with her sympathy and her indulgence, the divine offer of reconciliation.

Mary's motherhood is not only individual. It has a collective value that is expressed in her title of "Mother of the Church". On Calvary she was indeed united with the sacrifice of her Son who was looking to the formation of the Church; her motherly heart shared completely Christ's will « to gather into one all the dispersed children of God » (Jn 11:52). Having suffered for the Church, Mary deserved to become the mother of all her Son's disciples, the mother of their unity. For this reason the Council states that « the Catholic Church, taught by the Holy Spirit, honours her with filial affection and piety as a most beloved mother » (LG, 53).

The Church recognizes in her a mother who keeps watch over its development and does not cease to intercede with her Son to obtain for Christians more profound dispositions of faith, of hope, of love.

Mary seeks to promote the greatest possible unity of Christians, because a mother strives to ensure accord among her children. There is no ecumenical heart greater or more ardent than Mary's heart.

« THERE IS YOUR SON »

« Jesus said to his mother, "Woman, there is your son". In turn he said to the disciple, "There is your mother" » (Jn 19:26-27).

The circumstances under which this motherhood of Mary's was proclaimed show the importance that the Redeemer attributed to it. At the very moment when he was completing his sacrifice, Jesus spoke those basic words to his mother: « Woman, there is your son »; and to the disciple: « There is your mother » (Jn 19:26-27). And the Evangelist notes that after saying these words Jesus realized that everything was now finished. The gift of his mother was the final gift that he was giving mankind as the fruit of his sacrifice.

It is a quetion then of a gesture intended to crown his redemptive work. Asking Mary to treat the beloved disciple as her son, Jesus invites her to accept the sacrifice of his death and, as the price of this acceptance, he invites her to take on a new motherhood. As the Saviour of all mankind, he wants to give Mary's motherhood the greatest range. He therefore chooses John as the symbol of all the disciples whom he loves, and he makes it understood that the gift of his mother is the sign of a special intention of love, with which he embraces all who want to follow him as disciples, that is, all Christians and all men. Besides giving this motherhood an individual form, Jesus manifests the intention to make Mary not merely the mother of his disciples taken as a whole, but of each one of them in particular, as though each were her only son who is taking the place of her Only Son. This universal motherhood in the spiritual order was the final consequence of Mary's cooperation in the work of her divine Son, a cooperation begun in the fearful joy of the Annunciation and carried through right to the boundless sorrow of Calvary.

IN MARY THE MEANING
OF THE PASCHAL MISTERY

We wish to consider in Mary what could be called the « success » of the Paschal Mystery: its « result », its happy outcome. In fact, the Paschal Mystery, the glorification of life, is in time and space the perpetual source of life and, lived in the footsteps of Christ, always bears the fruits of life. Jesus did not die in vain: his death is like that of the seed thrown on the ground: it is fruitful in results. And its most beautiful and most exalting fruit is the glorious triumph of Mary, his mother. She is the most exquisite fruit of the seed of eternal life that God, in Jesus Christ, has sown in the heart of mankind in need of salvation after Adam's sin. Mary is the greatest « success » of the Paschal Mystery, she is the woman « resulting » perfectly in the order of nature as well as in the order of grace, because more than any other human creature she was able to meditate upon it, understand it, and live it. For the Christian it is impossible to taste the meaning of Easter prescinding from how Mary, victorious over the ancient adversary with Christ and through Christ, experienced it. In the mystery of her heavenly assumption in body and soul the whole Church will celebrate the plenary fulfilment of the Paschal Mystery, because in the Mother of God thus glorified she sees the ideal type and the destination of her journey through the course of the centuries.

It is therefore in Mary and with Mary that we can penetrate the meaning of the Paschal Mystery, allowing it to bear in us the immense richness of its effects and its fruits of eternal life. In her and with her, who did not pass from sin to grace, as we all did, but who through a singular privilege, in view of the merits of Christ, was preserved from sin, journeying toward the eternal Easter from the very first moment of her existence.

THE GOOD SHEPHERD

The passage from the Gospel according to John proposes to us the evocative image of the Good Shepherd. « He calls his own sheep by name and leads them out. When he has brought out all his own, he goes before them and the sheep follow him, for they know his voice » (Jn 10, 3-4). The Good Shepherd, the Risen Christ, guarantees in visible manner his perennial presence in renewed humanity by means of those whom throughout history he continually sends to carry out the work of salvation. Today also he is alive and present in the midst of us, and he makes each of us feel his voice and his love.

The Good Shepherd manifests his concern for the constant growth of this flock. There are in fact other sheep who are outside the fold (Jn 10:16). The dramatic experience of the multitudes of all times is ever before his gaze, « harassed and helpless, like sheep without a shepherd », which make him say « The harvest is plentiful, but the labourers are few! » (Mt 9:37). The grief-stricken lament of the Heart of Christ is repeated in time and profoundly touches our persons. Who in fact can remain insensitive in front of the dizzy increase of needs for evangelization? The Divine Redeemer calls to everyone for collaboration so that the labourers of the Gospel will not be lacking, so that there will always be men and women to consecrate themselves completely to the service of the People of God.

« THE GOOD SHEPHERD LAYS DOWN HIS LIFE FOR HIS SHEEP »

Christ tells us: « I am the Good Shepherd. The good shepherd lays down his life for his sheep » (Jn 10:11).
By means of this parable Jesus of Nazareth greatly wanted to reiterate that God – the Father – is good. He wanted to illustrate through a metaphor what in reality he accomplished with his passion and resurrection.
So, he laid down his life for his sheep: for those who with him and through him have become « children in the Son ». Laying down his life, he revealed most profoundly how good God is, how far the goodness of God goes. He not only gives us existence and the likeness to himself in creation; he not only gives us the grace of adoption as children in Jesus Christ, but over and above all this, through the death of his only-begotten Son he redeems every sin, so that men « may have life, and have it abundantly » (Jn 10:10).
The parable of the Good Shepherd speaks of this love, which does not draw back in the face of death in order to save man from evil and assure him of good. This is a particularly eloquent parable about Christ the Redeemer.

In man's history there continually is that « wolf that snatches the sheep » (Jn 10:12) — but there is also Christ, the Good Shepherd who continually watches over them. The Father, who is the source of all good, knows him as « he knows the Father » (Jn 10:15). And with this knowledge filled with giving, Christ embraces every man: « I know my sheep and they know me » (Jn 10:14).

The Good Sheperd knows each one of us with the knowledge of saving love, and he leads us to the Father. He leads even those sheep who are not « of this fold » (10:16). His love and saving concern are extended to all men.

« ...GOODNESS
AND MERCY SHALL FOLLOW ME... »

The words of Psalm 23, which in the Old Testament is, as it were, a preparation for the Gospel allegory of the Good Shepherd, are certainly very familiar to us.

It is rich in images, which belong to two different spheres. First of all it speaks of « pastures », which signify the certain spiritual nourishment which the Lord provides us; of « water », which quenches all our thirst; of « walking », which shows us how our life is moving toward a goal; and of a « dark valley », which represents the various difficulties we encounter. These images come from the sphere of the relationship between the shepherd and his flock. But then there are images which recall a joyful, convivial situation: therefore the Psalm speaks of a prepared « table », which signifies the abundance offered us by communion with the Lord; of « oil », in reference to his warm hospitality; and of an overflowing « cup », since the Lord is always magnanimous and generous with us.

The whole Psalm and particularly the last verse, « Surely goodness and mercy shall follow me all the days of my life, and I shall dwell in the house of the Lord for ever », expresses the boundless happiness brought forth by Christ the Good Shepherd, who guides man along the ways of « happines and grace » during earthly life in order to bring him definitively « to the house of the Lord ».

« HE MAKES ME LIE DOWN IN GREEN PASTURES... »

The image that emerges from Psalm 23 is a preparation in the Old Testament for the figure that Christ himself described with the parable of the Good Shepherd. The Psalm, evidently, reflects an Eastern mentality and is expressed in ways typical of the Jewish historical background and therefore would require a thorough exegesis. However, its message can be easily understood: Jesus, the Divine Word, became incarnate precisely to lead souls to Truth: « He makes me lie down in green pastures, he leads me beside still waters ». Jesus came to encourage us along the way of life, to guide us along the right way to salvation, to prepare for us the table of thanksgiving, to give us the joy of certainty. Jesus is with us, every day of our lives: faith in him gives us security and courage, even if we sometimes have to walk in a dark valley. Take heart, therefore. In spite of the sorrows and conflicts of life, in spite of social and public situations which may sometimes become tragic, do not lose confidence in Christ the Good Shepherd, the Redeemer of our souls, the Saviour of mankind!

Christ is precisely the Eternal Shepherd of the whole of mankind, because in him we have all been chosen by the Father as his adopted children. And through his work of redemption we have been united with the Holy Spirit, and so also participate in the mission of Christ « Priest, Prophet and King » (LG, 31).

CHRIST HAS ASCENDED TO THE FATHER

« Ascendit Deus in iubilatione! » Christ has ascended to the Father. Christ's earthly life concluded with his return to the Father on the day of the Ascension. Our ardent hearts follow him there, where he has gone « to prepare a place for us » (Jn 14:2); and with this faith he wishes to permeate human existence, in all its aspects.

Meanwhile the Church looks to the Upper Room in Jerusalem, and like the Apostles, with the Apostles, prays in union with Mary, waiting for the coming of the Holy Spirit. Let fervent prayers rise from our hearts to the Spirit, who descends to sanctify the Church, to vivify the world, to « renew the face of the earth », to elevate man. Let us wait together for the Paraclete, the Comforter!

CHRIST'S ASCENSION
IS THE CAUSE OF OUR ASCENSION

Reason for deep happiness for the entire Church, and also for mankind, is the liturgical celebration of the Ascension of Our Lord Jesus Christ, who was solemnly exalted and glorified by God. The Liturgy applies to Christ, who returns to the Father, the exultant words which the Psalmist dedicates to God:

« God mounts his throne amid shouts of joy;/the Lord, amid trumpet blasts,/Sing praise to God, sing praise; sing praise to our king, sing praise,/For the king of all the earth is God;/sing hymns of praise./God reigns over the nations,/God sits upon his holy throne » (Ps 46 [47]:6-9).

In this « mystery of the life of Christ » we meditate on the one hand on the glorification of Jesus of Nazareth, who died and rose again, and on the other, his departure from this earth and his return to the Father. This glorification, even in its cosmic aspect, is emphasized by St. Paul, who speaks to us of the extraordinary greatness of God's power on our behalf, manifested in Christ « when he raised Christ from the dead and seated him at his right hand in heaven, high above every principality, power... and every name that can be given in this age or in the age to come » (Eph 1:20-21). Christ's Ascension represents one of the fundamental stages of the « history of salvation », that is, the plan of God's merciful and salvific love for mankind. With his profound clarity, in his meditations on the « mysteries of the life of Christ », St Thomas Aquinas admirably emphasizes how the Ascension is the cause of our salvation under a twofold aspect: on our part, since our intellect moves towards Christ with faith, hope, charity; on his part, since, in ascending the throne, he has prepared the way for us also to ascend into heaven: « Christ's Ascension is the direct cause of our ascension, giving beginning to this in our head, with whom it is necessary for the members to unite » (*Summa Theol.* III, 57, 6, ad 2).

THE EXALTATION OF HUMAN NATURE

The Ascension is not only the definitive and solemn glorification of Jesus of Nazareth, but it is also the pledge and the guarantee of the exaltation, the elevation, of human nature. Our faith and our hope as Christians are strengthened and corroborated, since we are invited to meditate not only on our smallness, on our frailty, on our wretchedness, but also on that « transformation », even more admirable than creation itself, which Christ accomplishes in us when we are united with him through the sacraments and grace. « We commemorate and liturgically celebrate the day when the lowliness of our nature was raised in Christ above all the heavenly ranks – St Leo the Great tells us – above all the hierarchies of angels, beyond the height of the powers, right up to the throne of God the Father. Now in this fabric of divine operations we are established and built up: thus the grace of God will prove to be more wonderful when... faith does not doubt, hope does not waver, charity does not weaken. This is truly the power of great spirits, this is the light of authentically faithful souls: to believe without hesitation what does not appear to the eyes of the body and to direct desire where one's glance cannot reach » (Sermo LXXIV, I; PL 54, 597).

At the moment when Jesus leaves the Apostles, he gives them the mandate to be his witnesses in Jerusalem, throughout Judea and Samaria and even to the ends of the earth (Acts 1:8) and to preach « repentance and the forgiveness of sins » to all peoples (Lk 24:47).

« ...SO I SEND YOU »

The Church is born on the day of Pentecost. It is born under the powerful breathing of the Most Holy Spirit, who orders the Apostles to go out of the Upper Room and undertake their mission.

The evening of the Resurrection Christ said to them: « As the Father has sent me, so I send you ». The morning of Pentecost the Holy Spirit sees to it that they undertake this mission. So they go out among men and begin travelling throughout the world. Before that happened, the world – the human world – "had entered the Upper Room". Since: « All were filled with the Holy Spirit. They began to express themselves in foreign tongues and make bold proclamation as the Spirit prompted them » (Acts 2:4). "With this gift of tongues" the world of men also entered the Upper Room, men who speak various languages, and to whom it is necessary to speak in various languages so that the proclamation of the "marvels God has accomplished" (Acts 2:11) may be understood. Therefore, the Church was born on the day of Pentecost, under the powerful breathing of the Holy Spirit. It was born in a certain sense "in the whole world" inhabited by men, who speak various languages. It was born in order to go into the whole world teaching, in various languages, all the nations. It was born "so that", by teaching men and nations, "it may always be born anew" through the Word of the Gospel; so that it may always be born in them anew in the Holy Spirit, "by the sacramental power of the Eucharist". All those who accept the Word of the Gospel, all those who nourish themselves with the Body and Blood of Christ in the Eucharist, under the breathing of the Holy Spirit profess: « Jesus is Lord » (1 Cor 12:3).

JESUS, THE LORD

We are in the "Upper Room of Jerusalem" on the day of Pentecost. But at the same time the Liturgy of this solemnity leads us to the same Upper Room

« the evening of the day of the Resurrection ». In that very room, even though the doors were locked, "Jesus came" among the still frightened disciples assembled there.

After showing them his hands and side as proof that he was the same one who had been crucified, he said to them: « Peace be with you. As the Father has sent me, So I send you. Then he breathed on them and said: "Receive the Holy Spirit". If you forgive men's sins, they are forgiven them; if you hold them bound, they are held bound » (Jn 20:21-23).

So, therefore, the evening of the day of the Resurrection, locked in the silence of the Upper Room, the Apostles "received the same Holy Spirit", who descended upon them fifty days later so that, inspired by his power, they might become witnesses of the birth of the Church: « No one can say: "Jesus is Lord", except in the Holy Spirit » (1 Cor 12:3).

The evening of the day of the Resurrection the Apostles, through the power of the Holy Spirit, "confessed with all their hearts: 'Jesus is Lord'"; and it is the same truth which, beginning from the day of Pentecost, they proclaimed to all the people even to the spilling of their blood.

When the Apostles believed and confessed with their hearts that « Jesus is Lord », "the power of the Holy Spirit committed the Eucharist into their hands" – the Body and Blood of the Lord – that Eucharist which in the same Upper Room, during the Last Supper, Christ had entrusted to them before his passion.

While he gave them the bread he then said: « Take this, all of you, and eat it: "this is my body" which will be given up for you ». And then, giving them the cup of wine, he said: « Take this, all of you, and drink from it: this is the cup of my blood, the blood of the new and everlasting covenant. It will be shed for you and for all so that sins may be forgiven ». And having said this, he added: "Do this in memory of me".

THE POWER OF THE SPIRIT
IN THE WORK OF CREATION

« Lord, send forth your Spirit and renew the face of the earth! ».
Powerful is the breath of Pentecost.
In the power of the Holy Spirit, it raises the earth and the whole created world to God, through whom exists everything that is.
Therefore we sing together with the Psalmist: « How manifold are your works, O Lord! The earth is full of your creatures » (Ps 103 [104]:24).
Let us look at the "earthly globe", let us embrace the immensity of creation and let us continue to proclaim with the Psalmist: « If... you take away their breath, they perish and return to their dust. When you send forth your spirit, they are created, and you renew the face of the earth » (Ps 103 [104]:29-30).
Let us profess "the power of the Spirit in the work of creation": the visible world has its origin in invisible Wisdom, Omnipotence and Love. And we therefore desire to speak to creatures with the words they heard from their Creator at the beginning, when he saw that they were « good », « very good ». And therefore we sing:
« Bless the Lord, O my soul! O Lord, my God, you are great indeed!...
May the glory of the Lord endure forever; may the Lord be glad in his works! » (Ps 103 [104]:1, 31).

In the great and immense temple of creation, we repeat: « Lord, send forth your Spirit and renew the face of the earth! ».

Ande we repeat these words gathering again in the Upper Room of Pentecost: there, in fact, the Holy Spirit descended upon the Apostles, assembled with Christ's Mother, and there the Church was born "to serve the renewal of the face of the earth". At the same time, from among all the creatures that become the work of human hands, we choose bread and wine. We bring them to the altar. In fact, the Church, born on the day of Pentecost by the power of the Holy Spirit, "is constantly born" of the Eucharist, in which the bread and wine become the Body and Blood of the Redeemer. And this too happens thanks to the power of the Holy Spirit.

SPIRIT OF LOVE AND UNITY

Beginning with Pentecost the reconciliation of all people is no longer a dream of a distant future. It has become a reality, destined to grow ceaselessly with the universal expansion of the Church. The Holy Spirit, who is the Spirit of love and of unity, achieves in the concrete the scope of Christ's redemptive sacrifice, the reunion of the children of God who had at one time been separated. Two aspects of this unifying action can be distinguished. By causing men to adhere to Christ the Holy Spirit binds them together in the unity of one body, the Church, and in this way reconciles in one and the same friendship people who were very distant from each other by geographical and cultural situation. He makes the Church a perpetual centre of reunion and reconciliation.

It can be said, moreover, that the Holy Spirit esercises, in a certain way, a reconciling action even among those who remain outside the Church, by inspiring in them the desire of a greater unity of all nations and of all mankind, and by stimulating the efforts directed to overcome the numerous conflicts which continue to divide the world.

The Holy Spirit achieves this reconciliation of mankind with the help of Mary, the universal Mother of all men. At the beginning of the Church she, united in prayer with the Apostles and the first disciples, contributed to obtaining an abudant outpouring of the gifts of the Spirit. Today also Mary continues to collaborate with the Holy Spirit in reuniting men because her maternal love directed to each and every one calls for unity. May the Holy Spirit be pleased to support this deep yearning, making mankind ever more disposed to accepting her maternal invitations to brotherhood and solidarity.

THE GIFT OF THE HOLY SPIRIT

« Exalted at the right hand of God, and having received from the Father the promise of the Holy Spirit, he has poured out this which you see and hear » (Acts 2:33).

As a result of the pouring out of the Spirit the disciples were transformed interiorly and they began to proclaim the marvellous work of God. That outpouring was extended to persons of every race and tongue who were drawn to that place by the sound which accompanied the coming of the Spirit. When Peter explained the meaning of the event which manifested the sovereign power of him who a short time before had been crucified at the request of the people, the hearers « were cut to the heart ». The Spirit had touched to the very depths the souls of those who had cried out before Pilate:

« Crucify him », and had disposed them to conversion. At the invitation of Peter: « repent », three thousand had asked to be baptized (Acts 2:37-41). In the presence of this marvellous harvest of conversions we are led to recognize in the Holy Spirit him who works in human hearts the "reconciliation with Christ and with God". It is he who « cuts to the heart », to use the expression of the Acts of the Apostles, and he makes them pass from hostility to Christ to the embracing of his person and message in faith and love. It is he who inspires the words of Peter when he exhorts his hearers to repentance, and who causes them to produce a marvellous effect. In these first conversions there is inaugurated a movement which will never cease with the passage of the years and the centuries. At Pentecost the Holy Spirit launches the great undertaking of the regeneration of humanity. From that day he continues to attract men to Christ, arousing in them the desire of conversion and of the remission of sins and reconciling in this way more and more human hearts with God.

THE GIFT OF THE SPIRIT MAKES US FREE

In the very act in which God creates man he inscribes his law in man's heart. Man's personal being is endowed with his own proper order, it is directed to communion with God and with other human persons. In a word: it is endowed with its own "truth", to which liberty is subordinated. In the state of « original justice » this subordination was fully realized. Man enjoyed a perfect liberty because he willed the good: he willed it not by an "external" imposition, but by a kind of « interior coincidence » of his will with the truth of his being created by God.

As a result of his rebellion against God, the bond of liberty with truth was broken in the human person and the law of God is felt as a compulsion, a constraint of his liberty and contrary to it. It is the very « heart » of the person that is "divided". On the one hand, in fact, he is carried along and impelled, in his free subjectivity, to do evil, to construct an existence — as an individual and as community — contrary to the creative Wisdom of God. On the other hand, however, since sin has not completely destroyed that truth and that goodness of being which is the patrimony received in the act of creation, man feels the yearning to remain in harmony with the deep roots of his own being. Each one of us experiences this state of division which is manifested in our hearts as a struggle between good and evil.

And the result is that, in this condition, if man follows his evil inclinations, he becomes the slave of evil; if however he follows the law of God, he experiences this obedience as a submission to an extrinsic imposition and therefore not as an act of complete liberty.

It is the gift of the Spirit which makes us free with true liberty, he himself becoming our law!

SACRAMENT OF UNITY AND LOVE

The life of the Risen Christ is distinguished by its "power" and its "richness". He who communicates receives the spiritual power necessary to confront all obstacles and trials, remaining faithful to his commitments as a Christian. Besides, he draws from the sacrament, as from a superabundant source, continuous bursts of energy for the development of all his resources and qualities in a joyful fervour that arouses generosity.

« Love your enemies... To the man who slaps you on one cheek, present the other check too » (Lk 6:27. 29).
John Paul II with Ali Agca.

In particular, he draws the life-giving energy of charity. In the Church's Tradition, the Eucharist has always been considered and experienced as the sacrament "par excellence" of unity and love. St Paul once declared, « Because the loaf of bread is one, we, many though we are, are one body, for we all partake of the one loaf » (1 Cor 10:17). The Eucharistic celebration reunites all Christians, whatever their differences may be, in a unanimous offering and in a meal in which all participate. It gathers them all in the equal dignity of brothers and sisters of Christ and children of the Father. It urges them to respect, to mutual esteem, to mutual service. Communion further gives each one the moral strength necessary to place himself beyond reasons for division and opposition, to forgive injuries received, to give renewed effort in the direction of reconciliation and fraternal accord.

ORDINARY TIME

CHRISTIAN UNITY

Pope John XXIII set out the problem of Christian unity with evangelical clarity as a simple consequence of the will of Jesus Christ himself, our Master, the will that Jesus stated on several occasions but to which he gave expression in a special way in his prayer in the Upper Room the night before he died: « I pray... Father... that they may all be one » (Jn 17:21).

The Second Vatican Council responded concisely to this requirement with its Decree on ecumenism. Pope Paul VI, availing himself of the activities of the Secretariat for Promoting Christian Unity, began the first difficult steps on the road to the attainment of that unity.

Have we gone far along that road? Without wishing to give a detailed reply, we can say that we have made real and important advances.

And one thing is certain: we have worked with perseverance and consistency, and the representatives of other Christian Churches and Communities have also committed themselves together with us. It is also certain that in the present historical situation of Christianity and the world the only possibility we see of fulfilling the Church's universal mission, with regard to ecumenical questions, is that of seeking sincerely, perseveringly, humbly and also courageously the ways of drawing closer and of union. Pope Paul VI gave us his personal example for this.

We must therefore seek unity without being discouraged at the difficulties that can appear or accumulate along that road; otherwise we would be unfaithful to the word of Christ, we would fail to accomplish his testament. Have we the right to run this risk?

« BY THE GRACE OF GOD I AM WHAT I AM »

True ecumenical activity means openness, drawing closer, availability for dialogue, and a shared investigation of the truth in the full evangelical and Christian sense; but in no way does it or can it mean giving up or in any way diminishing the treasures of divine truth that the Church has constantly confessed and taught. To all who, for whatever motive, would wish to dissuade the Church from seeking the universal unity of Christians the question must once again be put: Have we the right not to do it? Can we fail to have trust — in spite of all human weakness and all the faults of past centuries — in our Lord's grace as revealed recently through what the Holy Spirit said and we heard during the Council? If we were to do so, we would deny the truth concerning ourselves that was so eloquently expressed by the Apostle: « By the grace of God I am what I am, and his grace towards me was not in vain » (1 Cor 15:10).

What we have just said must also be applied — although in another way and with the due differences — to activity for coming closer together with the representatives of the non-Christian religions, an activity expressed through dialogue, contacts, prayer in common, investigation of the treasures of human spirituality, in which, as we know well, the members of these religions also are not lacking. Does it not sometimes happen that the firm belief of the followers of the non-Christian religions — a belief that is also an effect of the Spirit of truth operating outside the visible confines of the Mystical Body — can make Christians ashamed at being often themselves so disposed to doubt concerning the truths revealed by God and proclaimed by the Church, and so prone to relax moral principles and open the way to ethical permissiveness. It is a noble thing to have a predisposition for understanding every person, analyzing every system and recognizing what is right; this does not at all mean losing certitude about one's own faith or weakening the principles of morality, the lack of which will soon make itself felt in the life of whole societies, with deplorable consequences besides.

WE WISH TO LOOK TOWARDS CHRIST

While the ways on which the Council of this century has set the Church going, ways indicated by the late Pope Paul VI in his first Encyclical, will continue to be for a long time the ways that all of us must follow, we can at the same time rightly ask at this new stage: How, in what manner should we continue? What should we do, in order that this new advent of the Church connected with the approaching end of the second millennium may bring us closer to him whom Sacred Scripture calls « Everlasting Father », "Pater futuri sæculi"? (Is 9:5). This is the fundamental question that the new Pope must put to himself on accepting in a spirit of obedience in faith the call corresponding to the command that Christ gave to Peter several times: « Feed my lambs » (Jn 21:15), meaning: Be the shepherd of my sheepfold, and again: « And you in turn, strengthen your brethren » (Lk 22:32).

To this question, a fundamental and essential response must be given. Our response must be: Our spirit is set in one direction, the only direction for our intellect, will and heart is — towards Christ our Redeemer, towards Christ, the Redeemer of man. We wish to look towards him because there is salvation in no one else but him, the Son of God

– repeating what Peter said: « Lord, to whom shall we go? You have the words of eternal life » (Jn 6:68).

Through the Church's consciousness, which the Council considerably developed, through all levels of this self-awareness, and through all the fields of activity in which the Church expresses, finds and confirms herself, we must constantly aim at him « who is the head » (Eph 1:22), « through whom are all things and through whom we exist » (1 Cor 8:6).

THE CHURCH:
SIGN OF INTIMATE UNION WITH GOD

« By her relationship with Christ, the Church is a kind of sacrament or sign and means of intimate union with God, and of the unity of all mankind » (LG, 1), and the source of this is he, he himself, he the Redeemer.

The Church does not cease to listen to his words. She rereads them continually. With the greatest devotion she reconstructs every detail of his life. These words are listened to also by non-Christians. The life of Christ speaks, also, to many who are not capable of repeating with Peter: « You are the Christ, the Son of the living God » (Mt 16:16). He, the Son of the living God, speaks to people also as Man: it is his life that speaks, his humanity, his fidelity to the truth, his all-embracing love. Furthermore, his death on the Cross speaks – that is to say the inscrutable depth of his suffering and abandonment. The Church never ceases to relive his death on the Cross and his Resurrection, which constitute the content of the Church's daily life. Indeed, it is by the command of Christ himself, her Master, that the Church unceasingly celebrates the Eucharist, finding in it the « fountain of life and holiness », the efficacious sign of grace and reconciliation with God, and the pledge of eternal life. The Church lives his mystery, draws unwearyingly from it and continually seeks ways of bringing this mystery of her Master and Lord to humanity – to the peoples, the nations, the succeeding generations, and every individual human being – as if she were ever repeating, as the Apostle did: « For I decided to know nothing among you except Jesus Christ and him crucified » (1 Cor 2:2). The Church stays within the sphere of the mystery of the Redemption, which has become the fundamental principle of her life and mission.

« GOD SO LOVED THE WORLD »

The Redeemer of the world! In him has been revealed in a new and more wonderful way the fundamental truth concerning creation to which the Book of Genesis gives witness when it repeats several times: « God saw that it was good » (Gn 1). The good has its source in Wisdom and Love. In Jesus Christ the visible world which God created for man (Gn 1:26-30) – the world that, when sin entered, « was subjected to futility » (GS, 2, 13) – recovers again its original link with the divine source of Wisdom and Love. Indeed, « God so loved the world that he gave his only Son » (Jn 3:16).

As this link was broken in the man Adam, so in the Man Christ it was reforged (cf. Rom 5:12-21). Are we of the twentieth century not convinced of the overpoweringly eloquent words of the Apostle of the Gentiles concerning the « creation (that) has been groaning and in agony even until now » (Rom 8:22) and « waits with eager longing for the revelation of the sons of God » (Rom 8:19), the creation that « was subjected to futility »? Does not the previously unknown immense progress – which has taken place especially in the course of this century in the field of man's dominion over the world itself – reveal, to a previously unknown degree, that manifold subjection « to futility »? It is enough to recall certain phenomena, such as the threat of pollution of the natural environment in areas of rapid industrialization, or the armed conflicts continually breaking out over and over again, or the prospects of self-destruction through the use of atomic, hydrogen, neutron and similar weapons, or the lack of respect for the life of the unborn. The world of the new age, the world of space flights, the world of the previously unattained conquests of science and technology – is it not also the world « groaning in agony » (Rom 8:22) that « waits with eager longing for the revealing of the sons of God »? (Rm 8:19).

CHRIST, OUR RECONCILIATION

We do not forget even for a moment that Jesus Christ, the Son of the living God, become our reconciliation with the Father. He it was, and he alone, who satisfied the Father's eternal love, that fatherhood which from the beginning found expression in creating the world, giving man all the riches of creation, and making him « little less than the angels » (Ps 8:6), in that he was created « in the image and after the likeness of God » (Gn 1:26). He and he alone also satisfied that fatherhood of God and that love which man in a way rejected by breaking the first Covenant and the later covenants that God « again and again offered to man ». The redemption of the world – this tremendous mystery of love in which creation is renewed – is, at its deepest root, the fullness of justice in a human Heart – the Heart of the First-born Son – in order that it may become justice in the hearts of many human beings, predestined from eternity in the Firstborn Son to be children of God and called to grace, called to love. The Cross on Calvary, through which Jesus Christ – a Man, the Son of the Virgin Mary, thought to be the son of Joseph of Nazareth – « leaves » this world, is also a fresh manifestation of the eternal fatherhood of God, who in him draws near again to humanity, to each human being, giving him the thrice holy « Spirit of truth » (Jn 16:13).

This revelation of the Father and outpouring of the Holy Spirit, which stamp an indelible seal on the mystery of the Redemption, explain the meaning of the Cross and death of Christ.

MAN CANNOT LIVE WITHOUT LOVE

Man cannot live without love. He remains a being that is incomprehensible for himself, his life is senseless, if love is not revealed to him, if he does not encounter love, if he does not experience it and make it his own, if he does not participate intimately in it. This is why Christ the Redeemer « fully reveals man to himself ». If we may use the expression, this is the human dimension of the mystery of the Redemption. In this dimension man finds again the greatness, dignity and value that belong to his humanity. In the mystery of the Redemption man becomes newly « expressed » and, in a way, is newly created. He is newly created! « There is neither Jew nor Greek, there is neither slave nor free, there is neither male nor female; for you are all one in Christ Jesus » (Gal 3:28). The man who wishes to understand himself thoroughly – and not just in accordance with immediate, partial, often superficial, and even illusory standards and measures of his being – he must with his unrest, uncertainty and even his weakness and sinfulness, with his life and death, draw near to Christ. He must, so to speak, enter into him with all his own self, he must « appropriate » and assimilate the whole of the reality of the Incarnation and Redemption in order to find himself. If this profound process takes place within him, he then bears fruit not only of adoration of God but also of deep wonder at himself.

THE GOOD NEWS

How precious must man be in the eyes of the Creator, if he « gained so great a Redeemer », and if God « gave his only Son » in order that man « should not perish but have eternal life » (Jn 3:16).
In reality, the name for that deep amazement at man's worth and dignity is the Gospel, that is to say: the Good News. It is also called Christianity. This amazement determines the Church's mission in the world and, perhaps even more so, « in the modern world ». This amazement, which is also a conviction and a certitude – at its deepest root it is the certainty of faith, but in a hidden and mysterious way it vivifies every aspect of authentic humanism – is closely connected with Christ. It also fixes Christ's place – so to speak, his particular right of citizenship – in the history of man and mankind. Unceasingly contemplating the whole of Christ's mystery, the Church knows with all the certainty of faith that the Redemption that took place through the Cross has definitively restored his dignity to man and given back meaning to his

life in the world, a meaning, that was lost to a considerable extent because of sin. And for that reason, the Redemption was accomplished in the paschal mystery, leading through the Cross and death to Resurrection.

The Church's fundamental function in every age and particularly in ours is to direct man's gaze, to point the awareness and experience of the whole of humanity towards the mystery of God, to help all men to be familiar with the profundity of the Redemption taking place in Christ Jesus. At the same time man's deepest sphere is involved — we mean the sphere of human hearts, consciences and events.

TO KNOW EACH OTHER

All of us who are Christ's follower must meet and unite around him. This unity in the various fields of the life, tradition, structures and discipline of the individual Christian Churches and ecclesial Communities cannot be brought about without effective work aimed at getting to know each other and removing the obstacles blocking the way to perfect unity. However, we can and must immediately reach and display to the world our unity in proclaiming the mystery of Christ, in revealing the divine dimension and also the human dimension of the Redemption, and in struggling with unwearying perseverance for the dignity that each human being has reached and can continually reach in Christ, namely the dignity of both the grace of divine adoption and the inner truth of humanity, a truth which — if in the common awareness of the modern world it has been given such fundamental importance — for us is still clearer in the light of the reality that is Jesus Christ.

THE VIOLENT PEOPLE OF GOD

Jesus Christ is the stable principle and fixed centre of the mission that God himself has entrusted to man. We must all share in this mission and concentrate all our forces on it, since it is more necessary than ever for modern mankind. If this mission seems to encounter greater opposition nowadays than ever before, this shows that today it is more necessary than ever and, in spite of the opposition, more awaited than ever. Here we touch indirectly on the mystery of the divine « economy » which linked salvation and grace with the Cross. It was not without reason that Christ said that « the kingdom of heaven has suffered violence, and men of violence take it by force » and moreover that « the children of this world are more astute... than are the children of light ». We gladly accept this rebuke, that we may be like those « violent people of God » that we have so often seen in the history of the Church and still see today, and that we may consciously join in the great mission of revealing Christ to the world, helping each person to find himself in Christ, and helping the contemporary generations of our brothers and sisters, the peoples, nations, States, mankind, developed and undeveloped countries – in short, helping everyone to get to know « the unsearchable riches of Christ », since these riches are for every individual and are everybody's property.

THE CHURCH'S MISSION

In this unity in mission, which is decided principally by Christ himself, all Christians must find what already unites them, even before their full communion is achieved. This is apostolic and missionary unity, missionary and apostolic unity. Thanks to this unity we can together come close to the magnificent heritage of the human spirit that has been manifested in all religions, as the Second Vatican Council's Declaration "Nostra Ætate" says. It also enables us to approach all cultures, all ideological concepts, all people of good will. We approach them with the esteem, respect and discernment that since the time of the Apostles has marked the "missionary" attitude, the attitude "of the missionary". Suffice it to mention Saint Paul and, for instance, his address in the Areopagus at Athens (Acts 17:22-31). The "missionary" attitude always begins with a feeling of deep esteem for « what is in man » (Jn 2:26), for what man has himself worked out in the depths of his spirit concerning the most profound and important problems. It is a question of respecting everything that has been brought about in him by the Spirit, which « blows where it wills » (Jn 3:8). The mission is never destruction, but instead is a taking up and fresh building, even if in practice there has not always been full correspondence with this high ideal.

HUMAN FREEDOM

We know well that the conversion that is begun by the mission is a work of grace, in which man must fully find himself again.
For this reason the Church in our time attaches great importance to all that is stated by the Second Vatican Council in its "Declaration on Religious Freedom", both the first and the second part of the document. We perceive intimately that the truth revealed to us by God imposes on us an obligation. We have, in particular, a great sense of responsibili-

ty for this truth. By Christ's institution the Church is its guardian and teacher, having been endowed with a unique assistance of the Holy Spirit in order to guard and teach it in its most exact integrity. In fulfilling this mission, we look towards Christ himself, the first evangelizer, and also towards his Apostles, martyrs and confessors. The "Declaration on Religious Freedom" shows us convincingly that, when Christ and, after him, his Apostles proclaimed the truth that comes not from men but from God (« My doctrine is not my own; it comes from him who sent me » (Jn 7:16), that is the Father's), they preserved, while acting with their full force of spirit, a deep esteem for man, for his intellect, his will, his conscience and his freedom.

THE SON OF GOD UNITED HIMSELF WITH EACH MAN

When we penetrate by means of the continually and rapidly increasing experience of the human family into the mystery of Jesus Christ, we understand with greater clarity that there is at the basis of all these ways that the Church of our time must follow, in accordance with the wisdom of Pope Paul VI, one single way: it is the way that has stood the test of centuries and it is also the way of the future. Christ the Lord indicated this way especially when, as the Council teaches, « by his Incarnation, he, the Son of God, in a certain way "united himself with each man" » (GS, 22). The Church therefore sees its fundamental task in enabling that union to be brought about and renewed continually. The Church wishes to serve this single end: that each person may be able to find Christ, in order that Christ may walk with each person the path of life, with the power of the truth about man and the world that is contained in the mystery of the Incarnation and the Redemption and with the power of the love that is radiated by that truth. Against a background of the ever increasing historical processes, which seem at the present time to have results especially within the spheres of various systems, ideological concepts of the world and regimes, Jesus Christ becomes, in a way, newly present, in spite of all his apparent absences, in spite of all the limitations of the presence and of the institutional activity of the Church. Jesus Christ becomes present with the power of the truth and the love that are expressed in him with unique unrepeatable fullness, in spite of the shortness of his life on earth and the even greater shortness of his public activity.

MAN IS THE FUNDAMENTAL WAY FOR THE CHURCH

The Church cannot abandon man, for his « destiny », that is to say his election, calling, birth and death, salvation or perdition, is so closely and unbreakably linked with Christ. We are speaking precisely of each man on this planet, this earth that the Creator gave to the first man, saying to the man and the woman: « subdue it and have dominion » (Gn 1:28). Each man in all the unrepeatable reality of what he is and what he does, of his intellect and will, of his conscience and heart. Man who in his reality has, because he is a « person », a history of his life that is his own and, most important, a history of his soul that is his own. Man who, in keeping with the openness of his spirit within and also with the many diverse needs of his body and his existence in time, writes this personal history of his through numerous bonds, contacts, situations, and social structures linking him with other men, beginning to do so from the first moment of his existence on earth, from the moment of his conception and birth. Man in the full truth of his existence, of his personal being and also of his community and social being – in the sphere of his own family, in the sphere of society and very diverse contexts, in the sphere of his own nation or people (perhaps still only that of his clan or tribe), and in the sphere of the whole of mankind – this man is the primary route that the Church must travel in fulfilling her mission: "he is the primary and fundamental way for the Church", the way traced out by Christ himself, the way that leads invariably through the mystery of the Incarnation and the Redemption.

A WEAK AND SINFUL BEING

It was precisely this man in all the truth of his life, in his conscience, in his continual inclination to sin and at the same time in his continual aspiration to truth, the good, the beautiful, justice and love that the Second Vatican Council had before its eyes when, in outlining his situation in the modern world, it always passed from the external elements of this situation to the truth within humanity: « In man himself many elements wrestle with one another. Thus, on the one hand, as a creature he experiences his limitations in a multitude of ways. On the other, he feels himself to be boundless in his desires and summoned to a higher life. Pulled by manifold attractions, he is constantly forced to choose among them and to renounce some. Indeed, as a weak and sinful being, he often does what he would not, and fails to do what he would. Hence he suffers from internal divisions, and from these flow so many and such great discords in society » (GS, 10).

This man is the way for the Church – a way that, in a sense, is the basis of all the other ways that the Church must walk – because man – every man without any exception whatever – has been redeemed by Christ, and because with man – with each man without any exception whatever – Christ is in a way united, even when man is unaware of it.

THE DRAMA OF PRESENT-DAY HUMAN EXISTENCE

The man of today seems ever to be under threat from what he produces, that is to say from the result of the work of his hands and, even more so, of the work of his intellect and the tendencies of his will. All too soon, and often in an unforeseeable way, what this manifold activity of man yields is not only subjected to « alienation », in the sense that it is simply taken away from the person who produces it, but rather it turns against man himself, at least in part, through the indirect consequences of its effects returning on himself. It is or can be directed against him. This seems to make up the main chapter of the drama of present-day human existence in its broadest and universal dimension. Man therefore lives increasingly in fear. He is afraid that what he produces – not all of it, of course, or even most of it, but part of it and precisely that part which contains a special share of his genius and initiative – can radically turn against himself; he is afraid that it can become the means and instrument for an unimaginable self-destruction, compared with which all the cataclysms and catastrophes of history known to us seem to fade away. This gives rise to a question: Why is it that the power given to man from the beginning by which he was to subdue the earth turns against himself, producing an understandable state of disquiet, of conscious or unconscious fear and of menace, which in various ways is being communicated to the whole of the present-day human family and is manifesting itself under various aspects?

THE EXPLOITATION OF THE EARTH DEMANDS RATIONAL AND HONEST PLANNING

This state of menace for man from what he produces shows itself in various directions and various degrees of intensity.

We seem to be increasingly aware of the fact that the exploitation of the earth, the planet on which we are living, demands rational and honest planning.

At the same time, exploitation of the earth not only for industrial but also for military purposes and the uncontrolled development of technology outside the framework of a long-range authentically humanistic plan, often bring with them a threat to man's natural environment, alienate him in his relations with nature and remove him from nature. Man often seems to see no other meaning in his natural environment than what serves for immediate use and consumption.

Yet it was the Creator's will that man should communicate with nature as an intelligent and noble « master » and « guardian », and not as a heedless « exploiter » and « destroyer ».

THE DEVELOPMENT OF TECHNOLOGY

The development of technology and the development of contemporary civilization, which is marked by the ascendancy of technology, demand a proportional development of morals and ethics. For the present, this last development seems unfortunately to be always left behind.

Accordingly, in spite of the marvel of this progress, in which it is difficult not to see also authentic signs of man's greatness, signs that in their creative seeds were revealed to us in the pages of the Book of Genesis, as early as where it describes man's creation, this progress cannot fail to give rise to disquiet on many counts.

The first reason for disquiet concerns the essential and fundamental question: Does this progress, which has man for its author and promoter, make human life on earth « more human » in every aspect of that life? Does it make it more « worthy of man »? There can be no doubt that in various aspects it does. But the question keeps coming back with regard to what is most essential — whether in the context of this progress man, as man, is becoming truly better, that is to say more mature spiritually, more aware of the dignity of his humanity, more responsible, more open to others, especially the neediest and the weakest, and readier to give and to aid all.

This question must be put by Christians, precisely because Jesus Christ has made them so universally sensitive about the problem of man. The same question must be asked by all men, especially those belonging to the social groups that are dedicating themselves actively to development and progress today.

ESSENTIAL QUESTIONS

Do all the conquests attained until now and those projected for technological future accord with man's moral and spiritual progress? In this context is man, as man, developing and progressing or is he regressing and being degraded in his humanity? In men and « in man's world », which in itself is a world of moral good and evil, does good prevail over evil? In men and among men is there a growth of social love, of respect for the rights of others – for every man, nation and people – or on the contrary is there an increase of various degrees of selfishness, exaggerated nationalism instead of authentic love of country, and also the propensity to dominate others beyond the limits of one's legitimate rights and merits and the propensity to exploit the whole of material progress and that in the technology of production for the exclusive purpose of dominating others or of favouring this or that imperialism?

These are the essential questions that the Church is bound to ask herself, since they are being asked with greater or less explicitness by the thousands of millions of people now living in the world. The subject of development and progress is on everybody's lips and appears in the columns of all the newspapers and other publications in all the languages of the modern world. Let us not forget however that this subject contains not only affirmations and certainties but also questions and points of anguished disquiet. The latter are no less important than the former. They fit in with the dialectical nature of human knowledge and even more with the fundamental need for solicitude by man for man, for his humanity, and for the future of people on earth.

MAN'S « KINGSHIP »

Man's situation in the modern world seems indeed to be far removed from the objective demands of the moral order, from the requirements of justice, and even more of social love. We are dealing here only with that which found expression in the Creator's first message to man at the moment in which he was giving him the earth, to « subdue » it (Gn 1:28).

This first message was confirmed by Christ the Lord in the mystery of the Redemption. This is expressed by the Second Vatican Council in these beautiful chapters of its teaching that concern man's « kingship », that is to say his call to share in the kingly function – the "munus regale" – of Christ himself (LG, 10; 36). The essential meaning of this « kingship » and « dominion » of man over the visible world, which the Creator himself gave man for his task, consists in the priority of ethics over technology, in the primacy of the person over things, and in the superiority of spirit over matter.

This is why all phases of present-day progress must be followed attentively. Each stage of that progress must, so to speak, be x-rayed from this point of view. What is in question is the advancement of persons, not just the multiplying of things that people can use. It is a matter – as a contemporary philosopher has said and as the Council has stated – not so much of « having more » as of « being more ».

Indeed there is already a real perceptible danger that, while man's dominion over the world of things is making enormous advances, he should lose the essential threads of his dominion and in various ways let his humanity be subjected to the world and become himself something subject to manipulation in many ways – even if the manipulation is often not perceptible directly – through the whole of the organization of community life, through the production system and through pressure from the means of social communication.

WHO IS MAN?

Man cannot relinquish himself or the place in the visible world that belongs to him; he cannot become the slave of things, the slave of economic systems, the slave of production, the slave of his own products.

A civilization purely materialistic in outline condemns man to such slavery, even if at times, no doubt, this occurs contrary to the intentions and the very premises of its pioneers.

It is not a matter here merely of giving an abstract answer to the question: Who is man?

It is a matter of the whole of the dynamism of life and civilization.

It is a matter of the meaningfulness of the various initiatives of everyday life and also of the premises for many civilization programmes, political programmes, economic ones, social ones, state ones, and many others.

If we make bold to describe man's situation in the modern world as far removed from the objective demands of the moral order, from the exigencies of justice, and still more from social love, we do so because this is confirmed by the well-known facts and comparisons that have already on various occasions found an echo in the pages of statements by the Popes, the Council and the Synod.

CONSUMER CIVILIZATION

Man's situation today is certainly not uniform but marked with numerous differences. These differences have causes in history, but they also have strong ethical effects. Indeed everyone is familiar with the picture of the consumer civilization, which consists in a certain surplus of goods necessary for man and for entire societies — and we are dealing precisely with the rich highly developed societies — while the remaining societies — at least broad sectors of them — are suffering from hunger, with many people dying each day of starvation and malnutrition. Hand in hand go a certain abuse of freedom by one group — an abuse linked precisely with a consumer attitude uncontrolled by ethics — and a limitation by it of the freedom of the others, that is to say those suffering marked shortages and being driven to conditions of even worse misery and destitution. This pattern, which is familiar to all, and the contrast referred to, in the documents giving their teaching, by the Popes of this century, most recently by John XXIII and by Paul VI, represent, as it were, the gigantic development of the parable in the Bible of the rich banqueter and the poor man Lazarus. So widespread is the phenomenon that it brings into question the financial, monetary, productive and commercial mechanisms that, resting on various political pressures, support the world economy. These are proving incapable either of remedying the unjust social situations inherited from the past or of dealing with the urgent challenges and ethical demands of the present. By submitting man to tensions created by himself, dilapidating at an accelerated pace material and energy resources, and compromising the geophysical environment, these structures unceasingly make the areas of misery spread accompanied by anguish, frustration and bitterness.

MAN'S TRUE FREEDOM

The principle of solidarity, in a wide sense, must inspire the effective search for appropriate institutions and mechanisms, whether in the sector of trade, where the laws of healthy competition must be allowed to lead the way, or on the level of a wider and more immediate redistribution of riches and of control over them, in order that the economically developing peoples may be able not only to satisfy their essential needs but also to advance gradually and effectively.

This difficult road of the indispensable transformation of the structures of economic life is one on which it will not be easy to go forward without the intervention of a true conversion of mind, will and heart. The task requires resolute commitment by individuals and peoples that are free and linked in solidarity. All too often freedom is confused with the instinct for individual or collective interest or with the instinct for combat and domination, whatever be the ideological colours with which they are covered. Obviously these instincts exist and are operative, but no truly human economy will be possible unless they are taken up, directed and dominated by the deepest powers in man, which decide the true culture of peoples. These are the very sources for the effort which will express man's true freedom and which will be capable of ensuring it in the economic field also.

« I WAS HUNGRY »

Economic development, with every factor in its adequate functioning, must be constantly programmed and realized within a perspective of universal joint development of each individual and people, as was convincingly recalled by my Predecessor Paul VI in "Populorum Progressio". Otherwise, the category of « economic progress » becomes in isolation a superior category subordinating the whole of human existence to its partial demands, suffocating man, breaking up society, and ending by entangling itself in its own tensions and excesses.

It is possible to undertake this duty. This is testified by the certain facts and the results, which it would be difficult to mention more analytically here. However, one thing is certain: at the basis of this gigantic sector it is necessary to establish, accept and deepen the sense of moral responsibility, which man must undertake. Again and always man.

This responsibility becomes especially evident for us Christians when we recall – and we should always recall it – the scene of the last judgment according to the words of Christ related in Matthew's Gospel.

This eschatological scene must always be « applied » to man's history; it must always be made the « measure » for human acts as an essential outline for an examination of conscience by each and every one: « I was hungry and you gave me no food... » (Mt 25:42).

HUMAN RIGHTS

This century has so far been a century of great calamities for man, of great devastations, not only material ones but also moral ones, indeed perhaps above all moral ones. Admittedly it is not easy to compare one age or one century with another under this aspect, since that depends also on changing historical standards. Nevertheless, without applying these comparisons, one still cannot fail to see that this century has so far been one in which people have provided many injustices and sufferings for themselves. Has this process been decisively curbed? In any case, we cannot fail to recall at this point, with esteem and profound hope for the future, the magnificent effort made to give life to the United Nations Organization, an effort conducive to the definition and establishment of man's objective and inviolable rights, with the member States obliging each other to observe them rigorously. This commitment has been accepted and ratified by almost all present-day States, and this should constitute a guarantee that human rights will become throughout the world a fundamental principle of work for man's welfare.

There is no need for the Church to confirm how closely this problem is linked with her mission in the modern world. After all, peace comes down to respect for man's inviolable rights – "Opus iustitiæ pax" – while war springs from the violation of these rights and brings with it still graver violations of them. If human rights are violated in time of peace, this is particularly painful and from the point of view of progress it represents an incomprehensible manifestation of activity directed against man, which can in no way be reconciled with any programme that describes itself as « humanistic ».

THE WELFARE OF MAN

The Declaration of Human Rights linked with the setting up of the United Nations Organization certainly had as its aim not only to depart from the horrible experiences of the last world war but also to create the basis for continual revision of programmes, systems and regimes precisely from this single fundamental point of view, namely the welfare of man – or, let us say, of the person in the community – which must, as a fundamental factor in the common good, constitute the essential criterion for all programmes, systems and regimes. If the opposite happens, human life is, even in time of peace, condemned to various sufferings and, along with these sufferings, there is a development of various forms of domination, totalitarianism, neocolonialism and imperialism, which are a threat also to the harmonious living together of the nations. Indeed, it is a significant fact, repeatedly confirmed by the experiences of history, that violation of the rights of man goes hand in hand with violation of the rights of the nation, with which man is united by organic links as with a larger family.

Already in the first half of this century, when various State totalitarianisms were developing, which, as is well known, led to the horrible catastrophe of war, the Church clearly outlined her position with regard to these regimes that to all appearances were acting for a higher good, namely the good of the State, while history was to show instead that the good in question was only that of a certain party, which had been identified with the State.

THE COMMON GOOD OF SOCIETY

The essential sense of the State, as a political community, consists in that the society and people composing it are master and sovereign of their own destiny. This sense remains unrealized if, instead of the exercise of power with the moral participation of the society or people, what we see is the imposition of power by a certain group upon all the other members of the society. This is essential in the present age, with its enormous increase in people's social awareness and the accompanying need for the citizens to have a right share in the political life of the community, while taking account of the real conditions of each people and the necessary vigour of public authority. These therefore are questions of primary importance from the point of view of the progress of man himself and the overall development of his humanity.

The Church has always taught the duty to act for the common good and, in so doing, has likewise educated good citizens for each State. Furthermore, she has always taught that the fundamental duty of power is solicitude for the common good of society; this is what gives power its fundamental rights. Precisely in the name of these premises of the objective ethical order, the rights of power can only be understood on the basis of respect for the objective and inviolable rights of man. The common good that authority in the State serves is brought to full realization only when all the citizens are sure of their rights. The lack of this leads to the dissolution of society, opposition by citizens to authority, or a situation of oppression, intimidation, violence, and terrorism, of which many exemples have been provided by the totalitarianisms of this century.

THE RIGHT TO RELIGIOUS FREEDOM

These rights are rightly reckoned to include the right to religious freedom together with the right to freedom of conscience. The Second Vatican Council considered especially necessary the preparation of a fairly long declaration on this subject. This is the document called "Dignitatis Humanæ", in which is expressed not only the theological concept of the question but also the concept reached from the point of view of natural law, that is to say from the « purely human » position, on the basis of the premises given by man's own experience, his reason and his sense of human dignity. Certainly the curtailment of the religious freedom of individuals and communities is not only a painful experience but it is above all an attack on man's very dignity, independently of the religion professed or of the concept of the world which these individuals and communities have. The curtailment and violation of religious freedom are in contrast with man's dignity and his objective rights. The Council document mentioned above states clearly enough what that curtailment or violation of religious freedom is. In this case we are undoubtedly confronted with a radical injustice with regard to what is particularly deep within man, what is authentically human. Indeed, even the phenomenon of unbelief, a-religiousness and atheism, as a human phenomenon, is understood only in relation to the phenomenon of religion and faith. It is therefore difficult, even from a « purely human » point of view, to accept a position that gives only atheism the right of citizenship in public and social life, while believers are, as though by principle, barely tolerated or are treated as second-class citizens or are even – and this has already happened – entirely deprived of the rights of citizenship.

THE CHURCH HAS ONLY ONE LIFE

This necessarily brief look at man's situation in the modern world makes us direct our thoughts and our hearts to Jesus Christ, and to the mystery of the Redemption, in which the question of man is inscribed with a special vigour of truth and love. If

Christ « united himself with each man », the Church lives more profoundly her own nature and mission by penetrating into the depths of this mystery and into its rich universal language. It was not without reason that the Apostle speaks of Christ's Body, the Church. If this Mystical Body of Christ is God's People – as the Second Vatican Council was to say later on the basis of the whole of the biblical and patristic tradition – this means that in it each man receives within himself that breath of life that comes from Christ. In this way, turning to man and his real problems, his hopes and sufferings, his achievements and falls – this too also makes the Church as a body, an organism, a social unit, perceive the same divine influences, the light and strength of the Spirit that come from the crucified and risen Christ, and it is for this very reason that she lives her life. The Church has only one life: that which is given her by her Spouse and Lord. Indeed, precisely because Christ united himself with her in his mystery of Redemption, the Church must be strongly united with each man.

« THE NEW MAN »

This union of Christ with man is in itself a mystery. From the mystery is born « the new man », called to become a partaker of God's life (2 Pt 1:4), and newly created in Christ for the fullness of grace and truth. Christ's union with man is power and the source of power, as Saint John stated so incisively in the prologue of his Gospel: « (The Word) gave power to become children of God » (Jn 1:12). Man is transformed inwardly by this power as the source of a new life that does not disappear and pass away but lasts to eternal life. This life, which the Father has promised and offered to each man in Jesus

Christ, his eternal and only Son, who, « when the time had fully come », became incarnate and was born of the Virgin Mary, is the final fulfilment of man's vocation. It is in a way the fulfilment of the « destiny » that God has prepared for him from eternity. This « divine destiny » is advancing, in spite of all the enigmas, the unsolved riddles, the twists and turns of « human destiny » in the world of time. Indeed, while all this, in spite of all the riches of life in time, necessarily and inevitably leads to the frontier of death and the goal of the destruction of the human body, beyond that goal we see Christ. « I am the resurrection and the life, he who believes in me... shall never die » (Jn 11:25-26).

« THE EYES
OF CHRIST HIMSELF »

In Jesus Christ, who was crucified and laid in the tomb and then rose again, « our hope of resurrection dawned... the bright promise of immortality », on the way to which man, through the death of the body, shares with the whole of visible creation the necessity to which matter is subject. We intend and are trying to fathom ever more deeply the language of the truth that man's Redeemer enshrined in the phrase « It is the spirit that gives life, the flesh is of no avail » (Jn 6:63). In spite of appearances, these words express the highest affirmation of man – the affirmation of the body given life by the Spirit. The Church lives these realities, she lives by this truth about man, which enables him to go beyond the bounds of temporariness and at the same time to think with particular love and solicitude of everything within the dimensions of this temporariness that affect man's life and the life of the human spirit, in which is expressed that never-ending restlessness referred to in the words of Saint Augustine: « You made us for yourself, Lord, and our heart is restless until it rests in you ». In this creative restlessness beats and pulsates what is most deeply human – the search for truth, the insatiable need for the good, hunger for freedom, nostalgia for the beautiful, and the voice of conscience. Seeking to see man as it were with « the eyes of Christ himself », the Church becomes more and more aware that she is the guardian of a great treasure, which she may not waste but must continually increase. Indeed, the Lord Jesus said: « He who does not gather with me scatters » (Mt 12:30). This treasure of humanity enriched by the inexpressible mystery of divine filiation and by the grace of « adoption as sons » (Gal 4:5) in the Only Son of God, through whom we call God « Abba, Father », (Gal 4:6), is also a powerful force unifying the Church above all inwardly and giving meaning to all her activity.

SIGN OF INTIMATE UNION WITH GOD

The appeal to the Spirit, intended precisely to obtain the Spirit, is the answer to all the « materialisms » of our age. It is these materialisms that give birth to so many forms of insatiability in the human heart. This appeal is making itself heard on various sides and seems to be bearing fruit also in different ways. Can it be said that the Church is not alone in making this appeal? Yes it can, because the « need » for what is spiritual is expressed also by people who are outside the visible confines of the Church. Is not this confirmed by the truth concerning the Church that the recent Council so acutely emphasized at the point in the Dogmatic Constitution "Lumen Gentium" where it teaches that the Church is a « sacrament or sign and means of intimate union with God, and of the unity of all mankind » (LG, 1)? This invocation addressed to the Spirit to obtain the Spirit is really a constant selfinsertion into the full magnitude of the mystery of the Redemption, in which Christ, united with the Father and with each man, continually communicates to us the Spirit who places within us the sentiments of the Son and directs us towards the Father.

« THE SON OF MAN CAME TO SERVE »

This is why the Church of our time — a time particularly hungry for the Spirit, because it is hungry for justice, peace, love, goodness, fortitude, responsibility, and human dignity — must concentrate and gather around that Mystery, finding in it the light and the strength that are indispensable for her mission. For if, as was already said, man is the way for the Church's daily life, the Church must be always aware of the dignity of the divine adoption received by man in Christ through the grace of the Holy Spirit and of his destination to grace and glory. By reflecting ever anew on all this, and by accepting it with a faith that is more and more aware and a love that is more and more firm, the Church also makes herself better fitted for the service to man to which Christ the Lord calls her when he says: « The Son of man came not to be served but to serve » (Mt 20:28). The Church performs this ministry by sharing in the « triple office » belonging to her Master and Redeemer. This teaching, with its biblical foundation, was brought fully to the fore by the Second Vatican

Council, to the great advantage of the Church's life. For when we become aware that we share in Christ's triple mission, his triple office as priest, as prophet and as king, we also become more aware of what must receive service from the whole of the Church as the society and community of the People of God on earth, and we likewise understand how each one of us must share in this mission and service.

THE CHURCH
AS RESPONSIBLE FOR TRUTH

In the light of the sacred teaching of the Second Vatican Council, the Church appears before us as the social subject of responsibility for divine truth. With deep emotion we hear Christ himself saying: « The word you hear is not mine; it comes from the Father who sent me » (Jn 14:24). In this affirmation by our Master do we not notice responsibility for the revealed truth, which is the « property » of God himself, since even he, « the only Son », who lives « in the bosom of the Father » (Jn 1:18), when transmitting that truth as a prophet and teacher, feels the need to stress that he is acting in full fidelity to its divine source? The same fidelity must be a constitutive quality of the Church's faith, both when she is teaching it and when she is professing it. Faith as a specific supernatural virtue infused into the human spirit makes us sharers in knowledge of God as a response to his revealed word. Therefore it is required, when the Church professes and teaches the faith, that she should adhere strictly to divine truth, and should translate it into living attitudes of « obedience in harmony with reason ». Christ himself, concerned for this fidelity to divine truth, promised the Church the special assistance of the Spirit of truth, gave the gift of infallibility to those whom he entrusted with the mandate of transmitting and teaching that truth — as has besides been clearly defined by the First Vatican Council and has then been repeated by the Second Vatican Council — and he furthermore endowed the whole of the People of God with a special sense of the faith.

Consequently, we have become sharers in this mission of the prophet Christ, and in virtue of that mission we together with him are serving divine truth in the Church. Being responsible for that truth also means loving it and seeking the most exact understanding of it, in order to bring it closer to ourselves and others in all its saving power, its splendour and its profundity joined with simplicity.

THE FUNDAMENTAL UNITY IN THE TEACHING OF FAITH

As in preceding ages, and perhaps more than in preceding ages, theologians and all men of learning in the Church are today called to unite faith with learning and wisdom, in order to help them to combine with each other. This task has grown enormously today because of the advance of human learning, its methodology, and the achievements in knowledge of the world and of man. This concerns both the exact sciences and the human sciences, as well as philosophy, which, as the Second Vatican Council recalled, is closely linked with theology (GS, 44).

In this field of human knowledge, which is continually being broadened and yet differentiated, faith too must be investigated deeply, manifesting the magnitude of revealed mystery and tending towards an understanding of truth, which has in God its one supreme source. If it is permissible and even desirable that the enormous work to be done in this direction should take into consideration a certain pluralism of methodology, the work cannot however depart from the fundamental unity in the teaching of Faith and Morals which is that work's end. Accordingly, close collaboration by theology with the Magisterium is indispensable. Every theologian must be particularly aware of what Christ himself stated when he said: « The word you hear is not mine; it comes from the Father who sent me » (Jn 14:24). Nobody, therefore, can make of theology as it were a simple collection of his own personal ideas, but everybody must be aware of being in close union with the mission of teaching truth for which the Church is responsible.

CATECHESIS

Catechesis constitutes a permanent and also fundamental form of activity by the Church, one in which her prophetic charism is manifested: witnessing and teaching go hand in hand. And although here we are speaking in the first place of priests, it is however impossible not to mention also the great number of men and women religious dedicating themselves to catechetical activity for love of the divine Master. Finally, it would be difficult not to mention the many lay people who find expression in this activity for their faith and their apostolic responsibility.

Furthermore, increasing care must be taken that the various forms of catechesis and its various fields – beginning with the fundamental field, family catechesis, that is the catechesis by parents of their children – should give evidence of the universal

WORDS OF APPRECIATION TO THE SOCIETY FOR THE PROPAGATION OF THE FAITH IN THE UNITED STATES

"I thank you for your partnership in the Gospel, for your sustained efforts in making the name of Jesus ever better known and loved.

"With your help the work of Jesus goes on; Jesus is present with his people, 'teaching and preaching the Gospel of the Kingdom and healing every disease and every infirmity.'"

—Pope John Paul II
Rome, April 24, 1981

THE SOCIETY FOR THE PROPAGATION OF THE FAITH

**1011 First Avenue
New York, N.Y. 10022
Rev. Thomas Modugno
ARCHDIOCESAN DIRECTOR**

"Remember me
always in your prayers!"

— Joannes Paulus pp. II

sharing by the whole of the People of God in the prophetic office of Christ himself. Linked with this fact, the Church's responsibility for divine truth must be increasingly shared in various ways by all. What shall we say at this point with regard to the specialists in the various disciplines, those who represent the natural sciences and letters, doctors, jurists, artists and technicians, teachers at various levels and with different specializations? As members of the People of God, they all have their own part to play in Christ's prophetic mission and service of divine truth, among other ways by an honest attitude towards truth, whatever field it may belong to, while educating others in truth and teaching them to mature in love and justice. Thus, a sense of responsibility for truth is one of the fundamental points of encounter between the Church and each man and also one of the fundamental demands determining man's vocation in the community of the Church.

« A ROYAL PRIESTHOOD »

By celebrating and also partaking of the Eucharist we unite ourselves with Christ on earth and in heaven who intercedes for us with the Father but we always do so through the redeeming act of his Sacrifice, through which he has redeemed us, so that we have been « bought with a price » (1 Cor 6:20). The « price » of our redemption is likewise a further proof of the value that God himself sets on man and of our dignity in Christ. For by becoming « children of God » (Jn 1:12), adopted sons, we also become in his likeness « a kingdom of priests » and obtain « a royal priesthood » (Rv 5:10; 1 Pt 2:9), that is to say we share in that unique and irreversible restoration of man and the world to the Father that was carried out once for all by him, who is both the eternal Son and also true Man. The Eucharist is the Sacrament in which our new being is most completely expressed and in which Christ himself unceasingly and in an ever new manner « bears witness » in the Holy Spirit to our spirit that each of us, as a sharer in the mystery of the Redemption, has access to the fruits of the filial reconciliation with God that he himself actuated and continually actuates among us by means of the Church's ministry.

THE EUCHARIST BUILDS THE CHURCH

It is an essential truth, not only of doctrine but also of life, that the Eucharist builds the Church, building it as the authentic community of the People of God, as the assembly of the faithful, bearing the same mark of unity that was shared by the Apostles and the first disciples of the Lord. The Eucharist builds ever anew this community and unity, ever building and regenerating it on the basis of the Sacrifice of Christ, since it commemorates his death on the Cross, the price by which he redeemed us. Accordingly, in the Eucharist we touch in a way the very mystery of the Body and Blood of the Lord, as is attested by the very words used at its institution, the words with which those called to this ministry in the Church unceasingly celebrate the Eucharist.

THE CHURCH
LIVES BY THE EUCHARIST

The Church lives by the Eucharist, by the fullness of this Sacrament, the stupendous content and meaning of which have often been expressed in the

Church's Magisterium from the most distant times down to our own days. However, we can say with certainty that, although this teaching is sustained by the acuteness of theologians, by men of deep faith and prayer, and by ascetics and mystics, in complete fidelity to the Eucharistic mystery, it still reaches no more than the threshold, since it is incapable of grasping and translating into words what the Eucharist is in all its fullness, what is expressed by it and what is actuated by it. Indeed, the Eucharist is the ineffable Sacrament! The essential commitment and, above all, the visible grace and source of supernatural strength for the Church as the People of God is to persevere and advance constantly in Eucharistic life and Eucharistic piety and to develop spiritually in the climate of the Eucharist.

THE MOST PROFOUND REVELATION OF THE HUMAN BROTHERHOOD

Eucharist is at one and at the same time a Sacrifice-Sacrament, a Communion-Sacrament, and a Presence-Sacrament. And, although it is true that the Eucharist always was and must continue to be the most profound revelation of the human brotherhood of Christ's disciples and confessors, it cannot be treated merely as an « occasion » for manifesting this brotherhood. When celebrating the Sacrament of the Body and Blood of the Lord, the full magnitude of the divine mystery must be respected, as must the full meaning of this sacramental sign in which Christ is really present and is received, the soul is filled with grace and the pledge of future glory is given. This is the source of the duty to carry out rigorously the liturgical rules and everything that is a manifestation of community worship offered to God himself, all the more so because in this sacramental sign he entrusts himself to us with limitless trust, as if not taking into consideration our human weakness, our unworthiness, the force of habit, routine, or even the possibility of insult. Every member of the Church, especially Bishops and Priests, must be vigilant in seeing that this Sacrament of love shall be at the centre of the life of the People of God, so that through all the manifestations of worship due to it Christ shall be given back « love for love » and truly become « the life of our souls » (Jn 6:51, 57). Nor can we, on the other hand, ever forget the following words of Saint Paul: « Let a man examine himself, and so eat of the bread and drink of the cup » (1 Cor 11:28).

« GO, AND DO NOT SIN AGAIN »

The Christ who calls to the Eucharistic banquet is always the same Christ who exhorts us to penance and repeats his « Repent ». Without this constant ever renewed endeavour for conversion, partaking of the Eucharist would lack its full redeeming effectiveness and here would be a loss or at least a weakening of the special readiness to offer God the spiritual sacrifice in which our sharing in the priesthood of Christ is expressed in an essential and universal manner. In Christ, priesthood is linked with his Sacrifice, his self-giving to the Father; and, precisely because it is without limit, that self-giving gives rise in us human beings subject to numerous limitations to the need to turn to God in an ever more mature way and with a constant, ever more profound conversion.

In the last years much has been done to high-light in the Church's practice — in conformity with the most ancient tradition of the Church — the community aspect of penance and especially of the sacrament of Penance. We cannot however forget that conversion is a particularly profound inward act in which the individual cannot be replaced by others and cannot make the community be a substitute for him. Although the participation by the fraternal community of the faithful in the penitential celebration is a great help for the act of personal conversion, nevertheless, in the final analysis, it is necessary that in this act there should be a pronouncement by the individual himself with the whole depth of his conscience and with the whole of his sense of guilt and of trust in God, placing himself like the Psalmist before God to confess: « Against you... have I sinned » (Ps 50 [51]:6). In faithfully observing the centuries-old practice of the Sacrament of Penance – the practice of individual confession with a personal act of sorrow and the intention to amend and make satisfaction – the Church is therefore defending the human soul's individual right: man's right to a more personal encounter with the crucified forgiving Christ, with Christ saying, through the minister of the sacrament of Reconciliation: « Your sins are forgiven » (Mk 2:5); « Go, and do not sin again » (Jn 8:11).

THE CHURCH OF THE DIVINE MISSION

By guarding the sacrament of Penance, the Church expressly affirms her faith in the mistery of the Redemption as a living and life-giving reality that fits in with man's inward truth, with human guilt and also with the desires of the human conscience. « Blessed are those who hunger and thirst for righteousness, for they shall be satisfied » (Mt 5:6). The sacrament of Penance is the means to satisfy man with the righteousness that comes from the Redeemer himself.

In the Church, gathering particularly today in a special way around the Eucharist and desiring that the authentic Eucharistic community should become a sign of the gradually maturing unity of all Christians, there must be a lively-felt need for penance, both in its sacramental aspect, and in what concerns penance as a virtue. This second aspect was expressed by Paul VI in the Apostolic Constitution "Paenitemini". One of the Church's tasks is to put into practice the teaching "Paenitemini" contains; this subject must be investigated more deeply by us in common reflection, and many more decisions must be made about it in a spirit of pastoral collegiality and with respect for the different traditions in this regard and the different circumstances of the lives of the people of today. Nevertheless, it is certain that the Church of the new Advent, the Church that is continually preparing for the new coming of the Lord, must be the Church of the Eucharist and of Penance. Only when viewed in this spiritual aspect of her life and activity is she seen to be the Church of the divine mission, the Church "in statu missionis", as the Second Vatican Council has shown her to be.

CHRIST'S MYSTICAL BODY

In building up from the very foundations the picture of the Church as the People of God — by showing the threefold mission of Christ himself, through participation in which we become truly God's People — the Second Vatican Council high-lighted, among other characteristics of the Christian vocation, the one that can be described as « kingly ». One element seems to stand out in the midst of all: the sharing in Christ's kingly mission, that is to say the fact of rediscovering in oneself and others the special dignity of our vocation that can be described as « kingship ». This dignity is expressed in readiness to serve, in keeping with the example of Christ, who « came not to be served but to serve » (Mt 20:28). If, in the light of this attitude of Christ's, « being a king » is truly possible only by « being a servant », then « being a servant » also demands so much spiritual maturity that it must really be described as « being a king ». In order to be able to serve others worthily and effectively we must be able to master ourselves, possess the virtues that make this mastery possible. Our sharing in Christ's kingly mission — his « kingly function » (munus) — is closely linked with every sphere of both Christian and human morality.

In presenting the complete picture of the People of God and recalling the place among that people held not only by priests but also by the laity, not only by the representatives of the Hierarchy but also by those of the Institutes of Consecrated Life, the Second Vatican Council did not deduce this picture merely from a sociological premise. The Church as a human society can of course be examined and described according to the categories used by the sciences with regard to any human society. But these categories are not enough. For the whole of the community of the People of God and for each member of it what is in question is not just a specific « social membership »; rather, for each and every one what is essential is a particular « vocation ». Indeed, the Church as the People of God is also — according to the teaching of Saint Paul mentioned above, of which Pius XII reminded us in wonderful terms — « Christ's Mystical Body ».

THE COMMUNITY OF THE PEOPLE OF GOD

If we wish to keep in mind the community of the People of God, which is so vast and so extremely differentiated, we must see first and foremost Christ saying in a way to each member of the community: « Follow me » (Jn 1:43). It is the community of the disciples, each of whom in a different way – at times very consciously and consistently, at other times not very consciously and very inconsistently – is following Christ. This shows also the deeply « personal » aspect and dimension of this society, which, in spite of all the deficiencies of its community life – in the human meaning of this word – is a community precisely because all its members form it together with Christ himself, at least because they bear in their souls the indelible mark of a Christian.

The Second Vatican Council devoted very special attention to showing how this « ontological » community of disciples and confessors must increasingly become, even from the « human » point of view, a community aware of its own life and activity. We must however always keep in mind the truth that every initiative serves true renewal in the Church and helps to bring the authentic light that is Christ insofar as the initiative is based on adequate awareness of the individual Christian's vocation and of responsibility for this singular, unique and unrepeatable grace by which each Christian in the community of the People of God builds up the Body of Christ. This principle, the key rule for the whole of Christian practice – apostolic and pastoral practice, practice of interior and of social life – must with due proportion be applied to the whole of humanity and to each human being.

FIDELITY TO ONE'S VOCATION

The fidelity to the vocation received from God through Christ involves the joint responsibility for the Church for which the Second Vatican Council wishes to educate all Christians. Indeed, in the Church as the community of the People of God under the guidance of the Holy Spirit's working, each member has « his own special gift », as Saint Paul teaches (1 Cor 7:7).

Although this « gift » is a personal vocation and a form of participation in the Church's saving work, it also serves others, builds the Church and the fraternal communities in the various spheres of human life on earth.

Fidelity to one's vocation, that is to say persevering readiness for « kingly service », has particular significance for these many forms of building, especially with regard to the more exigent tasks, which have more influence on the life of our neighbour and of the whole of society. Married people must be distinguished for fidelity to their vocation, as is demanded by the indissoluble nature of the sacramental institution of marriage. Priests must be distinguished for a similar fidelity to their vocation, in view of the indelible character that the sacrament of Orders stamps on their souls. In receiving this sacrament, we in the Latin Church knowingly and freely commit ourselves to live in celibacy, and each one of us must therefore do all he can, with God's grace, to be thankful for this gift and faithful to the bond that he has accepted for ever.

He must do so as married people must, for they must endeavour with all their strength to persevere in their matrimonial union, building up the family community through this witness of love and educating new generations of men and women, capable in their turn of dedicating the whole of their lives to their vocation, that is to say to the « kingly service » of which Jesus Christ has offered us the example and the most beautiful model.

THE BEST USE OF FREEDOM IS CHARITY

Mature humanity means full use of the gift of freedom received from the Creator when he called to existence the man made « in his image, after his likeness ». This gift finds its full realization in the unreserved giving of the whole of one's human person, in a spirit of the love of a spouse, to Christ and, with Christ, to all those to whom he sends men and women totally consecrated to him in accordance with the evangelical counsels. This is the ideal of the religious life, which has been undertaken by the Orders and Congregations both ancient and recent, and by the Secular Institutes. Nowadays it is sometimes held, though wrongly, that freedom is an end in itself, that each human being is free when he makes use of freedom as he wishes, and that this must be our aim in the lives of individuals and societies. In reality, freedom is a great gift only when we know how to use it consciously for everything that is our true good. Christ teaches us that the best use of freedom is charity, which takes concrete form in self-giving and in service. For this « freedom Christ has set us free » (Gal 5:1) and ever continues to set us free. The Church draws from this source the unceasing inspiration, the call and the drive for her mission and her service among all mankind. The full truth about human freedom is indelibly inscribed on the mystery of the Redemption. The Church truly serves mankind when she guards this truth with untiring attention, fervent love and mature commitment and when in the whole of her own community she transmits it and gives it concrete form in human life through each Christian's fidelity to his vocation.

THE CHURCH IS A MOTHER

The Church, uniting herself with all the riches of the mystery of the Redemption, becomes the Church of living people, living because given life from within by the working of « the Spirit of truth » (Jn 16:13) and visited by the love that the Holy Spirit has poured into our hearts. The aim of any service in the Church, whether the service is apostolic, pastoral, priestly or episcopal, is to keep up this dynamic link between the mystery of the Redemption and every man.

If we are aware of this task, then we seem to understand better what it means to say that the Church is a mother and also what it means to say that the Church always, and particularly at our time, has need of a Mother. We owe a debt of special gratitude to the Fathers of the Second Vatican Council, who expressed this truth in the Constitution "Lumen Gentium" with the rich mariological doctrine contained in it. Since Paul VI, inspired by that teaching, proclaimed the Mother of Christ « Mother of the Church », and that title has become known far and wide, may it be permitted to his unworthy Successor to turn to Mary as Mother of the Church at the close of these reflections which it was opportune to make at the beginning of his papal service. Mary is Mother of the Church because, on account of the Eternal Father's ineffable choice and due to the Spirit of Love's special action, she gave human life to the Son of God, « for whom and by whom all things exist » (Heb 2:10) **and from whom the whole of the People of God receives the grace and dignity of election. Her Son explicitly extended his Mother's maternity — in a way that could easily be understood by every soul and every heart — by designating, when he was raised on the Cross, his beloved disciple as her son.**

UNIQUE AND UNREPEATABLE MOTHERHOOD

All the generations of disciples, of those who confess and love Christ, like the Apostle John, spiritually took this Mother to their own homes, and she was thus included in the history of salvation and in the Church's mission from the very beginning, that is from the moment of the Annunciation. Accordingly, we who form today's generation of disciples of Christ, all wish to unite ourselves with her in a special way. We do so with all our attachment to our ancient tradition and also with full respect and love for the members of all the Christian Communities.

We do so at the urging of the deep need of faith, hope and charity. For if we feel a special need, in this difficult and responsible phase of the history of the Church and of mankind, to turn to Christ, who is Lord of the Church and Lord of man's history on account of the mystery of the Redemption, we believe that nobody else can bring us as Mary can into the divine and human dimension of this mystery. Nobody has been brought into it by God himself as Mary has. It is in this that the exceptional character of the grace of the divine Motherhood consists. Not only is the dignity of this Motherhood unique and unrepeatable in the history of the human race, but Mary's participation, due to this Maternity, in God's plan for man's salvation through the mystery of the Redemption is also unique in profundity and range of action.

We can say that the mystery of the Redemption took shape beneath the heart of the Virgin of Nazareth when she pronounced her « fiat ». From then on, under the special influence of the Holy Spirit, this heart, the heart of both a virgin and a mother, has always followed the work of her Son and has gone out to all those whom Christ has embraced and continues to embrace with inexhaustible love. For that reason her heart must also have the inexhaustibility of a mother.

The special characteristic of the motherly love that the Mother of God inserts in the mystery of the Redemption and the life of the Church finds expression in its exceptional closeness to man and all that happens to him.

«APART FROM ME YOU CAN DO NOTHING»

The Father's eternal love, which has been manifested in the history of mankind through the Son whom the Father gave, « that whoever believes in him should not perish but have eternal life » (Jn 3:16), comes close to each of us through this Mother and thus takes on tokens that are of more easy understanding and access by each person. Consequently, Mary must be on all the ways for the Church's daily life. Through her maternal presence the Church acquires certainty that she is truly living the life of her Master and Lord and that she is living the mystery of the Redemption in all its life-giving profundity and fullness. Likewise the Church, which has struck root in many varied fields of the life of the whole of present-day humanity, also acquires the certainty and, one could say, the experience of being close to man, to each person, of being each person's Church, the Church of the People of God.

Faced with these tasks that appear along the ways for the Church, those ways that Pope Paul VI clearly indicated in the first Encyclical of his pontificate, and aware of the absolute necessity of all these ways and also of the difficulties thronging them, we feel all the more our need for a profound link with Christ. We hear within us, as a resounding echo, the words that he spoke: « Apart from me you can do nothing » (Jn 15:5). We feel not only the need but even a categorical imperative for great, intense and growing prayer by all the Church. Only prayer can prevent all these great succeeding tasks and difficulties from becoming a source of crisis and make them instead the occasion and, as it were, the foundation for ever more mature achievements on the People of God's march towards the Promised Land.

THE EUCHARISTIC MEAL

« He who feeds on my flesh and drinks my blood has life eternal » (Jn 6:54). In instituting the Eucharist on the eve of his death, Christ wanted to give the Church a food that would continually nourish it and have it live the same life as the Risen One.

Some time before the institution, Jesus had announced this meal, the only one of its kind. In the Jewish religion there were not lacking sacred meals which were eaten in the presence of God and manifested the joy of divine favour. Jesus goes beyond all this: now it is he, in his flesh and blood, who becomes food and drink for mankind. "In the Eucharistic meal, man feeds on God".

When for the first time Jesus announces this food, he arouses the amazement of his listeners, who do not come to grasp such a high divine plan. Jesus therefore strongly emphasizes the objective truth of his words, affirming the necessity of the Eucharistic meal: « Let me solemnly assure you, if you do not eat the flesh of the Son of Man and drink his blood, you have no life in you » (Jn 6:53). It is not a question of a purely spiritual meal, in which the expressions « eat the flesh » of Christ and « drink his blood » would be vested with a metaphorical meaning. It is a true meal, as Jesus forcefully defines: « My flesh is real food and my blood real drink » (Jn 6:55). This food, moreover, is no less necessary to the development of the divine life in the faithful than material food is for the preservation and development of bodily life. "The Eucharist is not a luxury" offered to those who would want to live more intimately united with Christ: it is a necessity of Christian life. This necessity was understood by the disciples since, according to the testimony of the Acts of the Apostles, in the early times of the Church the « breaking of bread », that is, the Eucharistic meal, was practised every day in the homes of the faithful « with exultant and sincere hearts » (Acts 2:46).

GUARANTEE OF RESURRECTION

In the promise of the Eucharist, Jesus explains why this food is necessary: « I am the bread of life », he declares (Jn 6:48). « Just as the Father who has life sent me and I have life because of the Father, so the man who feeds on me will have life because of me » (Jn 6:57). The Father is the first source of life: this life he has given to the Son, who in turn communicates it to mankind. He who feeds on Christ in the

Eucharist does not have to wait until the hereafter to receive eternal life: he already possesses it on earth, and in it he possesses the guarantee of the resurrection of the body at the end of the world: « He who feeds on my flesh and drinks my blood has life eternal and I will raise him up on the last day » (Jn 6:54).

This guarantee of resurrection comes from the fact that the flesh of the Son of Man given as food "is his body in its glorious risen state". Those who heard the promise of the Eucharist did not accept this truth: they thought Jesus wanted to speak of his flesh in the state of its earthly life, and they therefore showed great repugnance for the announced meal. The Master corrects their way of thinking, making it definite that it is a question of the flesh of the Son of Man « ascended to where he was before » (Jn 6:62), that is, in the triumphant state of his ascension into heaven. This glorious body is filled with the life of the Holy Spirit, and this is why he can sanctify men who feed on it and give them the pledge of eternal glory.

In the Eucharist, therefore, we receive the life of the Risen Christ. In fact, when the sacrifice is effected sacramentally on the altar, there is made present not only the mystery of the Saviour's Passion and Death, but also the mystery of the Resurrection, in which the sacrifice finds its crowning. The Eucharistic celebration has us participate in the redemptive offering, but also in the triumphant life of the Risen Christ. This is the reason for the atmosphere of joy that characterizes every Eucharistic liturgy. Although commemorating the drama of Calvary, marked at one time by immense sadness, the priest and the faithful rejoice in uniting their offering to Christ's, because at the same time they can live the mystery of the Resurrection, inseparable from this offering.

« THIS IS MY BODY, WHICH IS FOR YOU »

« I received from the Lord what I handed on to you » (1 Cor 11:23). The testimony of Paul is the testimony of the other Apostles: they handed on what they received. And like them, their successors also faithfully continued to hand on what they had received.

From generation to generation, from century to century, without any break in continuity up to today.

And what the Apostles have handed on to us is Christ himself and his commandment to repeat and to hand down to all peoples what he, the Divine Master, said and did at the Last Supper: « This is my body, which is for you » (1 Cor 11:24). Having become part of a tradition which has lasted almost two thousand years, today we too repeat the act of the « breaking of bread ».

« This is my body, which is for you ». How can we not feel a profound thrill in our soul at the thought that in pronouncing that « you », Christ intended to refer "also to each one of us" and that he offered himself to death for each one of us?

And how can we not feel intimately moved at the thought that « offering of his own body » for us is not a long-ago act, committed to the cold pages of historical chronicles, "but it is an event that is still alive" even now, "although in an unbloody way", in the Sacrament of the Body and Blood, placed on the table of the altar? Christ returns to offer his Body and his Blood for us now, so that the purifying wave of divine "mercy" may spread once more over the "misery" of our condition as sinners, and that the seed of "immortal life" may be placed in the frailty of our "mortal" flesh.

THE LIVING BREAD

« I am the living bread come down from heaven, says the Lord; he who eats of this bread will live for ever ». Who does not want to live for ever? Is this not perhaps the deepest aspiration which pulses in the heart of every human being? But it is the aspiration which daily experience belies brutally and unappealably.

Why? The answer is given to us in the word of Scripture: « Sin entered into the world and with sin death » (Rom 5:12). So, is there no more hope for us? There is no hope as long as sin dominates; but hope can be reborn once sin is conquered. And this is precisely what has happened with the redemption by Christ. In fact, it is written: « If death began its reign through one man because of his offense, much more shall those who receive the overflowing grace and gift of justice live and reign through one man, Jesus Christ » (Rom 5:17). This is why Jesus says, « Whoever eats of this bread will live for ever ». Under the appearances of that bread he is present in person, the conqueror of sin and death, the Risen One! Whoever nourishes himself with that divine food, besides finding the strength to overcome within himself the suggestions of evil along the path of life, will also receive with it "the pledge of definitive victory over death" – « the last enemy to be destroyed is death » as the Apostle Paul says (1 Cor 15:26) – so that God can be « all in all » (1 Cor 15:28).

By reflecting on this mistery, how much one can understand the jealous love with which the Church guards this treasure of inestimable value! And how logical and natural it seems that Christians, during the course of their history, have felt the need to express, "even externally", their joy and gratitude for the reality of such a great gift.

THE TEMPLE OF THE HOLY SPIRIT

St Paul calls the human body « a temple of the Holy Spirit ». He writes: « Do you not know that your body is a temple of the Holy Spirit within you, which you have from God? You are not your own; you were bought with a price » (1 Cor 6:19-20). The Apostle points out the mistery of the « redemption of the body », carried out by Christ, as a source of a special moral duty wich commits the Christian to purity, to what Paul himself defines elsewhere as the necessity of « controlling his own body in holiness and honour » (1 Thes 4:4). However, we would not completely discover the riches of the thought contained in the Pauline texts, if we did not note that the mystery of redemption bears fruit in man also in a charismatic way. The Holy Spirit who, according to the Apostle's words, enters the human body as his own « temple », dwells there and operates together with his spiritual gifts. Among these gifts, known in the history of spirituality as the seven gifts of the Holy Spirit (Is 11:2), the one most congenial to the virtue of purity seems to be the gift of « piety » (eusebeia, donum pietatis). If purity prepares man to « control his own body in holiness and honour », as we read in the First Letter to the Thessalonians (4:3-5), piety, wich is a gift of the Holy Spirit, seems to serve purity in a particular way, making the human subject sensitive to that dignity which is characteristic of the human body by virtue of the mystery of creation and redemption. Thanks to the gift of piety, Paul's words: « Do you not know that your body is a temple of the Holy Spirit within you... You are not your own » (1 Cor 6:19), acquire the eloquence of an experience of the nuptial meaning of the body and of the freedom of the gift connected with it, in which the profound aspect of purity and its organic link with love is revealed.

THE EUCHARISTIC SACRIFICE

It is true that the sacrifice of Calvary sufficed to obtain for humanity all the graces of salvation: the Eucharistic Sacrifice does not do other than garner their fruits.

But Christ willed that his offering should be made continually present in order to associate the Christian community with it. In every Eucharist the Church is involved in the sacrifice of her Lord, and Christians are called to unite to it their own personal offering. The Eucharist is simultaneously the sacrifice of Christ and the sacrifice of the Church, because in the Eucharist Christ unites the Church with his own redemptive work, making it participate in his offering. How important it is, then, that the faithful, in taking part in the Eucharist, assume a personal attitude of offering. It does not suffice that they hear the word of God, nor that they pray together in community; it is necessary that they make Christ's offering their own by offering with him and in him their sufferings, their difficulties, their trials and still more, their very selves in order to make this their gift rise up to the Father together with that which Christ makes of himself.

Entering into the sacrificial offering of the Saviour, they participate in the victory which he won over the evil of the world. Every time that the words of consecration are pronounced in the Mass and the Body and Blood of the Lord are made present in the act of sacrifice, there is also present the triumph of love over hatred, of holiness over sin. Every Eucharistic celebration is more powerful than all the evil of the universe; it signifies a real concrete fulfilment of the Redemption and an ever deeper reconciliation of sinful humanity with God in the perspective of a better world. By extending the application of the work of redemption to humanity, the Eucharistic Sacrifice contributes to the building up of the Church.

« THIS IS MY BODY
WHICH WILL BE GIVEN UP FOR YOU »

In the Eucharist the Redemption is re-lived in an actual manner: the sacrifice of Christ, becoming the sacrifice of the Church, produces in humanity today its fruits of reconciliation and salvation.
When the priest, in the name and person of Christ, pronounces the words: « This is my body which will be given up for you », he does not merely affirm the presence of the Body of Christ; he expresses, moreover, the sacrifice by which Jesus gave his life for the salvation of all.
Christ indeed intended this in instituting the Eucharist. Already in his discourse at Capernaum, after the multiplication of the bread, in order to make them understand the excellence of the Bread which he wished to provide for the starving crowds, declared: « The bread which I shall give you is my flesh for the life of the world » (Jn 6:51). The gift of the Eucharistic bread cost Jesus the immolation of his own flesh. Thanks to the sacrifice, this flesh would be able to communicate life.

« THIS IS THE CUP OF MY BLOOD »

The words of consecration over the wine are still more explicit: « This is the cup of my blood of the new and everlasting covenant. It will be shed for you and for all, so that sins may be forgiven ». The blood given as drink is the blood which was shed on Calvary for the establishment of the New Covenant.

The first covenant was broken by sin: Christ sets up a new Covenant which cannot be again broken, because it is accomplished in his very person in whom mankind has been definitively reconciled with God.

Thus, in the consecration of the bread and wine, the redemptive sacrifice is made present. Through the mediation of the priest Christ offers himself in a mysterious way, presenting to the Father the gift of his own life made in its own time on the Cross. In the Eucharist there is not merely a memorial of the sacrifice offered once for all on Calvary. That sacrifice becomes present by renewing itself sacramentally in every community which offers it by means of the consecrated minister.

« WHO DO YOU SAY THAT I AM? »

At the same time, along with Peter, we confess him to be the « Son of the living God ». And this title places him in a most special relationship with God himself, whom time and again calls « Father », or rather « my Father » (Mt 11:25-27). God in fact sent him as a sing of his love for the world (Jn 3:16); and he had no other food than doing his will (Jn 4:31), proclaiming himself « one » with him (Jn 10:30). Truly, in Jesus, « God is with us » (Mt 1:23) being himself God. Therefore, when we say « You are the Son of the living God », we recognize in Jesus not only the one who gives a meaning to history, but also the one who essentially surpasses it, because his more profound essence is not reducible to it. He in fact participates in the divinity, and it is precisely for this reason that there opens to us a glimpse of the inexhaustible mystery of the communion which characterizes the divine life and which on our part can only be the object of contemplation and adoration.

All these things Peter confessed at Caesarea Philippi when Jesus asked the Twelve, « Who do you say that I am? ». And after hearing his response, Jesus called him « blessed » because of the non-human origin of his declaration. In particular, Matthew reports some solemn words of investiture with which the Lord, attributing to Simon the singular epithet of « Peter-Rock », inseparably links his role and his destiny to the configuration of the Church and its supernatural and at the same time historical existence. Through his confession of faith, Simon became the foundation rock on which Christ perennially builds his Church, thus becoming the point of support and unity for all the power lines that stimulate the Christian community.

« YOU ARE THE CHRIST »

« Simon Peter answered, "You are the Christ, the Son of the living God" » (Mt 16:16).

This open confession of faith by the Apostle Simon Peter in the name of the Twelve makes its specific mark on today's feast on which we are celebrating the blessed memory of Saints Peter and Paul. Yes, Paul of Tarsus also shared with the fisherman from Bethsaida the same christological faith. In fact, he writes, « He who... called me by his favour chose to reveal his Son to me, that I might spread among the Gentiles the good tidings concerning him » (Gal 1:15-16).

Well, then, we too wish to make our own and to repeat the same confession that, beginning on that long-ago day in the neighbourhood of Caesarea

Philippi, has resounded for two millennia now: « You are the Christ, the Son of the living God »! We say this to that Jesus of Nazareth, the Incarnate Word of the Father, who lived and died for love of man, in total obedience to God. We say it to him with all our heart, since he, our Redeemer, is the only one worthy of such a proclamation: he is the Christ, the Son of the living God.

TO CONFESS JESUS AS « CHRIST »

To confess Jesus as « Christ » means to recognize and accept his role as Messiah. This is a title that places him in a particular relationship with history, be it the history of Israel or of all mankind, inasmuch as he fulfils its expectations, liberates it from tensions, in a word, he constitutes its goal. He is the one who was to come (Mt 11:3); and as such « he will return » (Acts 1:11). In fact, according to the seer of the Book of Revelation, he is « the First and the Last and the One who lives » (Rv 1:17 f.). Therefore, when we say « You are the Christ », we not only place Jesus over human existence, but above all, we proclaim his incomparable relation with the daily and at the same time centuries-long happenings of human existence on this earth.

Besides becoming a sharer in this human existence, he constitutes its secret dynamism, he is the solution to its multiple anxieties, the sure landing place of its every uncertain wandering. As in the case of old Simeon who was awaiting the consolation of Israel, our prayer for everyone is, therefore, that he will not see death « until he has seen the Anointed of the Lord » (Lk 2:26), and that each one can say with interior exultation, like Andrew, « We have found the Messiah » (Jn 1:41).

JESUS: PRINCIPLE OF UNITY

Ecclesial unity, is a deep mystery which transcends our conceptions, our efforts, our desires. The Fathers of the Second Vatican Council meditated at length on this mystery of the Church, of the People of God, as the Constitution "Lumen Gentium" and other texts bear witness. « Christ bestowed the unity of the one and only Church on his Church from the beginning » (Decree on Ecumenism, 4). And at the same time, it must constantly be sought, reconstructed, for Christians as a whole.

In a certain sense, Christians do not exist before the Church, and they do not continue to exist, as such, independently of the Church. Let us say rather: men join the Church to become Christians, her who was born as one people from the plan of God the Father, the sacrifice of Christ, and the gift of the Holy Spirit. « All those who in faith look towards Jesus, the author of salvation and the principle of unity and peace, God has gathered together and established as the Church, that it may be for each and every one the visible sacrament of this saving unity » (LG, 9).

SEED OF UNITY, HOPE AND SALVATION

Unity does not come merely from listening to the same evangelical message, which, moreover, is transmitted to us by the Church; it takes on a mystical depth: we are joined to the very Body of Christ through faith and baptism in the name of the Father, the Son and the Holy Spirit; it is the Spirit himself who justifies us and animates our Christian life: « There is one body and one Spirit, just as you were called to the one hope that belongs to your call, one Lord, one faith, one baptism » (Eph 4:4-5).

Such is the one source that involves and requires, today as at the dawn of the Church, « unity in the teaching of the apostles, and fellowship in the breaking of bread and in prayer » (LG, 13). The very structure of the Church, with her hierarchy and her sacraments, merely expresses and realizes this essential unity received from Christ the Head. Finally this unity within the Church of Christ constitutes « a most sure seed of unity, hope and salvation for the whole human race » (LG, 9).

« THAT THEY MAY ALL BE ONE »

But that does not mean that all the sons and daughters of the Church live according to this grace and this vocation. Christ, who merited this unified people through his cross, and who set the conditions and the ways of this unity, himself recalled the risks of division among those who believed in him. That was why he prayed so insistently that these threats might be overcome: « That they may all be one; even as you, Father, are in me, and I in you... so that the world may believe that you have sent me » (Jn 17:21). Unity therefore appears as a fundamental characteristic of the Church, but its realization is difficult, strewn with dangers, at least if we consider the deep unity that Christ wishes. And it is a fact that certain scissions appeared in this one Church of God right from the beginning (UR, 3). Subsequently the Church experienced more serious disagreements, which our generation inherits and from which it suffers, even if it sometimes provokes new ones. Faithfulness to Christ makes it an urgent duty for us to reconstruct full unity. It is true that we share a common heritage in a certain number of things. And there is

And carrying his own cross he went
out... (Jn 19:17).
The Way of the Cross in Colosseum.

considerable progress in understanding, charity and common prayer, even if, out of honesty and loyalty to ourselves and to our brothers and sisters, we cannot celebrate the Lord's Eucharist together, for it is the Sacrament of Unity. It is impossible, in fact, to separate eucharistic communion and ecclesial communion in one and the same faith.

With fervour and humility, each one must, therefore, make his own contribution to this work of reconstructing unity, according to his responsibilities in the Church. There is the level of theological research, which is necessary, and whose loyal and patient approaches we know. There is the level of prayer and charity in which you are engaged. But Christians must seek « purification and renewal so that the sign of Christ may shine more brightly over the face of the Church » (LG, 15).

ENTRUSTED TO PETER

Conversion of heart and holiness of life are, with prayer, the soul of the whole of ecumenism (UR, 8). It is not a question of any kind of unity whatsoever, but of the one that corresponds to the ways laid down by the Lord in the foundation of his Church and followed by the most venerable tradition of the Church.

And in the first place, this unity of the Church, given by Christ, marred by Christians and therefore ceaselessly to be rebuilt, was especially entrusted to the Apostle Peter, who had come from the shores of Lake Tiberias to the banks of the Tiber and who died as a martyr in this very place in the reign of Nero. It was not to John, the great contemplative, nor to Paul, the incomparable theologian and preacher, that Christ gave the task of strengthening the other Apostles, his brethren (Lk 2:31-32), of feeding the lambs and the sheep (Jn 21:15-17) but to Peter alone. It is always enlightening and moving to meditate on the Gospel texts expressing the unique and irreducible role of Peter in the College of Apostles and in the Church at her beginning. It is even overwhelming, for each of us, to see how much Christ continues to put all his trust in Peter, in spite of his momentary weakness. And Peter took this role seriously, even to the supreme witness of shedding his blood. His First Letter certainly seems to prove that he meditated deeply upon the astonishing words that Jesus had said to him. It reveals the personal spirituality of the one who had received the charge of gathering together the flock of the one Shepherd: « Tend the flock of God that is your charge... not for shameful gain but eagerly... And when the chief Shepherd is manifested you will obtain the unfading crown of glory » (1 Pt 5:2-4; 2:25). Peter remembers that he is the rock but also the shepherd. And when he exhorts the Elders to carry out their pastoral task eagerly, it is because he remembers having received his own pastoral task in response to a threefold protestation of love.

« I SHOULD BE BAPTIZED BY YOU »

In the act of baptism "Jesus' humility" is seen. This humility is particularly stressed in the Gospel of St Matthew, who records the words of John the Baptist: « I should be baptized by you, yet you come to me! » (Mt 3:14). Jesus answers by making it understood that in this gesture there is reflected his mission to "establish a reign of justice", that is, a reign of divine sanctity in the world: « Give in for now. We must do this if we would fulfil all of God's demands » (Mt 3:15).

The intention to carry out in humanity a work of sanctification enlivens the act of baptism and makes its profound significance understood. The baptism administered by John the Baptist was a baptism of repentance for the remission of sins. It was suited to those who, acknowledging their faults, wanted to convert and turn to God. Jesus, absolutely holy and innocent, is in a different situation. He cannot be baptized for the remission of his sins. If he undergoes a baptism of repentance and conversion, it is for the remission of the sins of mankind. What had been announced in the oracle of the Book of Isaiah about the suffering servant began to be fulfilled already in the baptism: the servant was represented there as a just man who bore the weight of the sins of mankind and offered himself in sacrifice to obtain divine forgiveness for sinners (Is 53:4-12).

The baptism of Jesus is therefore "a symbolic gesture" that signifies his commitment to sacrifice for the purification of mankind. The fact that at that moment the heavens were opened enables us to understand that the work of reconciliation between God and man began. Sin had caused heaven to be closed; Jesus re-establishes communication between heaven and earth. The Holy Spirit descends upon Jesus to guide his whole mission, which will consist in restoring the covenant between God and man.

THE DIVINE SONSHIP

As the Gospels tell us, the baptism sheds light on "Jesus' divine sonship": the Father proclaims his beloved Son in whom he is well pleased. It is clearly a call to believe in the mistery of the Incarnation, and especially in the mystery of the "redemptive" Incarnation, because it is "intended for the sacrifice" that will obtain the remission of sins and will offer reconciliation to the world. Indeed, we must not ignore the fact that Jesus will later describe this sacrifice "as a baptism" when he asks two of his disciples: « Can you be baptized in the same bath of pain as I? » (Mk 10:38). At the Jordan, his baptism is only figurative; on the cross he will receive the baptism that will purify the world.

THE DIGNITY OF SONSHIP

Through his baptism, first expressed in the waters of the Jordan and then fulfilled on Calvary, the Saviour laid the foundation for Christian Baptism. The Baptism that the Church uses is derived from the sacrifice of Christ. It is the sacrament by which the fruit of this sacrifice is applied to anyone who becomes a Christian and enters the Church: communication of divine life with liberation from the state of sin.

The rite of Baptism, the rite of purification in water, recalls for us the baptism of Jesus in the Jordan. In a certain way it reproduces that first baptism, the baptism of the Son of God, to confer "the dignity of divine sonship" to the newly baptized. However, we must not forget that the baptismal rite actually produces its effect in virtue of the sacrifice offered on the cross. It is the reconciliation achieved on Calvary that is applied to whoever receives Baptism.

Here, therefore, is the great truth: Baptism, by making us sharers in the death and resurrection of the Saviour, fills us with new life. As a result, we must avoid sin or, according to the expression of the Apostle Paul, we must « be dead to sin » and « alive for God in Christ Jesus » (Rom 6:11).

Throughout our whole Christian life Baptism is the source of a higher life that comes to those who, as children of the Father in Christ, must bear in themselves the divine likeness.

THE SOURCE
OF ALL THE MORAL RESPONSIBILITIES

In the life of the Church, "the actuation of the Paschal Mystery is intimately linked by Christ's will to the Sacrament of Baptism" and to the other sacraments of Christian initiation. For each Christian, Baptism is a sacramental introduction to the Church that is herself the sacrament of salvation and the household of the faith. Moreover, from the Council of Trent we know that Baptism is not only a sign of faith but also a cause of faith (DS 1606). Baptism is of supreme importance for our people for many reasons. It is the sacrament of interior enlightenment, spiritual liberation and new life. Through Baptism our people are given a vital participation in the redemptive death and Resurrection of Christ and are called to « walk in newness of life » (Rom 6:4). "Baptism is also the source of all the moral responsibilities incumbent on Christians".

It is by reason of their Baptism that they must consider themselves « dead to sin and alive to God in Christ Jesus » (Rom 6:11). Through Baptism the very power of the Paschal Mystery is sacramentally brought to bear on human weakness and sinfulness, so that Christ's victory over sin and death actually enters into individual lives and triumphs in individual hearts. "God's gift of Baptism is the basis of all Christian dignity", because it is the origin of incorporation into Christ.

DRAWN INTO THE COMMUNITY OF FAITH

Through Baptism we are "incorporated into the Church".

The minister, our parents and godparents sign us with the sign of the Cross, Christ's proud standard. This shows that it is the whole assembly of the faithful, the whole community of Christ, that supports us in the new life of faith and obedience that follows from our Baptism, our new birth in Christ.

In Baptism wer are drawn into the community of faith. We become part of the pilgrim People of God which, in all times and in all places, goes forward in hope towards the fulfilment of the « promise ». Baptism creates "a sacramental bond of unity" linking all who have been reborn by means of it. But Baptism, of itself, is only a beginning, a point of departure, for it is wholly directed towards the fullness of life in Christ (UR 22).

Baptism is the foundation of the unity that all Christians have in Christ: a unity we must seek to perfect.

When we set out clearly the privilege and the duty of the Christian, we feel ashamed that we have not all been capable of maintaining the full unity of faith and charity that Christ willed for his Church. We the baptized have work to do together as brothers and sisters in Christ.

The world is in need of Jesus Christ and his Gospel – the Good News that God loves us, that God the Son was born, was crucified and died to save us, that he rose again and that we rose with him, and that in baptism he has sealed us with the Spirit for the first time, gathered us into "a community of love and of witness to his truth".

« HOW GLORIOUS IS YOUR NAME OVER ALL THE EARTH »

« O Lord, our Lord, how glorious is your name over all the earth! » (Ps 8:2).
These words of the Psalm place us, trembling and adoring, before the great mystery of the Most Holy Trinity. « How glorious is your name over all the earth! » But the expanse of the world and the universe, as endless as it is, does not equal the immeasurable reality of God's life. Before him it is more than ever necessary to accept humbly the invitation of the biblical sage when he warns: « Be not hasty in your utterance and let not your heart be quick to make a promise in God's presence. God is in heaven and you are on earth » (Eccl 5:1). In fact, God is the only reality that escapes our capacity to measure, to control, to dominate, to understand completely. This is why he is God: because it is he who measures us, supports us, guides us, and understands us, even when we are unaware of it. But if this is true for the Divinity in general, how much more true it is for the Trinitarian mystery, that is, the typically Christian one, of God himself. He is at once Father, Son and Holy Spirit. But it is not a matter of three separate gods — that would be blasphemy — nor of simply different and impersonal ways of a sole divine person's presenting himself — that would mean radically impoverishing his wealth of interpersonal communion. We are able to say more about what the One and Triune God is not, than about what he is. Moreover, if we were able to explain him adequately with our reason, it would mean that we had captured him and reduced him to the size of our minds, had imprisoned him as it were in the web of our thought. But then we would have reduced him to the paltry dimensions of an idol!

« ALL MANKIND
SHALL SEE THE SALVATION OF GOD »

The Prophet Isaiah, seven centuries before Christ, and John the Baptist on the banks of the Jordan, proclaimed such salvation. They proclaimed it using the future tense: « All mankind "shall see" the salvation of God ». With these words they express what constitutes the very substance of Advent. In fact, Advent speaks of the salvation which comes to man from God: from God alone. What was the "credibility" of these words "then", during the time of Isaiah? At the time of John the Baptist?

What is the "credibility" of these words "today"? In a certain sense, it is the same as then. Man, today as then, knows through experience, through the general experience of all men, that his existence in the visible world "does not make him participate" in the immutable and definitive good. And if this earthly existence offers man different goods, and if the total of the goods which exist in the world and those which are produced by the human race increase and grow in power, at the same time, "taken all together", they are not capable of « saving » man, that is, of freeing him from every evil and of strengthening him in the fulness of good. Rather, modern man, in the cosmic dimension of his existence, feels "threatened on the part of a multiple evil" perhaps more greatly and in a more painful way than the contemporaries of the Prophet Isaiah or of John the Baptist on the banks of the Jordan. This is, however, an "exclusively negative argument". It says: « the world does not save ». It says: « man does not find salvation in his earthly destiny ». Under this aspect, the credibility of the words of Isaiah and of John the Baptist is today similar to that of long ago. Perhaps even more dramatic.

THE SALVATION OF GOD

« God will save you » – « all mankind shall see the salvation of God ». The Prophet "uses the language of faith", the argument of faith. And, if he tacitly presupposes the credibility which derives from the general experience of men, he does this to invoke, also upon this basis, the "credibility of the word of God himself".

God said that he wants to save man.

God constantly says that he is man's salvation. He said so through Isaiah and all the prophets. He said so through John the Baptist. Above all, he said so through Jesus Christ. And with the power of Christ, he constantly says so through the Church.

« Make ready the way of the Lord, clear him a straight path ...all mankind shall see the salvation of God! » (Lk. 3:4-6).

I beg you, dear brothers and sisters, to accept this invitation with all the simplicity of your faith. Man prepares the way of the Lord and clears straight paths for him when he examines "his conscience", when he examines his deeds, his words, his thoughts, when he calls good and evil by their proper name, when he does not hesitate to confess his sins in the Sacrament of Penance, repenting of them and making the resolution to sin no more.

This is precisely what « clearing straight paths » means.

It also means to welcome the good news of salvation.

Every one of us can "see the salvation of God" in our own heart and in our conscience when we participate in the mystery of the remission of sins, as in our own Advent.

THE DIALOGUE BETWEEN FAITH AND CULTURE

We are all aware that man can be truly man only through his culture, through his freedom to grow integrally and with all his specific capabilities. And man who rightly seeks such growth is also endowed with supreme dignity and freedom, as befits a being created in the image of God and redeemed by Christ.

The Second Vatican Council gave new impetus to the "dialogue between faith and culture". For it had become evident that a dramatic distance threatened to develop between the Church and the various cultural movements developing around the world. While the modern world was fascinated with its own conquests and achievements in science and technology, it has at times lost its bearings and given credence to ideologies and ethical criteria out of harmony with the Gospel. That is why the Council wished to commit the whole Church "to listening to modern man" in order to understand him, and to looking for a new form of dialogue that would enable the originality of the Gospel message to penetrate contemporary minds and hearts.

There are two main and complementary aspects of the question that correspond to the two dimensions in which the Church acts. One is the dimension of "the evangelization of cultures" and the other is that of the "defence of man and his cultural advancement".

The Church must become all things to all peoples. There is a long and "important process of inculturation" ahead of us in order that the Gospel may penetrate the very soul of living cultures. By promoting this process, the Church responds to peoples deep aspiration and helps them come to the sphere of faith itself.

THE BEAUTY OF MAN AT WORK

The age-old experience of many peoples, the progress of science ad technology, the evolution of social institutions, the unfolding of the arts: these are all ways in which "the nature of man becomes more fully revealed". They open up new avenues towards truth and deepen for us the understanding of God's mysteries. Advances in the cosmic sciences, life sciences, communications, medicine, mass-education, psychology, means of production, electronic data processing – all this can help bring about a deeper appreciation of man. Indeed, these splendid achievements of the human race are a sign of God's greatness and the flowering of his own mysterious design. Through them a door is opened on God's creation, and on the meaning of his gift of redemption. In this context we can see so clearly how dangerous is any dichotomy between the Gospel and authentic cultures. We all do well to recall those important words of Paul VI: « The split between the Gospel and culture is without a doubt the drama of our time, just as it was of other times » (EN, 20).

We should justly welcome and admire the God-given power and beauty of man at work. Yet precisely because the power that he wields is so very great, man is also in great need of a lucid sense of discernment. This power produces wonders; it can also destroy the one who uses it unwisely.

« MAN MUST BE AFFIRMED FORM HIMSELF »

Because he lacks authentic « wisdom » in the use of his capabilities, "man is threatened" in his biological existence by irreparable pollution, by genetic manipulation, by the suppression of unborn life. His moral being can be made the prey of nihilistic hedonism, indiscriminate consumerism, and the erosion of a sense of values. And in our day, on a scale hitherto unknown, unjust economic systems exploit whole population, political and ideological policies victimize the very soul of entire peoples, with the result that they are forced into uniform apathy or an attitude of total distrust of others. As Christians we cannot remain silent in the face of so many threats to man's dignity, to peace, to genuine progress. Our faith obliges us "to resist" whatever prevents individuals, groups and entire peoples from being their true selves according to their deeper calling. Our Christian faith obliges us above all to go beyond mere condemnation: it leads us to build, to love! « Man must "be affirmed for himself", and not for any other motive or reason: solely for himself! What is more, man must be loved because he is man; love must be claimed for man by reason of the particular dignity he possesses. The body of the affirmations concerning man belongs to the very substance of Christ's message and of the mission of the Church..." Similarly, « man is and always becomes the "way" of the Church's daily life ». Yes, man is « the way of the Church », for without this loving respect for man and for his dignity, how could anyone proclaim the words of truth and life?

THE MISTERY OF MAN

The passage from Sirach calls upon us to reflect on the "mystery of man": this being who was « created from the earth », to which he is « destined to return again », and yet « made in the image of God » (Sir 17:1, 3); this ephemeral creature, to whom « limited days of life » have been assigned (Sir 17:2), and who nonetheless has eyes capable of « beholding God's majestic glory » (Sir 17:11). In this primary mystery of man is rooted the existential tension which lies at the heart of his every experience. The desire for eternity, present in him through the divine reflection that shines on his countenance, clashes with his radical inability to satisfy it, and this undermines his every effort. One of the great Christian thinkers of the beginning of this century, Maurice Blondel, who dedicated a great part of his life to reflecting on this mysterious aspiration of man's for eternity, wrote: « We are compelled to want to become what by ourselves we can neither achieve nor possess... It is because I have the ambition to be infinite that I feel my impotence: I have not made myself, I am incapable of what I want, I am compelled to go beyond myself » (M. Blondel, "L'Action", Paris, 1982). When in concrete existence man perceives this radical inability that characterizes him, he discovers that he is alone, with a profound and insatiable loneliness. It is an original loneliness that comes to him from the acute, and sometimes dramatic, awareness that no one, neither he nor anyone like him, can definitively answer his need and satisfy his desire.

THE EXPERIENCE OF LONELINESS

Paradoxically, this primary loneliness, which the person knows he can count on nothing purely human to overcome, gives rise to the most profound and genuine "community among men". It is this very experience of loneliness that he suffers that is the origin of a true sociality, ready to give up the violence of ideology and the abuse of power.

We are dealing here with a paradox: in fact, if it were not for this profound « compassion » for the other, which one discovers only if he understands in himself this total loneliness, whoever would urge man, aware of this state of his, to venture society? By the same token, how could society not be the place of domination by the strongest, by the « man who is a wolf to man », as the modern conception of the State not only has theorized but also tragically has practised?

Thanks to a glance at himself that is so laden with truth, man can feel joined with all other men, seeing in them similar subjects frustrated by the same inability and the same desire for complete fulfilment.

The experience of loneliness thus becomes the decisive step on the road toward the discovery of the answer to the radical question. In fact, it creates a profound bond with other men who share the same destiny and are inspired by the same hope. Thus from this abyssal loneliness is born man's serious commitment to his own humanity, a commitment that becomes passion for the other and solidarity with each and every one. An autentic society is the possible for man, because it is not based on selfish calculation but on the attachment to what is most true in himself and in all others.

MAN'S CONSTITUTIVE DIMENSIONS

Solidarity with the other becomes more properly an encounter with the other through the various existential expressions that characterize human relationships. Of these, the "affectionate relationship between man and woman" seems to be the principal one, because it is based on a value judgment in which man invests in a most original way all his vital dynamisms: his intellect, his will, his sensitivity. He then has the experience of that radical intimacy, but not deprived of pain, which the Creator placed in his very nature "in the beginning": « The Lord God built up into a woman the rib that he had taken from the man. When he brought her to the man, the man said, "This one, at last, is bone of my bones and flesh of my flesh" » (Gn 2:22-23).

Guided by this primary experience of communion, man applies himself with others to the building of a "society" understood as an ordered life in common. The acquired sense of solidarity with all mankind is made concrete above all in a fabric of relationships in which man primarily is called to live and to express himself, bringing his own contribution to them, and receiving from them in return a considerable influence on the development of his own personality. It is in the various environments in which his growth takes place that man is educated to perceive the value of belonging to a people as the indispensable condition for living the dimensions of the world.

The pairs of terms, man-woman, person-society, and more basically, soul-body, are "man's constitutive dimensions". The whole « pre-Christian » anthropology can be easily seen as reduced to these three dimensions, in the sense that they represent all that man can say of himself aside from Christ.

THE DANGERS OF GENETIC MANIPULATION

The rights of the human being when confronted with certain new possibilities in medicine, particularly in the matter of "genetic manipulation" pose a serious question to every individual's moral conscience.

How, in fact, can such manipulation be reconciled with a concept that credits man with an innate dignity and an untouchable autonomy?

A strictly therapeutic intervention whose explicit objective is the healing of various illnesses such as those stemming from deficiencies of chromosomes will, in principle, be considered desirable, provided it is directed to the true promotion of the personal wellbeing of man and does not infringe on his integrity or worsen his conditions of life. Such an intervention indeed would fall within the logic of the Christian moral tradition.

But here the question returns. Indeed, it is of great interest to know if an intervention on genetic inheritance that goes beyond the limits of the therapeutic in the strict sense should be regarded likewise as morally acceptable. For this to be realized, several conditions must be respected and certain premises accepted.

TO RESPECT THE DIGNITY OF MAN

The biological nature of each person is untouchable in the sense that it is constitutive of the personal identity of the individual throughout the whole course of his history. Each human person, in his absolutely unique singularity, is constituted not only by his spirit, but by his body as well. Thus, in the body and through the body, one touches the person himself in his concrete reality. To respect the dignity of man consequently amounts to safeguarding this identity of the man « corpore et anima unus ». It is on the basis of this anthropological vision that one should find the fundamental criteria for decision-making in the case of not strictly therapeutic interventions, for example those aimed at the amelioration of the human biological condition.

In particular, this kind of intervention must not infringe on the origin of human life, that is, procreation linked to the union, not only biological but also spiritual, of the parents, united by the bond of marriage. It must consequently respect the fundamental dignity of men and the common biological nature which is at the base of liberty, avoiding manipulations that tend to modify genetic inheritance and to create groups of different men at the risk of causing new cases of marginality in society.

THE COMMAND TO LOVE

To be faithful to their vocation, the followers of Christ must give concrete proof that the Gospel is life both for souls and for the whole of society. The communion of the faithful in the Spirit must take shape in a community such that, in breaking the one Bread of Life, it also shares the bread of the earth, acting with concrete forms of involvement, according to the social and cultural conditions in which the Christians live. The free articulation of the many according to the entire breadth of human expressions, but in the sphere of the one body of Christ, brilliantly demonstrates the possibility of the most profound peace in civil and international society. Charity, which firmly joins the members of the Body of Christ, modelled after the measure of the merciful love of God, cannot but point out the most just and most fruitful mechanisms for the dialogue of peace. In the light of the universality of the Christian vocation (Gal 3:28), the commandment of love thus extends to the community of peoples, making it possible to love not only one's homeland, but also the very identity of others as one's own.

The free sharing of goods among the members of the Christian community, where it is practised according to the Gospel, will effectively demonstrate the possibility of sharing the goods of the earth on the part of all the members of the political community on a national and international level; in this way a contribution will be made to find those « mechanisms and instruments of "authentic participation in the economic and social fields, with the possibility offered to everyone to have access to the goods of the earth", with the possibility to "fulfil oneself in work"; in a word, with "the application of the social doctrine" of the Church ».

« FAITH WITHOUT WORKS IS DEAD »

« Faith without works is dead ». What good is it if someone says « I have faith » if he does not do good works? Man is justified by his good works and not by faith alone (Jas 2:24).

Faith teaches us that man is the image and likeness of God (Gn 1:27): this means that he is endowed with immense dignity and that when man is abused, when his rights are violated, when flagrant injustices are committed against him, when he is subjected to torture, when violence is done to him by unlawful restraint or his right to life is violated, a criminal and most grave offence is committed against God. At that moment, Christ retraces the steps of his Passion and suffers the horrors of the crucifixion in the victimized and the oppressed. Let us remember, nevertheless, that you can make your brother die little by little, day by day, when you block his access to the goods which God created for everyone's benefit and not just for the advantage of the few.

A RELATIONSHIP
OF FATHER TO SON

The Letter to the Ephesians opens with these solemn and exultant words: « Praised be the God and Father of our Lord Jesus Christ, who has bestowed on us in Christ every spiritual blessing in the heavens... he predestined us through Jesus Christ to be his adopted sons... » (Eph 1:3-5). God-Love wanted to establish with man a relationship of Father to son. For this reason he intervenes in his history, individual and collective, in various ways. A particular mode of presence is the pact which he entered into with Israel, freeing it from oppression and constituting it as a people. This fatherhood towards Israel is like a sign of the broader and very real fatherhood which he intends to demonstrate to all of humanity and which he manifests fully in the gift which he makes to us of his Son: « God so loved the world that he gave his only Son » (Jn 3:16). It is a solicitous Father who is revealed, a Father who is not interested only in our spiritual salvation; he, who clothes the lilies of the field and looks after the fate of the smallest among the birds (Mt 6:26-29), also takes care of man's daily material problems (Mt 6:31-34). This universal divine fatherhood is further specified in the relationship to the baptized, inasmuch as they, by sharing in the one and incomparable sonship of Jesus (Gal 4:1-7; Col 1:13), truly become by new title children of God (1 Jn 3:1). Since Christ is « first-born of many brothers » (Rom 8:29), it derives from this that all those who are a part of him find that they are brethren among themselves (Mt 23:8), and what is more, they are under a new requirement of love with regard to all men (Mt 5:43-48).

THE PROFOUND LINKS
BETWEEN EVANGELIZATION
AND HUMAN ADVANCEMENT

The human advancement is an integral part of evangelization and faith.

Paul VI, in the Apostolic Exhortation "Evangelii Nuntiandi", spoke with extreme clarity concerning this: « Between evangelization and human advancement – development and liberation – there are in fact profound links. These include links of an anthropological order, because the man who is to be evangelized is not an abstract being but is subject to social and economic questions. They also include links in the theological order, since one cannot dissociate the plan of creation from the plan of redemption. The latter plan touches the very concrete situations of injustice to be combatted and of justice to be restored. They include links of the eminently evangelical order, which is that of charity: how in fact can one proclaim the new commandment without promoting in justice and in peace the true, authentic advancement of man?

NEW MEN

« Those who believe shared all things in common » (Acts 2:44). In the passage from the Acts of the Apostles which we have just heard, and in other similar texts (Acts 4:32-36; 5:12-16), there is vividly expressed a fundamental reality of our faith. Christian newness clothes the totality of the person and mutually involves those who encounter it, suggesting to them a new way of leading their daily life.

In this way, the Christian community, from the very earliest times, becomes a well distinguishable public fact within society: « They used to meet in Solomon's Portico » (Acts 5:12), the Book of Acts tells us. The most common aspects of human life are met according to a new logic, communion, and each one, with freedom, is called to alleviate the needs, including material ones, of everyone.

The Book of Acts is often concerned with pointing out how conversion implies belonging publicly to the community of believers: « Day by day the Lord added to their number those who were being saved » (Acts 2:47). This "social dimension" is the inevitable result of the presence of Christians in the world as new men and women who give rise to a renewed society. In fact, the encounter with Christ touches man at his roots and determines in him a new religious identity, which cannot but overflow into his cultural and social sphere as well.

The Church, in her make-up as a communion, is thus placed as an efficacious sign of the Redemption of Christ active in the world. The Church, according to the words of the Second Vatican Council, « is a lasting and sure seed of unity, hope and salvation » (LG, 9). This seed is the sum total of the People of God who as a visibly expressed communion faces life.

« GOD CREATED MAN IN HIS OWN IMAGE »

Ever and anew, man must look in upon himself in order to discover, in his capability to transcend himself as a person, that is, to decide on his life in all freedom and truth, the proof of his dignity. It is impossible to grasp this dignity without considering "the person's connection with the truth". The truth of man lies in his intimate relationship with God, above all through the seal that God, in creating him, impressed in his natural makeup. « God created man in his own image: in the image of God he created him... » (Gn 1:27).

The great patristic and scholastic tradition from Augustine to John Damascene and Thomas, has investigated in depth the doctrine of the « image of God » and has reached two important conclusions. First of all, man, made in the image of God, is structurally placed in relation with the truth through his 'mens' (mind), the singular seat of his intellectual and volitional faculty. The intellectual energy with which he searches truth and the volitional energy with which he reaches for it are the elementary and universal expression of his dignity. In the second place, in his daily life man experiences his dependence resulting from his limitations and his sin. He then realizes that he is "in the image" of God and not indeed "the image" of God. The image of God is the Word only, the Son in whom the Father is totally pleased. Man is only a very imperfect image of God (cf. Thomas Aquinas, "Scriptum super Sententiis", I c. 3, q. 3 a 1 resp. ad 5). The expression « in the image » indicates for man a tension toward full openness to the truth; it maps out for him an ethical and ascetical path made up of virtues and laws, duties and rights. He cannot but meet on this path, sooner or later, the One who is the full image of God, Christ who has « united himself » to each one of us.

THE FOUNDATION OF HUMAN DIGNITY

In Christ, the most rejected among men can say with Paul: « he loved me and gave himself for me » (Gal 2:20). Truly, one must recognize that, with an unstoppable crescendo from the Old to the New Testament, there is manifested in Christianity the authentic conception of man "as a person" and no longer merely "as an individual". If an individual perishes, the species remains unaltered: in the logic established by Christianity, however, when a person dies, something unique and unrepeatable is lost. "The foundation of human dignity", which every person can grasp by reflecting on his nature of being gifted with freedom, that is, with intellect, will, and affective energy, is fully intelligible in Christ's Redemption. In the Encyclical "Redemptor Hominis" I wrote that « ...the name for that deep amazement at man's worth and dignity is the Gospel, that is to say, the Good News. It is also called Christianity » (RH, 10). This does not make sterile the effort that from all time man has made and continues to make to base his dignity as a person in his nature and to establish the fundamental rights that must be guaranteed to every one by his fellow human beings and by all institutions. One can say rather that this effort becomes exalted, according to the logic through which the « Christian » enables « the human » to be discovered and so grace its nature.

The rooting of man's dignity in that ultimate level, achieved by Christ on the Cross, does not destroy, therefore, but completes and climaxes the "rational search" by wich man of every era, and modern man in particular, strives toward the ever clearer definition of the values inherent in his reality that is composed of soul and body.

RESPECT MATERNAL VOCATION OF WOMAN WHO WORKS

The problem of juridical equality between man and woman must be solved by a social legislation which recognizes the equality of working men and working women and at the same time, as « Pacem in

Terris » states, protects the right of the latter « to conditions of work reconcilable with the requirements and with their duties as wives and mothers » (n. 10). It is necessary to construct a society in which woman can attend to the upbringing of her children, who are the hope of future society.

The Church is sensitive to this point, and, « the family must be able to live in a fitting manner even when the mother dedicates herself completely to it ».

This does not mean the exclusion of woman from the world of work and social and public activity. « The true advancement of women requires that labour should be structured in such a way that women do not have to pay for their advancement by abandoning what is specific to them and at the expense of the family, in which women as mothers have an irreplaceable role ».

In a society which wishes to be just and human it is absolutely necessary that the spiritual and material requirements of the person should occupy the first place in the hierarchy of values.

It is to be hoped, therefore, that, while respecting the equality of rights to work of all – both men and women – it will be made possible for every mother, « without inhibiting her freedom, without psychological or practical discrimination, and without penalizing her as compared with other women, to devote herself to taking care of her children and educating them in accordance with their needs, which vary with age ».

The Church recognizes and praises the specific contribution, a necessary and irreplaceable one, that woman, particularly today, can and does make to the promotion of the common good in public order and in the area of work.

THE PROBLEMS OF THE ELDERLY

The problems of the elderly today differ considerably from those with which they had to contend in the past. There is, firstly, the fact that the numbers of old people have been steadily increasing; in countries with a high standard of living the increase is accounted for by the improvement in health services and medical care, by better working conditions and general welfare. Then there are certain factors proper to the modern industrial society, the principal being the alteration in the pattern of the family, which is now generally reduced to a small nucleus, whereas in a peasant society it was a patriarchal grouping. Further, it is often isolated and unstable, sometimes even broken up. Various things have contributed to bring this about, such as the flight from the land and the rush to the cities; and to these may be added in our times the (sometimes immoderate) search for comforts and tendency towards consumerism. In this kind of context, the elderly, often enough, finish by becoming an encumbrance.

And so there come about those conditions that far too often make the lives of the elderly a misery: abject poverty, especially in countries where there are no social security provisions for the old; forced inaction for the pensioners, particularly those who have worked in industry, or who are now very old; desolate loneliness for those deprived of the affection of family or the company of friends. Then, as the years pass and their strength fails and illness comes to debilitate them further, they are made to feel increasingly conscious of their physical fragility and, above all, of the burden of life.

There can be no adequate solution to these problems unless they are taken to heart by everybody and accepted as a matter with which the whole of humanity must concern itself.

MASTERS OF LIFE

In the Old Testament, the old person is regarded as a master of life: « How attractive is wisdom in the aged! Rich experience is the crown of the aged, and their boast is the fear of the Lord » (Sir 25:5-6). What is more, the old have another important task: to pass on the word of God to the new generations: « We have heard with our ears, O God, our fathers have told us, what deeds you did perform in their days » (Ps 44:1). Announcing to the young their own faith in God, they preserve a fecundity of the spirit which suffers no decline with the weakening of their physical powers: « They still bring forth fruit in old age, they are ever full of sap and green, to show that the Lord is upright » (Ps 92:15-16). For these tasks of the aged there are corresponding duties for the young. They must "listen to them": « Do not disregard the discourse of the aged » (Sir 8:9), « ask your father, and he will show you; your elders, and they will tell you » (Dt 32:7); and they must "assist them": « Help your father in his old age, and do not grieve him as long as he lives; even if he is lacking in understanding, show forbearance; in all your strength do not despise him » (Sir 3:12-13). No less rich is the teaching of the New Testament, where St Paul gives « evangelical » counsels for an ideal of life in old age, prescribing sobriety, dignity, judiciousness, soundness in the faith, in love and patience (Ti 2:2). A very striking example is given by the old man Simeon, who lived in the hope and expectation of meeting the Messiah, and for whom the Christ became the fullness of life and the hope of the future. Having prepared himself in faith and humility, he was able to recognize the Lord, and joyfully sang, not a farewell to life, but a hymn of thanks to the Saviour of the world, on the threshold of eternity (Lk 2:25-32).

OLD AGE AS A GIFT OF GOD
TO THE SOCIETY

Workers in the social communications profession have a mission to fulfil in favour of the elderly which is ever so important. I should say, in fact, there is nothing else which can substitute for it. The media instruments in their hands, with their worldwide range of action and with their immediacy in getting messages across, can quickly and eloquently concentrate general attention and excite general reflection on the elderly and on their conditions of life. It is only when it is jerked into awareness, given a salutary shock, and then mobilized into taking appropriate action, that society can go about seeking ways and means to give effective solutions to the new needs.

Another contribution from the communications fraternity will be to correct among the young certain modes of thinking regarding the old, restoring to those of mature years and to the old a confidence of their own usefulness, and re-modelling the attitudes of society so that it will see the elderly at their true value. It is also in their power to give opportune reminders to public opinion that, alongside the problem of a "just wage", there also exists the problem of a "just pension" which equally requires attention as a demand of "social justice".

The fact is that modern cultural patterns in which an unbalanced emphasis is often given to economic productivity, efficiency, physical strength and beauty, personal comfort, can have the effect of making the elderly seem burdensome, superfluous and useless, and of emarginating them from family and social life. A careful examination reveals that part of the responsibility for this situation may be attributed to certain attitudes of the mass media: if it is true that the media reflect the society in which they operate, it is no less true that they contribute to making in the sort of society as well, and therefore cannot be exempted from taking their share of the responsibility.

Media people are particularly well qualified to communicate widely a vision of the old, as outlined above, which is genuinely human and therefore also Christian: a vision of old age as a gift of God to the individual, to the family and to society.

OUR NEEDY BROTHER

The civil society will be stimulated to adopt adequate systems of social security and assistance, which will take account not only of physical and material needs but also of those which are psychological and spiritual, so as to integrate the elderly once and for all into the community's benefits and allow them a full life. Generous persons will feel themselves called upon to give their time and energies to this cause, having recognized Christ Himself in their needy brother.

Beyond this work of animation, the media workers, well aware that the elderly form a large and stable proportion of their public, especially as readers and users of radio and television, will take care to see that there are programmes and publications suitable for them, thus offering them not only recreational material, but also an assistance in their continuing education, a thing that is required at every age. Communicators will merit the special gratitude of the housebound and the sick for making it possible for them to participate with the People of God in liturgical services and other Church events. In such transmissions it will naturally be necessary to keep in mind the needs and special sensibilities of the old, avoiding novelties which may upset them and showing respect for the sense of the sacred which old people possess in large measure and which constitutes in the Church a good which is worth preserving intact.

CHURCH'S CONTINUED INTEREST IN SCHOOLS

Why has the Church always linked its own survival as a Church to the reality of the school? The reason is clear: to be faithful to the example of Christ the Lord and to carry out his mandate to « teach » all the nations (Mt 28:19).

The school is an essential instrument for spreading and deepening the faith, for the expansion of Christianity and the Kingdom of God. For this reason the school is the lifeline for the Church. The Church cannot live without teaching, without making use of the school method. Certainly the school as such does not have a supernatural aim but rather a natural one: to educate man in the intellectual and moral virtues, to lead man to his perfection as man.

On the other hand, the « teaching » which Christ proposes has quite higher objectives than those of building a mere humanism; certainly it has to do with leading man to his fullness, but also and above all with making him a « child of God », « moved by the Spirit », a « sharer in the divine nature » and an heir to eternal life. Christian teaching is therefore essentially « evangelization » and « catechesis ». But at the same time, the Church wants to and must always be the promoter of man's culture and education. This too falls within the mandate which she received from Christ. She cannot separate the proclamation of the Gospel from a generous work of man's elevation and education. Because of this, the school, even as a merely human and cultural reality, is one of the indispensable « ways of the Church ». The ecclesial community has gained an even greater awareness of this truth during these years after the Second Vatican Council and therefore asks all the religious families for a renewed commitment in this special field of the apostolate, and asks a more active and responsible participation of the laity.

THE DOUBLE DIMENSION
OF THE CATHOLIC SCHOOL

The Catholic school is at the same time an ecclesial reality and a component of civil society. It must never lose sight of its double dimension. As an ecclesial reality, it gives witness of Christ to the world. As a part of civil society by full right, it must be exemplarily committed to the service of man, of culture, and of the common good, without privileges, but also aware of its just right. This double dimension of the Catholic school – spiritual and at the same time temporal – makes it a choice area for a profound collaboration between the Catholic laity and religious institutions, and for that matter this is what happens. However, the awareness of this composite reality must always be alive, not in order to foster opposition or competition, but rather for a greater reciprocal complementarity, on the basis of the charisms and the duties proper to each one. This reality of the Catholic school also signifies something else: that all the People of God, not only the bishops and the pastors of souls, but all its members, religious and lay, according to each one's ability, must feel they are sharers and co-responsible in the promotion and – if necessary – in the defence of the Catholic school. Neither the inevitable difficulties nor the temptation to find new and more modern forms of witness must lead to abandoning such a tested instrument of evangelization and human advancement. Rather, efforts must be intensified that the most suitable and prepared subjects be destined for educational work. This is one of the principal ways by which the school will be able to enjoy the full prestige it deserves in a democratic society and fulfil its ecclesial role with complete freedom and credibility.

« YOUR BODIES
ARE MEMBERS OF CHRIST »

The Church cannot but encourage ·everything that serves the harmonious development of the human body, rightly considered the masterpiece of the whole of creation, not only because of its proportion, vigour and beauty, but also and especially because God has made it his dwelling and the instrument of an immortal soul, breathing into it that « breath of life » (Gn 2:7) by which man is made in his image and likeness. If we then consider the supernatural aspect, St Paul's words are an illuminating admonition: « Do you not know that your bodies are members of Christ?... Do you not know that your body is a temple of the Holy Spirit within you, which you have from God?... So glorify God in your body » (1 Cor 6:15; 19-20). These are some features of what Revelation teaches us about the greatness and dignity of the human body, created by God and redeemed by Christ. For this reason the Church does not cease to recommend the best use of this marvellous instrument by a suitable physical education which, while it avoids on the one hand the deviations of body worship, on the other hand it trains both body and spirit for effort, courage, balance, sacrifice, nobility, brotherhood, courtesy and, in a word, fair play.

THE JOY OF LIFE

In the first place sport is "making good use of the body", an effort to reaching optimum physical condition, which brings marked consequences of psychological wellbeing. From our Christian faith we know that, through Baptism, the human person, in his or her totality and integrity of soul and body, becomes a temple of the Holy Spirit: « Do you not know that your body is a temple of the Holy Spirit within you, which you have from God? You are not your own; you were bought with a price (that is, with the blood of Christ the Redeemer). So glorify God in your body » (1 Cor 6:19-20).

Sport is "competitiveness", a contest for winning a crown, a cup, a title, a first place. But from the Christian faith we know that the « imperishable crown », the « eternal life » which is received from God as a gift but which is also the goal of a daily victory in the practice of virtue is much more valuable. And if there is a really important form of striving, again according to Saint Paul it is this: « But earnestly desire the higher gifts » (1 Cor 12:31), which means the gifts that best serve the growth of the Kingdom of God in yourselves and in the world!

Sport is the "joy of life, a game, a celebration" and as such it must be properly used and perhaps, today, freed from excessive technical perfection and professionalism, through a recovery of its free nature, its ability to strengthen bonds of friendship, to foster dialogue and openness to others, as an

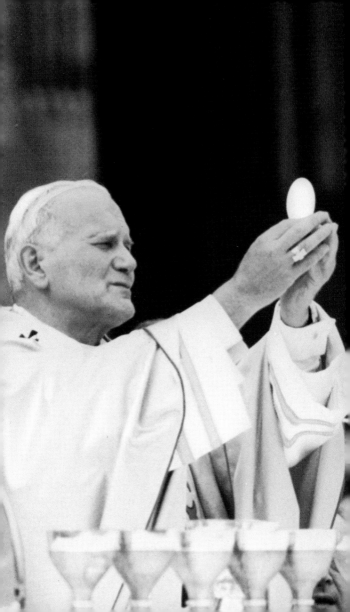

« This is my body which will be given up for you; do this in memory of me » (Lk 22:19).

expression of the "richness of being", much more valid and to be prized than "having", and hence far above the harsh laws of production and consumption and all other purely utilitarian and hedonistic considerations in life.

THE NEED TO UNDERSTAND
THE SITUATION

Since God's plan for marriage and the family touches men and women in the concreteness of their daily existence in specific social and cultural situations, the Church ought to apply herself to understanding the situations within which marriage and the family are lived today, in order to fulfil her task of serving.

This understanding is, therefore, an inescapable requirement of the work of evangelization. It is, in fact, to the families of our times that the Church must bring the unchangeable and ever new Gospel of Jesus Christ, just as it is the families involved in the present conditions of the world that are called to accept and to live the plan of God that pertains to them. Moreover, the call and demands of the Spirit resound in the very events of history, and so the Church can also be guided to a more profound understanding of the inexhaustible mystery of marriage and the family by the circumstances, the questions and the anxieties and hopes of the young people, married couples and parents of today. To this ought to be added a further reflection of particular importance at the present time. Not infrequently ideas and solutions which are very appealing, but which obscure in varying degrees the truth and the dignity of the human person, are offered to the men and women of today, in their sincere and deep search for a response to the important daily problems that affect their married and family life. These views are often supported by the powerful and pervasive organization of the means of social communication, which subtly endanger freedom and the capacity for objective judgement.

THE SITUATION OF THE FAMILY IN THE WORLD TODAY

The situation in which the family finds itself presents positive and negative aspects: the first are a sign of the salvation of Christ operating in the world; the second, a sign of the refusal that man gives to the love of God.

On the one hand, in fact, there is a more lively awareness of personal freedom and greater attention to the quality of interpersonal relationships in marriage, to promoting the dignity of women, to responsible procreation, to the education of children. There is also an awareness of the need for the development of interfamily relationships, for reciprocal spiritual and material assistance, the rediscovery of the ecclesial mission proper to the family and its responsibility for the building of a more just society. On the other hand, however, signs are not lacking of a disturbing degradation of some fundamental values: a mistaken theoretical and practical concept of the independence of the spouses in relation to each other; serious misconceptions regarding the relationship of authority between parents and children; the concrete difficulties that the family itself experiences in the transmission of values; the growing number of divorces; the scourge of abortion; the ever more frequent recourse to sterilization; the appearance of a truly contraceptive mentality.

At the root of these negative phenomena there frequently lies a corruption of the idea and the experience of freedom, conceived not as a capacity for realizing the truth of God's plan for marriage and the family, but as an autonomous power of self-affirmation, often against others, for one's own selfish well-being.

Worthy of our attention also is the fact that, in the countries of the so-called Third World, families often lack both the means necessary for survival, such as food, work, housing and medicine, and the most elementary freedoms. In the richer countries, on the contrary, excessive prosperity and the consumer mentality, paradoxically joined to a certain anguish and uncertainty about the future, deprive married couples of the generosity and courage needed for raising up new human life: thus life is often perceived not as a blessing, but as a danger from which to defend oneself.

A CONFLICT BETWEEN TWO LOVES

The historical situation in which the family lives appears as an interplay of light and darkness. This shows that history is not simply a fixed progression towards what is better, but rather an event of freedom, and even a struggle between freedoms that are in mutual conflict, that is, according to the well-known expression of Saint Augustine, a conflict between two loves: the love of God to the point of disregarding self, and the love of self to the point of disregarding God.

It follows that only an education for love rooted in faith can lead to the capacity of interpreting « the signs of the times », which are the historical expression of this twofold love.

Living in such a world, under the pressures coming above all from the mass media, the faithful do not always remain immune from the obscuring of certain fundamental values, nor set themselves up as the critical conscience of family culture and as active agents in the building of an authentic family humanism.

Among the more troubling signs of this phenomenon, the Synod Fathers stressed the following, in particular: the spread of divorce and of recourse to a new union, even on the part of the faithful; the acceptance of purely civil marriage in contradiction to the vocation of the baptized to « be married in the Lord »; the celebration of the marriage sacrament without living faith, but for other motives; the rejection of the moral norms that guide and promote the human and Christian exercise of sexuality in marriage.

THE « NEW HUMANISM »

The whole Church is obliged to a deep reflection and commitment, so that the new culture now emerging may be evangelized in depth, true values acknowledged, the rights of men and women defended, and justice promoted in the very structures of society. In this way the « new humanism » will not distract people from their relationship with God, but will lead them to it more fully.

Science and its technical applications offer new and immense possibilities in the construction of such a humanism. Still, as a consequence of political choices that decide the direction of research and its applications, science is often used against its original purpose, which is the advancement of the human person.

It becomes necessary, therefore, on the part of all, to recover an awareness of the primacy of moral values, which are the values of the human person as such. The great task that has to be faced today for the renewal of society is that of recapturing the ultimate meaning of life and its fundamental values.

THE COVENANT OF CONJUGAL LOVE

Christian revelation recognizes two specific ways of realizing the vocation to love of the human person in its entirety: marriage and virginity or celibacy. Either one is, in its own proper form an actuation of the most profound truth of man, of his being « created in the image of God ». Consequently, sexuality, by means of which man and woman give themselves to one another through the acts which are proper and exclusive to spouses, is by no means something purely biological, but concerns the innermost being of the human person as such. It is realized in a truly human way only if it is an integral part of the love by which a man and a woman commit themselves totally to one another until death. The total physical self-giving would be a lie if it were not the sign and fruit of a total personal self-giving, in which the whole person, including the temporal dimension, is present: if the person were to withhold something or reserve the possibility of deciding otherwise in the future, by this very fact he or she would not be giving totally. This totality which is required by conjugal love also corresponds to the demands of responsible fertility. This fertility is directed to the generation of a human being, and so by its nature it surpasses the purely biological order and involves a whole series of personal values. For the harmonious growth of these values a persevering and unified contribution by both parents is necessary.

The only « place » in which this self-giving in its whole truth is made possible is marriage, the covenant of conjugal love freely and consciously chosen, whereby man and woman accept the intimate community of life and love willed by God himself. Only in this light the marriage manifests its true meaning.

JESUS CHRIST,
BRIDEGROOM OF THE CHURCH

The communion between God and his people finds its definitive fulfilment in Jesus Christ, the Bridegroom who loves and gives himself as the Saviour of humanity, uniting it to himself as his body. He reveals the original truth of marriage, the truth of the « beginning » (Eph 5:32-33), and, freeing man from his hardness of heart, he makes man capable of realizing this truth in its entirety. This revelation reaches its definitive fullness in the gift of love which the Word of God makes to humanity in assuming a human nature, and in the sacrifice which Jesus Christ makes of himself on the Cross for his bride, the Church. In this sacrifice there is entirely revealed that plan which God has imprinted on the humanity of man and woman since their creation; the marriage of baptized persons thus becomes a real symbol of that new and eternal covenant sanctioned in the blood of Christ. The Spirit which the Lord pours forth gives a new heart, and renders man and woman capable of loving one another as Christ has loved us. Conjugal love reaches that fullness to which it is interiorly ordained, conjugal charity, which is the proper and specific way in which the spouses participate in and are called to live the very charity of Christ who gave himself on the Cross.

Receiving and meditating faithfully on the word of God, the Church has solemnly taught and continues to teach that the marriage of the baptized is one of the seven sacraments of the New Covenant. Indeed, by means of baptism, man and woman are definitively placed within the new and eternal covenant, in the spousal covenant of Christ with the Church.

WITNESS TO THE SALVATION

By virtue of the sacramentality of their marriage, spouses are bound to one another in the most profoundly indissoluble manner. Their belonging to each other is the real representation, by means of the sacramental sign, of the very relationship of Christ with the Church.

Spouses are therefore the permanent reminder to the Church of what happened on the Cross; they are for one another and for the children witnesses to the salvation in which the sacrament makes them sharers. Of this salvation event marriage, like every sacrament, is a memorial, actuation and prophecy: « As a memorial, the sacrament gives them the grace and duty of commemorating the great works of God and of bearing witness to them before their children. As actuation, it gives them the grace and duty of putting into practice in the present, towards each other and their children, the demands of a love which forgives and redeems. As prophecy, it gives them the grace and duty of living and bearing witness to the hope of the future encounter with Christ ».

Like each of the seven sacraments, so also marriage is a real symbol of the event of salvation, but in its own way. « The spouses participate in it as spouses, together, as a couple, so that the first and immediate effect of marriage (res et sacramentum) is not supernatural grace itself, but the Christian conjugal bond, a typically Christian communion of two persons because it represents the mystery of Christ's incarnation and the mystery of his covenant. The content of participation in Christ's life is also specific: conjugal love involves a totality, in which all the elements of the person enter – appeal of the body and instinct, power of feeling and affectivity, aspiration of the spirit and of will.

THE PERMANENT SIGN
OF CONJUGAL UNITY

In its most profound reality, love is essentially a gift; and conjugal love, while leading the spouses to the reciprocal « knowledge » which makes them « one flesh » (Gn 2:24), does not end with the couple, because it makes them capable of the greatest possible gift, the gift by which they become cooperators with God for giving life to a new human person. Thus the couple, while giving themselves to one another, give not just themselves but also the reality of children, who are a living reflection of their love, a permanent sign of conjugal unity and a living and inseparable synthesis of their being a father and a mother. When they become parents, spouses receive from God the gift of a new responsibility. Their parental love is called to become for the children the visible sign of the very love of God, « from whom every family in heaven and on earth is named » (Eph 3:15). It must not be forgotten however that, even when procreation is not possible, conjugal life does not for this reason lose its value. Physical sterility in fact can be for spouses the occasion for other important services to the life of the human person, for example, adoption, various forms of educational work, and assistance to other families and to poor or handicapped children.

THE FAMILY, A COMMUNION

In matrimony and in the family a complex of interpersonal relationships is set up – married life, fatherhood and motherhood, filiation and fraternity – through which each human person is introduced into the « human family » and into the « family of God », which is the Church.

Christian marriage and the Christian family build up the Church: for in the family the human person is not only brought into being and progressively introduced by means of education into the human community, but by means of the rebirth of baptism and education in the faith the child is also introduced into God's family, which is the Church.

The human family, disunited by sin, is reconstituted in its unity by the redemptive power of the death and Resurrection of Christ. Christian marriage, by participating in the salvific efficacy of this event, constitutes the natural setting in which the human person is introduced into the great family of the Church.

The commandment to grow and multiply, given to man and woman in the beginning, in this way reaches its whole truth and full realization.

The Church thus finds in the family, born from the sacrament, the cradle and the setting in which she can enter the human generations, and where these in their turn can enter the Church.

MARRIAGE AND VIRGINITY

Virginity or celibacy for the sake of the Kingdom of God not only does not contradict the dignity of marriage but presupposes it and confirms it. Marriage and virginity or celibacy are two ways of expressing and living the one mystery of the covenant of God with his people. When marriage is not esteemed, neither can consecrated virginity or celibacy exist; when human sexuality is not regarded as a great value given by the Creator, the renunciation of it for the sake of the Kingdom of Heaven loses its meaning. Rightly indeed does Saint John Chrysostom say: « Whoever denigrates marriage also diminishes the glory of virginity. Whoever praises it makes virginity more admirable and resplendent. What appears good only in comparison with evil would not be particularly good. It is something better than what is admitted to be good that is the most excellent good ». In virginity or celibacy, the human being is awaiting, also in a bodily way, the eschatological marriage of Christ with the Church, giving himself or herself completely to the Church in the hope that Christ may give himself to the Church in the full truth of eternal life. The celibate person thus anticipates in his or her flesh the new world of the future resurrection. By virtue of this witness, virginity or celibacy keeps alive in the Church a consciousness of the mystery of marriage and defends it from any reduction and impoverishment.

THE ROLE OF THE CHRISTIAN FAMILY

The family finds in the plan of God the Creator and Redeemer not only its "identity", what it "is", but also its "mission", what it can and should "do".

The role that God calls the family to perform in history derives from what the family is; its role represents the dynamic and existential development of what it is. Each family finds within itself a summons that cannot be ignored, and that specifies both its dignity and its responsibility: family, "become" what you "are". Accordingly, the family must go back to the « beginning » of God's creative act, if it is to attain self-knowledge and self-realization in accordance with the inner truth not only of what it is but also of what it does in history. And since in God's plan it has been established as an « intimate community of life and love » (GS, 48), the family has the mission to become more and more what it is, that is to say, a community of life and love, in an effort that will find fulfilment, as will everything created and redeemed, in the Kingdom of God. Looking at it in such a way as to reach its very roots, we must say that the essence and role of the family are in the final analysis specified by love. Hence the family has "the mission to guard, reveal and communicate love", and this is a living reflection of and a real sharing in God's love for humanity and the love of Christ the Lord for the Church his bride.

Every particular task of the family is an expression and concrete actuation of that fundamental mission. We must therefore go deeper into the unique riches of the family's mission and probe its contents, which are both manifold and unified. Thus, with love as its point of departure and making constant reference to it, the recent Synod emphasized four general tasks for the family:
1) forming a community of persons;
2) serving life;
3) participating in the development of society;
4) sharing in the life and mission of the Church.

LOVE AS THE PRINCIPLE
OF COMMUNION

The family, which is founded and given life by love, is a community of persons: of husband and wife, of parents and children, of relatives. Its first task is to live with fidelity the reality of communion in a constant effort to develop an authentic community of persons.

The inner principle of that task, its permanent power and its final goal is love: without love the family is not a community of persons and, in the same way, "without love the family cannot live, grow and perfect itself as a community of persons". What I wrote in the Encyclical "Redemptor Hominis" applies primarily and especially within the family as such: « Man cannot live without love. He remains a being that is incomprehensible for himself, his life is senseless, if love is not revealed to him, if he does not encounter love, if he does not experience it and make it his own, if he does not participate intimately in it » (RH, 10).

THE COMMUNITY OF MARRIAGE

The love between husband and wife and, in a derivative and broader way, the love between members of the same family – between parents and children, brothers and sisters and relatives and members of the household – is given life and sustenance by an unceasing inner dynamism leading the family to ever deeper and more intense "communion", which is the foundation and soul of the "community" of marriage and the family. The first communion is the one which is established and which develops between husband and wife: by virtue of the covenant of married life, the man and woman « are no longer two but one flesh » (Mt 19:6) and they are called to grow continually in their communion through day-to-day fidelity to their marriage promise of total mutual self-giving.

« THE DOMESTIC CHURCH »

The Christian family is also called to experience a new and original communion which confirms and perfects natural and human communion. In fact the grace of Jesus Christ, « the first-born among many brethren » (Rom 8:29), is by its nature and interior dynamism « a grace of brotherhood », as Saint Thomas Aquinas calls it.

The Holy Spirit, who is poured forth in the celebration of the sacraments, is the living source and inexhaustible sustenance of the supernatural communion that gathers believers and links them with Christ and with each other in the unity of the Church of God.

The Christian family constitutes a specific revelation and realization of ecclesial communion, and for this reason too it can and should be called « the domestic Church » (LG, 11).

All members of the family, each according to his or her own gift, have the grace and responsibility of building, day by day, the communion of persons, making the family « a school of deeper humanity »: (GS, 52) this happens where there is care and love for the little ones, the sick, the aged; where there is mutual service every day; where there is a sharing of goods, of joys and of sorrows. A fundamental opportunity for building such a communion is constituted by the educational exchange between parents and children, in which each gives and receives.

By means of love, respect and obedience towards their parents, children offer their specific and irreplaceable contribution to the construction of an authentically human and Christian family.

« THAT THEY MAY BE ONE »

Family communion can only be preserved and perfected through a great spirit of sacrifice. It requires, in fact, a ready and generous openness of each and all to understanding, to forbearance, to pardon, to reconciliation. There is no family that does not know how selfishness, discord, tension and conflict violently attack and at times mortally wound its own communion: hence there arise the many and varied forms of division in family life. But, at the same time, every family is called by the God of peace to have the joyous and renewing experience of « reconciliation », that is, communion reestablished, unity restored. In particular, participation in the sacrament of Reconciliation and in the banquet of the one Body of Christ offers to the Christian family the grace and the responsibility of overcoming every division and of moving towards the fullness of communion willed by God, responding in this way to the ardent desire of the Lord: « that they may be one » (Jn 17:21).

WOMEN AND SOCIETY

There is no doubt that the equal dignity and responsibility of men and women fully justifies women's access to public functions. On the other hand the true advancement of women requires that clear recognition be given to the value of their maternal and family role, by comparison with all other public roles and all other professions. Furthermore, these roles and professions should be harmoniously combined, if we wish the evolution of society and culture be truly and fully human. This will come about more easily if, in accordance with the wishes expressed by the Synod, a renewed « theology of work » can shed light upon and study in depth the meaning of work in the Christian life and determine the fundamental bond between work and the family, and therefore the original and irreplaceable meaning of work in the home and in rearing children. Therefore the Church can and should help modern society by tirelessly insisting that the work of women in the home be recognized and respected by all in its irreplaceable value. This is of particular importance in education: for possible discrimination between the different types of work and professions is eliminated at its very root once it is clear that all people, in every area, are working with equal rights and equal responsibilities. The image of God in man and in woman will thus be seen with added lustre.

While it must be recognized that women have the same right as men to perform various public functions, society must be structured in such a way that wives and mothers are "not in practice compelled" to work outside the home, and that their families can live and prosper in a dignified way even when they themselves devote their full time to their own family.

MEN AS HUSBANDS AND FATHERS

Within the conjugal and family communion-community, the man is called upon to live his gift and role as husband and father.

In his wife he sees the fulfilment of God's intention: « It is not good that the man should be alone; I will make him a helper fit for him », (Gn 2:18) and he makes his own the cry of Adam, the first husband: « This at last is bone of my bones and flesh of my flesh » (Gn 2:23). Authentic conjugal love presupposes and requires that a man have a profound respect for the equal dignity of his wife: « You are not her master », writes Saint Ambrose, « but her husband; she was not given to you to be your slave, but your wife... Reciprocate her attentiveness to you and be grateful to her for her love ». With his wife a man should live « a very special form of personal friendship ». As for the Christian, he is called upon to develop a new attitude of love, manifesting towards his wife a charity that is both gentle and strong like that which Christ has for the Church. Love for his wife as mother of their children and love for the children themselves are for the man the natural way of understanding and fulfilling his own fatherhood. As experience teaches, the absence of a father causes psychological and moral imbalance and notable difficulties in family relationships, as does, in contrary circumstances, the oppressive presence of a father, especially where there still prevails the phenomenon of « machismo », or a wrong superiority of male prerogatives which humiliates women and inhibits the development of healthy family relationships.

« LET THE CHILDREN COME TO ME »

In the family, which is a community of persons, special attention must be devoted to the children, by developing a profound esteem for their personal dignity, and a great respect and generous concern for their rights. This is true for every child, but it becomes all the more urgent the smaller the child is and the more it is in need of everything, when it is sick, suffering or handicapped.

By fostering and exercising a tender and strong concern for every child that comes into this world, the Church fulfils a fundamental mission: for she is called upon to reveal and put forward anew in history the example and the commandment of Christ the Lord, who placed the child at the heart of the Kingdom of God: « Let the children come to me, and do not hinder them; for to such belongs the kingdom of heaven » (Lk 18:16).

FECUNDITY IS THE SIGN OF CONJUGAL LOVE

With the creation of man and woman in his own image and likeness, God crowns and brings to perfection the work of his hands: he calls them to a special sharing in his love and in his power as Creator and Father, through their free and responsible cooperation in transmitting the gift of human life: « God blessed them, and God said to them, "Be fruitful and multiply, and fill the earth and subdue it" » (Gn 1:28).

Thus the fundamental task of the family is to serve life, to actualize in history the original blessing of the Creator — that of transmitting by procreation the divine image from person to person. Fecundity is the fruit and the sign of conjugal love, the living testimony of the full reciprocal self-giving of the spouses: « While not making the other purposes of matrimony of less account, the true practice of conjugal love, and the whole meaning of the family life which results from it, have this aim: that the couple be ready with stout hearts to cooperate with the love of the Creator and the Saviour, who through them will enlarge and enrich his own family day by day » (GS, 50). However, the fruitfulness of conjugal love is not restricted solely to the procreation of children, even understood in its specifically human dimension: it is enlarged and enriched by all those fruits of moral, spiritual and supernatural life which the father and mother are called to hand on to their children, and through the children to the Church and to the world.

THE VIRTUE OF CONJUGAL CHASTITY

In the context of a culture which seriously distorts or entirely misinterprets the true meaning of human sexuality, because it separates it from its essential reference to the person, the Church more urgently feels how irreplaceable is her mission of presenting sexuality as a value and task of the whole person, created male and female in the image of God. In this perspective the Second Vatican Council clearly affirmed that « when there is a question of harmonizing conjugal love with the responsible transmission of life, the moral aspect of any procedure does not depend solely on sincere intentions or on an evaluation of motives. It must be determined by "objective standards". These, "based on the nature of the human person and his or her acts", preserve the full sense of mutual self-giving and human procreation in the context of true love. Such a goal cannot be achieved unless the virtue of conjugal chastity is sincerely practised » (GS, 51).

It is precisely by moving from « an integral vision of man and of his vocation, not only his natural and earthly, but also his supernatural and eternal vocation », that Paul VI affirmed that the teaching of the Church « is founded upon the inseparable connection, willed by God and unable to be broken by man on his own initiative, between the two meanings of the conjugal act: the unitive meaning and the procreative meaning ». And he concluded by re-emphasizing that there must be excluded as intrinsically immoral « every action which, either in anticipation of the conjugal act, or in its accomplishment, or in the development of its natural consequences, proposes, whether as an end or as a means, to render procreation impossible ».

THE MORAL PROGRESS OF MARRIED PEOPLE

Married people are called upon to progress unceasingly in their moral life, with the support of a sincere and active desire to gain ever better knowledge of the values enshrined in and fostered by the law of God. They must also be supported by an upright and generous willingness to embody these values in their concrete decisions. They cannot however look on the law as merely an ideal to be achieved in the future: they must consider it as a command of Christ the Lord to overcome difficulties with constancy. « And so what is known as "the law of gradualness" or step-by-step advance cannot be identified with "gradualness of the law", as if there were different degrees or forms of precept in God's law for different individuals and situations. In God's plan, all husbands and wives are called in marriage to holiness, and this lofty vocation is fulfilled to the extent that the human person is able to respond to God's command with serene confidence in God's grace and in his or her own will ». On the same lines, it is part of the

Church's pedagogy that husbands and wives should first of all recognize clearly the teaching of "Humanae Vitae" as indicating the norm for the exercise of their sexuality, and that they should endeavour to establish the conditions necessary for observing that norm.

As the Synod noted, this pedagogy embraces the whole of married life.

Accordingly, the function of transmitting life must be integrated into the overall mission of Christian life as a whole, which without the Cross cannot reach the Resurrection. In such a context it is understandable that sacrifice cannot be removed from family life, but must in fact be wholeheartedly accepted if the love between husband and wife is to be deepened and become a source of intimate joy.

THE MISSION TO EDUCATE

The mission to educate demands that Christian parents should present to their children all the topics that are necessary for the gradual maturing of their personality from a Christian and ecclesial point of view.

They will therefore follow the educational lines mentioned above, taking care to show their children the depths of significance to which the faith and love of Jesus Christ can lead. Furthermore, their awareness that the Lord is entrusting to them the growth of a child of God, a brother or sister of Christ, a temple of the Holy Spirit, a member of the Church, will support Christian parents in their task of strengthening the gift of divine grace in their children's souls.

THE CHRISTIAN TRANSFORMATION
OF THE WORLD

The Second Vatican Council describes the content of Christian education as follows: « Such an education does not merely strive to foster maturity... in the human person. Rather, its principal aims are these: that as baptized persons are gradually introduced into a knowledge of the mystery of salvation, they may daily grow more conscious of the gift of faith which they have received; that they may learn to adore God the Father in spirit and in truth (Jn 4:23), especially through liturgical worship; that they may be trained to conduct their personal life in true righteousness and holiness, according to their new nature (Eph 4:22-24), and thus grow to maturity, to the stature of the fullness of Christ (Eph 4:13), and devote themselves to the upbuilding of the Mystical Body. Moreover, aware of their calling, they should grow accustomed to giving witness to the hope that is in them (1 Pt 3:15), and to promoting the Christian transformation of the world.

GOD'S PROVIDENT FATHERHOOD

Christian families, recognizing with faith all human beings as children of the same heavenly Father, will respond generously to the children of other families, giving them support and love not as outsiders but as members of the one family of God's children. Christian parents will thus be able to spread their love beyond the bonds of flesh and blood, nourishing the links that are rooted in the spirit and that develop through concrete service to the children of other families, who are often without even the barest necessities.

Christian families will be able to show greater readiness to adopt and foster children who have lost their parents or have been abandoned by them. Rediscovering the warmth of affection of a family, these children will be able to experience God's loving and provident fatherhood witnessed to by Christian parents, and they will thus be able to grow up with serenity and confidence in life. At the same time the whole family will be enriched with the spiritual values of a wider fraternity.

THE FIRST AND VITAL CELL OF SOCIETY

« Since the Creator of all things has established the conjugal partnership as the beginning and basis of human society », the family is « the first and vital cell of society » (AA, 11).

The family has vital and organic links with society, since it is its foundation and nourishes it continually through its role of service to life: it is from the family that citizens come to birth and it is within the family that they find the first school of the social virtues that are the animating principle of the existence and development of society itself.

Thus, far from being closed in on itself, the family is by nature and vocation open to other families and to society, and undertakes its social role. The very experience of communion and sharing that should characterize the family's daily life represents its first and fundamental contribution to society.

The relationships between the members of the family community are inspired and guided by the law of « free giving ». By respecting and fostering personal dignity in each and every one as the only basis for value, this free giving takes the forme of heartfelt acceptance, encounter and dialogue, disinterested availability, generous service and deep solidarity.

Thus the fostering of authentic and mature communion between persons within the family is the first and irreplaceable school of social life, an example and stimulus for the broader community relationships marked by respect, justice, dialogue and love.

THE SOCIAL ROLE OF THE FAMILY

The social role of the family certainly cannot stop short at procreation and education, even if this constitutes its primary and irreplaceable form of expression. Families therefore, either singly or in association, can and should devote themselves to manifold social service activities, especially in favour of the poor, or at any rate for the benefit of all people and situations that cannot be reached by the public authorities' welfare organization.

The social contribution of the family has an original character of its own, one that should be given greater recognition and more decisive encouragement, especially as the children grow up, and actually involving all its members as much as possible.

« PRACTISE HOSPITALITY »

In particular, note must be taken of the ever greater importance in our society of hospitality in all its forms, from opening the door of one's home and still more of one's heart to the pleas of our brothers and sisters, to concrete efforts to ensure that every family has its own home, as the natural environment that preserves it and makes it grow. In a special way the Christian family is called upon to listen to the Apostle's recommendation: « Practise hospitality », (Rom 12:13) and therefore, imitating Christ's example and sharing in his love, to welcome the brother or sister in need: « Whoever gives to one of these little ones even a cup of cold water because he is a disciple, truly I say to you, he shall not lose his reward » (Mt 10:42). The social role of families is called upon to find expression also in the form of "political intervention": families should be the first to take steps to see that the laws and institutions of the State not only do not offend but support and positively defend the rights and duties of the family.

THE RIGHTS OF THE FAMILY

The Synod Fathers mentioned the following rights of the family:
— the right to exist and progress as a family, that is to say, the right of every human being, even if he or she is poor, to found a family and to have adequate means to support it;
— the right to exercise its responsibility regarding the transmission of life and to educate children;
— the right to the intimacy of conjugal and family life;
— the right to the stability of the bond and of the institution of marriage;
— the right to believe in and profess one's faith and to propagate it;
— the right to bring up children in accordance with the family's own traditions and religious and cultural values, with the necessary instruments, means and institutions;
— the right, especially of the poor and the sick, to obtain physical, social, political and economic security;

– the right to housing suitable for living family life in a proper way;
– the right to expression and to representation, either directly or through associations, before the economic, social and cultural public authorities and lower authorities;
– the right to form associations with other families and institutions, in order to fulfil the family's role suitably and expeditiously;
– the right to protect minors by adequate institutions and legislation from harmful drugs, pornography, alcoholism, etc.;
– the right to wholesome recreation of a kind that also fosters family values;
– the right of the elderly to a worthy life and a worthy death;
– the right to emigrate as a family in search of a better life.

THE FAMILY
WITHIN THE MYSTERY OF THE CHURCH

Among the fundamental tasks of the Christian family is its ecclesial task: the family is placed at the service of the building up of the Kingdom of God in history by participating in the life and mission of the Church.

In order to understand better the foundations, the contents and the characteristics of this participation, we must examine the many profound bonds linking the Church and the Christian family and establishing the family as a « Church in miniature » (Ecclesia domestica) (LG, 11) in such a way that in its own way the family is a living image and historical representation of the mystery of the Church.

It is, above all, the Church as Mother that gives birth to, educates and builds up the Christian family, by putting into effect in its regard the saving mission which she has received from her Lord.

By proclaiming the word of God, the Church reveals to the Christian family its true identity, what it is and should be according to the Lord's plan; by celebrating the sacraments, the Church enriches and strengthens the Christian family with the grace of Christ for its sanctification to the glory of the Father; by the continuous proclamation of the new commandment of love, the Church encourages and guides the Christian family to the service of love, so that it may imitate an relive the same self-giving and sacrificial love that the Lord Jesus has for the entire human race.

« PROFESSION OF FAITH »

The celebration of the sacrament of marriage is the basic moment of the faith of the couple.

This sacrament, in essence, is the proclamation in the Church of the Good News concerning married love. It is the word of God that « reveals » and « fulfils » the wise and loving plan of God for the married couple, giving them a mysterious and real share in the very love with which God himself loves humanity.

Since the sacramental celebration of marriage is itself a proclamation of the word of God, it must also be a « profession of faith » within and with the Church, as a community of believers, on the part of all those who in different ways participate in its celebration.

THE PLAN OF GOD

The profession of faith demands that it be prolonged in the life of the married couple and of the family. God, who called the spouses "to" marriage, continues to call them "in" marriage. In and through the events, problems, difficulties and circumstances of everyday life, God comes to them, revealing and presenting the concrete « demands » of their sharing in the love of Christ for his Church in the particular familial, social and ecclesial situation in which they find themselves.
The discovery of and obedience to the plan of God on the part of the conjugal and family community must take place in « togetherness », through the human experience of love between husband and wife, between parents and children, lived in the Spirit of Christ. Thus the little domestic Church, like the greater Church, needs to be constantly and intensely evangelized: hence its duty regarding permanent education in the faith.

MARRIAGE AS A SACRAMENT
OF MUTUAL SANCTIFICATION

The sacrament of marriage is the specific source and original means of sanctification for Christian married couples and families. It takes up again and makes specific the sanctifying grace of Baptism. By virtue of the mystery of the death and Resurrection of Christ, of which the spouses are made part in a new way by marriage, conjugal love is purified and made holy: « This love the Lord has judged worthy of special gifts, healing, perfecting and exalting gifts of grace an of charity » (GS, 49).
The gift of Jesus Christ is not exhausted in the actual celebration of the sacrament of marriage, but

rather accompanies the married couple throughout their lives. This fact is explicitly recalled by the Second Vatican Council when it says that Jesus Christ « abides with them so that, just as he loved the Church and handed himself over on her behalf, the spouses may love each other with perpetual fidelity through mutual self-bestowal... For this reason, Christian spouses have a special sacrament by which they are fortified and receive a kind of consecration in the duties and dignity of their state. By virtue of this sacrament, as spouses fulfil their conjugal and family obligations, they are penetrated with the Spirit of Christ, who fills their whole lives with faith, hope and charity. Thus they increasingly advance towards their own perfection, as well as towards their mutual sanctification, and hence contribute jointly to the glory of God ».

THE EUCHARIST
IS THE SOURCE OF CHRISTIAN MARRIAGE

The Christian family's sanctifying role is grounded in Baptism and has its highest expression in the Eucharist, to which Christian marriage is intimately connected.

The Second Vatican Council drew attention to the unique relationship between the Eucharist and marriage by requesting that « marriage normally be celebrated within the Mass ». To understand better and live more intensely the graces and responsibilities of Christian marriage and family life, it is altogether necessary to rediscover and strengthen this relationship.

The Eucharist is the very source of Christian marriage. The Eucharistic Sacrifice, in fact, represents Christ's covenant of love with the Church, sealed with his blood on the Cross.

A FOUNTAIN OF CHARITY

In the sacrifice of the New and Eternal Covenant, Christian spouses encounter the source from which their own marriage covenant flows, is interiorly structured and continuously renewed. As a representation of Christ's sacrifice of love for the Church, the Eucharist is a fountain of charity. In the Eucharistic gift of charity the Christian family finds the foundation and soul of its « communion » and its « mission »: by partaking in the Eucharistic bread, the different members of the Christian family become one body, which reveals and shares in the wider unity of the Church. Their sharing in the Body of Christ that is « given up » and in his Blood that is « shed » becomes a never-ending source of missionary and apostolic dynamism for the Christian family.

A FRUIT OF THE SPIRIT

The law of Christian life is to be found not in a written code, but in the personal action of the Holy Spirit who inspires and guides the Christian. It is the « law of the Spirit of life in Christ Jesus » (Rom 8:2): « God's love has been poured into our hearts through the Holy Spirit who has been given to us » (Rom 5:5).
This is true also for the Christian couple and family. Their guide and rule of life is the Spirit of Jesus poured into their hearts in the celebration of the sacrament of Matrimony. In continuity with Baptism in water and the Spirit, marriage sets forth anew the evangelical law of love, and with the gift of the Spirit engraves it more profoundly on the hearts of Christian husbands and wives. Their love, purified

and saved, is a fruit of the Spirit acting in the hearts of believers and constituting, at the same time, the fundamental commandment of their moral life to be lived in responsible freedom.

« SERVICE » OF LOVE

Thus the Christian family is inspired and guided by the new law of the Spirit and, in intimate communion with the Church as kingly people, it is called to exercise its « service » of love towards God and towards its fellow human beings. Just as Christ exercises his royal power by serving us, so also the Christian finds the authentic meaning of his participation in the kingship of his Lord in sharing his spirit and practice of service to man. « Christ has communicated this power to his disciples that they might be established in royal freedom and that by self-denial and a holy life they might conquer the reign of sin in themselves (Rom 6:12). Further, he has shared this power so that by serving him in their fellow human beings they might through humility and patience lead their brothers and sisters to that King whom to serve is to reign.

TOWARDS THE FULL REVELATION OF THE KINGDOM OF GOD

In the light of faith and by virtue of hope, the Christian family too shares, in communion with the Church, in the experience of the earthly pilgrimage towards the full revelation and manifestation of the Kingdom of God. Therefore, it must be emphasized once more that the pastoral intervention of the Church in support of the family is a matter of urgency. Every effort should be made to strengthen and develop pastoral care for the family, which should be treated as a real matter of priority, in the certainty that future evangelization depends largely on the domestic Church. The Church's pastoral concern will not be limited only to the Christian families closest at hand; it will extend its horizons in harmony with the Heart of Christ, and will show itself to be even more lively for families in general and for those families in particular which are in difficult or irregular situations. For all of them the Church will have a word of truth, goodness, understanding, hope and deep sympathy with their sometimes tragic difficulties. To all of them she will offer her disinterested help so that they can come closer to that model of a family which the Creator intended from « the beginning » and which Christ has renewed with his redeeming grace.

THE CHURCH'S PASTORAL ACTION

The Church's pastoral action must be progressive, also in the sense that it must follow the family, accompanying it step by step in the different stages of its formation and development.

More than ever necessary in our times is preparation of young people for marriage and family life. In some countries it is still the families themselves that, according to ancient customs, ensure the passing on to young people of the values concerning married and family life, and they do this through a gradual process of education or initiation. But the changes that have taken place within almost all modern societies demand that not only the family but also society and the Church should be involved in the effort of properly preparing young people for their future responsibilities. Many negative phenomena which are today noted with regret in family life derive from the fact that, in the new situations, young people not only lose sight of the correct hierarchy of values but, since they no longer have certain criteria of behaviour, they do not know how to face and deal with the new difficulties. But experience teaches that young people who have been well prepared for family life generally succeed better than others.

PREPARATION FOR MARRIAGE

Marriage preparation has to be seen and put into practice as a gradual and continuous process. It includes three main stages: remote, proximate and immediate preparation. "Remote preparation" begins in early childhood, in that wise family training which leads children to discover themselves as beings endowed with a rich and complex psychology and with a particular personality with its own strengths and weaknesses. It is the period when esteem for all authentic human values is instilled, both in interpersonal and in social relationships, with all that this signifies for the formation of character, for the control and right use of one's inclinations, for the manner of regarding and meeting people of the opposite sex, and so on. Also necessary, especially for Christians, is solid spiritual and catechetical formation that will show that marriage is a true vocation and mission, without excluding the possibility of the total gift of self to God in the vocation to the priestly or religious life.

Upon this basis there will subsequently and gradually be built up the "proximate preparation", which — from the suitable age and with adequate catechesis, as in a catechumenal process — involves a more specific preparation for the sacraments, as it be a rediscovery of them. This renewed cathechesis of young people and others preparing for Christian marriage is absolutely necessary in order that the sacrament may be celebrated and lived with the right moral and spiritual dispositions.

THE RELIGIOUS FORMATION

The religious formation of young people should be integrated, at the right moment and in accordance with the various concrete requirements, with a preparation for life as a couple.

This preparation will present marriage as an interpersonal relationship of a man and a woman that has to be continually developed, and it will encourage those concerned to study the nature of conjugal sexuality and responsible parenthood, with the essential medical and biological knowledge connected with it. It will also acquaint those concerned with correct methods for the education of children, and will assist them in gaining the basic requisites for well-ordered family life, such as stable work, sufficient financial resources, sensible administration, notions of housekeeping.

Finally, one must not overlook preparation for the family apostolate, for fraternal solidarity and collaboration with other families, for active membership in groups, associations, movements and undertakings set up for the human and Christian benefit of the family.

THE IMMEDIATE PREPARATION

The "immediate preparation" for the celebration of the sacrament of Matrimony should take place in the months and weeks immediately preceding the wedding, so as to give a new meaning, content and form to the so-called premarital enquiry required by Canon Law. This preparation is not only necessary in every case, but is also more urgently needed for engaged couples that still manifest shortcomings or difficulties in Christian doctrine and pratice. Among the elements to be instilled in this journey of faith, which is similar to the catechumenate, there must also be a deeper knowledge of the mystery of Christ and the Church, of the meaning of grace and of the responsibility of Christian marriage, as well as preparation for taking an active and conscious part in the rites of the marriage liturgy.

A MUTUAL EXCHANGE OF PRESENCE

In order that the family may be ever more a true community of love, it is necessary that all its members should be helped and trained in their responsibilities as they face the new problems that arise, in mutual service, and in active sharing in family life. This holds true especially for young families, which, finding themselves in a context of new values and responsibilities, are more vulnerable, especially in the first years of marriage, to possible difficulties, such as those created by adaptation to life together or by the birth of children. Young married couples should learn to accept willingly, and make good use of the discreet, tactful and generous help offered by other couples that already have more experience of married and family life. Thus, within the ecclesial community – the great family made up of Christian families – there will take place a mutual exchange of presence and help among all the families, each one putting at the service of the others its own experience of life, as well as the gifts of faith and grace. Animated by a true apostolic spirit, this assistance from family to family will constitute one of the simplest, most effective and most accessible means for transmitting from one to another those Christian values which are both the starting-point and goal of all pastoral care. Thus young families will not limit themselves merely to receiving, but in their turn, having been helped in this way, will become a source of enrichment for other longeer established families, through their witness of life and practical contribution.

THE PASTORAL CARE OF THE FAMILY

Still within the Church, which is the subject responsible for the pastoral care of the family, mention should be made of the various groupings of members of the faithful in which the mystery of Christ's Church is in some measure manifested and lived. One should therefore recognize and make good use of – each one in relationship to its own characteristics, purposes, effectiveness and methods – the different ecclesial communities, the various groups and the numerous movements engaged in various ways, for different reasons and at a different levels, in the pastoral care of the family.

For this reason the Synod expressly recognized the useful contribution made by such associations of spirituality, formation and apostolate. It will be their task to foster among the faithful a lively sense of solidarity, to favour a manner of living inspired by the Gospel and by the faith of the Church, to form consciences according to Christian values and not according to the standards of public opinion; to stimulate people to perform works of charity for one another and for others with a spirit of openness which will make Christian families into a true source of light and a wholesome leaven for other families.

FOR THE BUILDING
OF A MORE JUST WORLD

It is similarly desirable that, with a lively sense of
the common good, Christian families should become actively engaged, at every level, in other non-ec-
clesial associations as well. Some of these associations work for the preservation, transmission and
protection of the wholesome ethical and cultural values of each people, the development of the human
person, the medical, juridical and social protection
of mothers and young children, the just advancement of women and the struggle against all that is
detrimental to their dignity, the increase of mutual
solidarity, knowledge of the problems connected
with the responsible regulation of fertility in accordance with natural methods that are in conformity
with human dignity and the teaching of the Church.
Other associations work for the building of a more
just and human world; for the promotion of just
laws favouring the right social order with full respect for the dignity and every legitimate freedom
of the individual and the family, on both the national and the international level; for collaboration
with the school and with the other institutions that
complete the education of children, and so forth.

BISHOPS AND PRIESTS

The person principally responsible in the diocese
for the pastoral care of the family is the Bishop. As
father and pastor, he must exercise particular solicitude in this clearly priority sector of pastoral care.
He must devote to it personal interest, care, time,
personnel and resources, but above all personal support for the families and for all those who, in the
various diocesan structures, assist him in the pasto-

ral care of the family. It will be his particular care to make the diocese ever more truly a « diocesan family », a model and source of hope for the many families that belong to it. The setting up of the Pontifical Council for the Family is to be seen in this light: to be a sign of the importance that I attribute to pastoral care for the family in the world, and at the same time to be an effective instrument for aiding and promoting it at every level.

The Bishops avail themselves especially of the priests, whose task – as the Synod expressly emphasized – constitutes an essential part of the Church's ministry regarding marriage and the family. The same is true of deacons to whose care this sector of pastoral work may be entrusted. Their responsibility extends not only to moral and liturgical matters but to personal and social matters as well. They must support the family in its difficulties and sufferings, caring for its members and helping them to see their lives in the light of the Gospel. It is not superfluous to note that from this mission, if it is exercised with due discernment and with a truly apostolic spirit, the minister of the Church draws fresh encouragement and spiritual energy for his own vocation too and for the exercise of his ministry.

MEN AND WOMEN RELIGIOUS

The contribution that can be made to the apostolate of the family by men and women religious and consecrated persons in general finds its primary, fundamental and original expression precisely in their consecration to God. By reason of this consecration, « for all Christ's faithful religious recall that wonderful marriage made by God, which will be fully manifested in the future age, and in

which the Church has Christ for her only spouse »,
and they are witnesses to that universal charity
which, through chastity embraced for the Kingdom
of heaven, makes them ever more available to
dedicate themselves generously to the service of
God and to the works of the apostolate. Hence the
possibility for men and women religious, and
members of Secular Institutes and other institutes
of perfection, either individually or in groups, to
develop their service to families, with particular
solicitude for children, especially if they are abandoned, unwanted, orphaned, poor or handicapped.
They can also visit families and look after the sick;
they can foster relationships of respect and charity
towards one-parent families or families that are in
difficulties or are separated; they can offer their
own work of teaching and counselling in the
preparation of young people for marriage, and in
helping couples towards truly responsible parenthood; they can open their own houses for simple
and cordial hospitality, so that families can find
there the sense of God's presence and gain a taste
for prayer and recollection, and see the practical
examples of lives lived in charity and fraternal joy
as members of the larger family of God. I would
like to add a most pressing exhortation to the heads
of institutes of consecrated life to consider – always
with substantial respect for the proper and original
charism of each one – the apostolate of the family
as one of the priority tasks, rendered even more
urgent by the present state of the world.

LAY SPECIALISTS

Considerable help can be given to families by lay
specialists (doctors, lawyers, psychologists, social
workers, consultants, etc.) who either as indivi-

duals or as members of various associations and undertakings offer their contribution of enlightenment, advice, orientation and support. To these people one can well apply the exhortations that I had the occasion to address to the Confederation of Family Advisory Bureaux of Christian Inspiration: « Yours is a commitment that well deserves the title of mission, so noble are the aims that it pursues, and so determining, for the good of society and the Christian community itself, are the results that derive from it... All that you succeed in doing to support the family is destined to have an effectiveness that goes beyond its own sphere and reaches other people too and has an effect on society. The future of the world and of the Church passes through the family ».

THE FAMILIES OF MIGRANT WORKERS

An even more generous, intelligent and prudent pastoral commitment, modelled on the Good Shepherd, is called for in the case of families which, often independently of their own wishes and through pressures of various other kinds, find themselves faced by situations which are objectively difficult.
In this regard it is necessary to call special attention to certain particular groups which are more in need not only of assistance but also of more incisive action upon public opinion and especially upon cultural, economic and juridical structures, in order that the profound causes of their needs may be eliminated as far as possible.
Such for example are the families of migrant workers; the families of those obliged to be away for long periods, such as members of the armed forces, sailors and all kinds of itinerant people; the

families of those in prison, of refugees and exiles; the families in big cities living practically speaking as outcasts; families with no home; incomplete or single-parent families; families with children that are handicapped or addicted to drugs; the families of alcoholics; families that have been uprooted from their cultural and social environment or are in danger of losing it; families discriminated against for political or other reasons; families that are ideologically divided; families that are unable to make ready contact with the parish; families experiencing violence or unjust treatment because of their faith; teenage married couples; the elderly, who are often obliged to live alone with inadequate means of subsistence.

IDEOLOGICALLY DIVIDED

A difficult problem is that of the family which is "ideologically divided". In these cases particular pastoral care is needed. In the first place it is necessary to maintain tactful personal contact with such families. The believing members must be strengthened in their faith and supported in their Christian lives. Although the party faithful to Catholicism cannot give way, dialogue with the other party must always be kept alive. Love and respect must be freely shown, in the firm hope that unity will be maintained. Much also depends on the relationship between parents and children. Moreover, ideologies which are alien to the faith can stimulate the believing members of the family to grow in faith and in the witness of love. Other difficult circumstances in which the family needs the help of the ecclesial community and its pastors are: the children's adolescence, which can be disturbed, rebellious and sometimes stormy; the childrens' marriage, which takes them away from their family; lack of understanding or lack of love on the part of those held most dear; abandonment by one of the spouses, or his or her death, which brings the painful experience of widowhood, or the death of a family member, which breaks up and deeply transforms the original family nucleus. Similarly, the Church cannot ignore the time of old age, with all its positive and negative aspects. In old age married love, which has been increasingly purified and ennobled by long and unbroken fidelity, can be deepened. There is the opportunity of offering to others, in a new form, the kindness and the wisdom gathered over the years, and what energies remain. But there is also the burden of loneliness, more often psychological and emotional rather than physical, which results from abandonment or neglect on the part of children and relations. There is also suffering caused by ill-health, by the gradual loss of strength, by the humiliation of having to depend on others, by the sorrow of feeling that one is perhaps a burden to one's loved ones, and by the approach of the end of life.

MIXED MARRIAGES

There must be borne in mind the particular difficulties inherent in the relationships between husband and wife with regard to respect for religious freedom: this freedom could be violated either by undue pressure to make the partner change his or her beliefs, for by placing obstacles in the way of the free manifestation of these beliefs by religious practice. With regard to the liturgical and canonical form of marriage, Ordinaries can make wide use of their faculties to meet various necessities. In dealing with these special needs, the following points should be kept in mind:

— In the appropriate preparation for this type of marriage, every reasonable effort must be made to ensure a proper understanding of Catholic teaching on the qualities and obligations of marriage, and also to ensure that the pressures and obstacles mentioned above will not occur.

— It is of the greatest importance that, through the support of the community, the Catholic party should be strengthened in faith and positively helped to mature in understanding and practising that faith, so as to become a credible witness within the family through his or her own life and through the quality of love shown to the other spouse and the children.

INTELLECTUAL PREPARATION

Application to study — an effective means of growth and personal improvement — is, together with piety, the great daily duty of the seminarian, his professional work. For students of the philosophical and theological courses, study takes on a particularly full and profound dimension, because it must now serve as an aid and enrichment of the life of faith and as an indispensable instrument for the future ministry. It is necessary in particular that knowledge of the movements of philosophical thought and of literature, the reading of the events of history and of the cultural and social formation of peoples, and the whole humanistic formation in general should give the future pastor of souls that capacity of interpreting the oustanding stages of human civilization in a Christian key, in order to be truly a spiritual guide for his contemporaries, especially for youth. On this basis there must be inserted the study of theology in all its branches, which opens to the seminarian a complete view of the divine plan of salvation, and offers him the irreplaceable instruments of his ministerial and catechetical activity, at which he is aiming with all his strength.

DISCIPLINARY PREPARATION

In seminary life discipline is required not only by the need to shape the personality of the young men, and to subordinate spontaneity to duty, but it is also indispensable for the requirements of community life to be respected. It must be considered, furthermore, as an integrating element of all formation, to help the students to acquire self control, to ensure the harmonious development of the personality, facilitating the capacity of control and collaboration, and to form all those other states of mind which are so useful to make the activity of the Church orderly and fruitful (OT, 11).

There is no doubt that in this framework the essential part is constituted by the action of the rector, the representative of the bishop, since he is « the first person responsible for the life of the seminary » (Italian Ratio Institutionis, 102). Since the rector performs his task in communion and collaboration with other educators, it is opportune that he meet them periodically to meditate, pray together, celebrate the Eucharist as a community, and to discuss problems regarding the individual students and the whole community. With the young men he will always be a father who is able to listen, dialogue, and advise, and so encourage that climate of confidence and mutual trust which is the indispensable condition for useful and serene work.

He will not fail, however, to demand of them, after having duty explained the reasons, generous availability for sacrifice and renunciation, since only on these premises it is possible to construct that austerity of life and behaviour which is indispensable for the future ministry to be really incisive and fruitful.

SPIRITUAL PREPARATION

The educational effort of the seminary must aim at bringing the youth to the knowledge and personal experience of the Lord, in order to mould in him a pastor of souls, who, in his person and in his activity, will appear and really be « a servant of Christ and a steward of the mysteries of God » (1 Cor 4:1).

Among the aspects that seem to deserve particular consideration in the spiritual preparation of future priests, I would like to submit to your attention those so opportunely indicated in the circular letter of the Sacred Congregation for Catholic Education on « Some more urgent aspects of spiritual formation in the seminaries » (January 6, 1980). They can be summed up in the following points:

a) to train priests who will accept and deeply love Christ, the Word of God, our Brother, Friend and Saviour;

b) to train priests who can see in the Paschal Mystery the supreme expression of the love that the Word had for us, sacrificing himself for the Church — "in finem dilexit eos";

c) to train priests who are not afraid to recognize that real communion and concrete friendship with Christ entail an asceticism, and therefore a commitment to renunciation and sacrifice;

d) to make the seminary a school of filial love for her who is the Mother of Jesus and our mother. In this field the work of the spiritual director, who has the task of contributing to the formation of truly priestly men, is still determinant and irreplaceable. His action is to be considered fundamental in educational work, since it constitutes a decisive moment to create in the student's heart that image of Christ to which he will have to refer as his supreme ideal throughout his life. To be such, spiritual direction must take the shape of a serious relationship, clear, open, assiduous and continuous. It cannot be reduced, therefore, to mere listening, to an exchange of ideas or opinions, nor can it be confused with group dialogue, nor be conceived as a personal, though spontaneous, dialogue which springs from the intimacy of friendship.

TO PROCLAIM THE GOSPEL OF SALVATION

The priest is sent by Christ and his Church "to proclaim the Gospel of salvation", above all in the celebration of the Eucharist. The priest is ordained to offer the Sacrifice of the Mass, and thus to renew the Paschal Mystery of our Lord Jesus Christ. As a minister of Christ, the priest is called to sanctify the People of god by word and sacrament. He shares the pastoral solicitude of the Good Shepherd, which is frequently expressed in prayer for the flock.

UNION WITH CHRIST

No priest can carry out his ministry well unless he lives in "union with Christ". His life, like Christ's life, must be marked by self-sacrifice, zeal for the spreading of the Kingdom of God, unblemished chastity, unstinted charity. All this is possible only when the priest is a man of prayer and Eucharistic devotion. By praying the Liturgy of the Hours in union with the Church he will find strength and joy for the apostolate. In silent prayer before the Blessed Sacrament he will be constantly renewed in his consecration to Jesus Christ and confirmed in his permanent commitment to priestly celibacy. By invoking Mary the Mother of Jesus, the priest will be sustained in his generous service to all Christ's brothers and sisters in the world. Yes, the priest must not allow the passing needs of the active apostolate to elbow out or eat into his prayer life. He must not be so engrossed with working for God that he is in danger of forgetting God himself. He will remember that our Saviour warned us that without him we can do nothing. Without him, we can fish all night and still catch nothing.

UNDER THE LEADERSHIP OF THE BISHOP

No priest can work all by himself. He works with his brother priests and "under the leadership of the bishop", who is their father, brother, co-worker and friend. The authentic priest will maintain the love and unity of the presbyterium. He will reverence and obey his bishop as he solemnly promised on ordination day. The presbyterium of the bishop with all his priests, diocesan and religious, should function as a family, as an apostolic team marked with joy, mutual understanding and fraternal love. The presbyterium exists so that, through the renewal of Christ's Sacrifice, the mystery of Christ's saving love may enter the lives of God's people. Priests must not forget to help their brother priests who are in difficulty: moral, spiritual, financial or otherwise. And the sick and the old priests find in your warmth of brotherly charity both solace and support.

The priest must be a leaven in the community of today. The priest by word and example must call attention to higher values. Man does not live by bread alone. The priest must "identify with the poor", so as to be able to bring them the uplifting Gospel of Christ.

The priests who work in the mass media have a wonderful opportunity to share Christ with others, as do the spiritual directors of the religious and laity, the chaplains of all lay apostolate organizations, and the priests who recruit vocations to the priesthood and the religious life.

« HIGHER VALUES »

In a society which gives value only to having, in which a constant desire for personal well-being and comfort seems to rule, and which is so often fascinated with luxury, in direct contrast with evident misery, in this society — poverty, and especially the spirit of poverty, is a challenge. A challenge for all, for the rich and the poor in material goods, and a challenge especially for those who have made a « profession » of evangelical poverty.

Evangelical poverty is something more than the simple renunciation of material possession; it is to abandon oneself, to « lose oneself » in God. Christ spoke one day about a merchant who chose a precious pearl and exchanged all that he had to buy it (Mt 13:46). He valued the choice of higher goods, those « of great value » given to those who can proceed with wisdom. Peter, after making this choice, dared to ask Christ about these « higher values », for which he had left everything to follow his Master; and he received the famous reply: a hundredfold in this life and life everlasting (Mt 19:27-29).

Thinking back to this exchange which we also make, in the light of the explanation obtained by St Peter, could we or others hesitate to verify the fulfilment of the Lord's promise? Our internal attitude and external behaviour which others see will always be that of serene possession of this « hundredfold » and of the hope of eternal life. Or will it more easily appear that we do not abandon everything – questions, « hypotheses » without hypotheses, human « security », « ties » which do not allow us to throw aside all risks, etc. – and receive nothing more than any other « non-chosen » who totally commits himself to living this present life?

« THE POOR WILL EAT... »

« Jesus took the loaves, and when he had given thanks, he distributed them to those who were seated » (Jn 6:11). The Gospel scene of the multiplication of the loaves has a particularly meaningful precedent in the Old Testament.

There too, a few loaves of barley and wheat, offered as first fruits to the prophet Eliseus, were enough to feed a hundred people, and moreover, after the meal was finished, there were even loaves left over. Likewise in the Gospel, after the crowd – in this case, it involved several thousands of people – had eaten their fill, they were able to fill a good twelve baskets with the remaining pieces of bread.

An abundance, therefore; the possibility offered to everyone to eat their fill. Here is the essential message. There reechoes in it a characteristic announcement of the prophets, who has spoken of the time of the coming Messiah as a period of great abundance: « The poor will eat and will have their fill », said Psalm 21 (v. 27). And the prophet Isaiah in his turn had predicted, « On this mountain the Lord of hosts will make for all peoples a feast of fat things, a feast of excellent wine, of succulent foods, of well-refined wines » (Is 25:6).

This is the message. We welcome it into our hearts and there we reflect on it in an attitude of faith. We know that the full confirmation of this prophetic prediction would happen only at the conclusion of the eschatological period, when Christ's coming on earth has just begun. When Christ returns in glory to solemnly conclude the world's history, then mankind will finally attain that abundance of every good in which will be found the fulfilment of all the expectations of the « poor ».

The « full satisfaction » is therefore a goal toward which mankind of today, as well mankind of the messianic era, is still on its way. This however does not take away from the fact that some of that fulness is to be experienced in the present time. The eschatological period, in fact, has already begun, even if it is not yet fully realized.

WORLD HUNGER TODAY

It is a duty of Christians, the « children of the Kingdom » (Mt 13:38), to commit themselves with generous concern that right now anyone who lacks the goods necessary for life may come to have them as soon as possible, so as to be able to satisfy himself and the members of his family.

The problem of world hunger is posed today with tragic urgency, because its solution, rather than being closer with the passing of time, seems rather to be getting further and further away. The economic imbalance between the developed nations and the others in fact continues to register a disturbing progression.

There are now many voices raised to denounce the scandal of this situation in which a minority of fortunate people prosper and grow rich while ignoring a majority of unfortunate people often exposed, besides the humiliation of underdevelopment or economic dependence, to the very experience of physically wasting away and of premature death for lack of sufficient nourishment. It is now necessary and urgent to pass from words to deeds with practical initiatives, among which must not be neglected that of « gathering the fragments left over », according to the Gospel warning, because one of the reasons for the frightening imbalances is to be sought in the squandering of available resources, to which rich people have been abandoning themselves for years, dazed by the habit of unbridled consumerism. It is necessary to go into action, as individuals and as a community. Jesus satisfied in a practical way the people who were hungry, offering with this gesture an exemplary norm to his Church, which through the centuries has felt that it cannot ignore those who are hungry and thirsty, those who are naked or away from home, those who are sick or in prison (Mt 25:35-36).

MAN CAN TURN AGAINST HIMSELF

The Apostle writes: « God has sent the Spirit of his Son into our hearts, crying, "Abba! Father!" So through God you are no longer a slave but a son, and if a son then an heir » (Gal 4:6-7).

In the dephts of the human heart a great struggle is going on: the « son » fights the « slave ». This struggle takes place at the same time in the history of man on earth.

Man can become a « slave » in various ways. He can be a « slave » when his freedom is restricted, when he is deprived of objective human rights: but he can also become a slave due to an abuse of freedom which is specifically his.

Modern man is threatened by a « slavery » derived from the products of his own thought and his will, products which may serve mankind, but can also be turned against man.

This is what would happen, in particular, in the hypothesis of a nuclear conflict.

PREVENTION IS OUR ONLY RECOURSE

Apart, in fact, from the mass destruction of human lives, « the suffering of the surviving population would be without parallel. There would be complete interruption of communications, of food supplies and of water. Help would be given only at the risk of mortal danger from radiation for those venturing outside of buildings in the first days. The social disruption following such an attack would be unimaginable...

« The medical facilities of any nation would be inadequate to care for the survivors... prevention is our only recourse ».

PEACE IS A DUTY

Peace is a duty — "and it is also possible". Are we not led to consider it as such by that special gift of man, thanks to which he is placed over all creatures, thus meriting the title of « king of creation »? That gift is reason: the capacity to distinguish good from evil: the capacity to recognize one's own rights, and at the same time the rights of others, and therefore the duties that these rights involve; the capacity to direct one's life towards the right goals, and if necessary to correct any errors that one may have committed.

Recourse to reason makes man a civilized being, one who is not reduced to being able to settle differences only by the use of force. It makes him able to seek and find the solution through dialogue, meetings and negotiations.

This was the thought of the great Augustine when, writing to a Roman magistrate, he said that the highest title to glory is « to kill war with the words of negotiation, instead of killing men with the sword »: « ipsa bella verbo occidere, quam homines ferro » (Ep 229, "Ad Darium").

ELUSIVE PEACE

Peace! Much is said about it: yet genuine peace is ever more elusive. On the one hand, the instruments of war — tools of death and destruction — constantly increase. On the other hand, the available structures of dialogue, whether between the bigger nations and alliances or between the parties to limited and localized disputes, have shown themselves to be extremely fragile and vulnerable. Should we then cease to speak out about peace? Or should we not rather find words that will evoke a response of "serious reflection" on the part of all those who have responsibility for the decisions and policies that affect peace? Would it not be a crime to remain silent when what is needed is an effective appeal for a real « conversion of heart » on the part of individuals, governments and nations?

« From a new heart, peace is born ». As I pointed

out, I believe that a serious reflection on this theme « permits us to go to the very depths of the problem and is capable of calling into question "the presuppositions that" precisely constitute a threat to peace. Humanity's helplessness to resolve the existing tensions reveals that the obstacles, and likewise the hopes, come from something deeper than the systems themselves ». This change or « conversion » of heart is not an exclusively Christian or even religious ideal. It is a very fundamental and original human experience, and it applies to nations as well as to individuals.

PEACE IS THREATENED

Peace is threatened wherever the human spirit is oppressed by poverty or constrained by socio-political or ideological dictates. In our world, peace is seriously threatened by the tensions arising out of ideological differences "between East and West"; and by the growing contrast between the developed countries of "the North" and the developing countries of "the South".

Peace is threatened wherever the fundamental rights of man are ignored or trampled upon, especially the right of religious liberty. Peace is threatened where the integral well-being of the human person is not recognized, promoted and safeguarded; where human beings are not respected in their unique dignity and worth; where they are subordinated to preconceived interests and to the ambition of power in any of its forms; where the poor are exploited by the rich, the weak by the strong, the uneducated by the clever and unscrupulous. Peace is threatened where the human person is made the "victim" of scientific and technological processes, rather than the "beneficiary" of the marvellous capabilities for genuine progress and development which man wrests from the universe. Peace is threatened by events; but these events themselves mirror deeper causes connected with the attitude of the human heart.

There is a serious need for "rethinking basic policies and priorities". At this time in history there is a great need for wisdom. There is less and less room for gambling with the well-being of the human family. The only option is "sincere dialogue and mutual collaboration" for the construction of a more just order in the world. What this just order is, still remains, to some extent, to be discovered through a trust-filled exchange of ideas and values without preconceived bias; a dialogue that has as its object the common good of all and the inalienable rights of every human being.

A NEW CLIMATE OF TRUST

"That a new way of thinking may be found", together with the courage to make a new beginning! The basic moral and psychological conditions underlying the present world situation need to be carefully and impartially reexamined. Perhaps the greatest difficulty in achieving a constructive dialogue is the "lack of mutual trust" between individuals, groups, nations and alliances. There exists "an atmosphere of suspicion" that causes one side to doubt the good will of the other. This is a serious, objective obstacle to peace, one that follows from the real circumstances affecting the lives of nations. It has to be recognized that this atmosphere of fear, suspicion, distrust and uncertainty is extremely difficult to dispel. The feeling of insecurity is real, and sometimes justified. This leads, in turn, to ever higher levels of tension aggravated by the inevitable search, by every means and by all sides, "to ensure military superiority" – even to gain the upper hand by acts of naked terrorism – or predominance through economic and ideological control. The aspirations of hundreds of millions of human beings for a better life, the hopes of the young for a better world, will inevitably be frustated unless there is a change of heart and a new beginning!

In a re-examination of the basic moral and psychological presuppositions that constitute a threat to peace, to development and to justice, a fundamental requisite is "the achievement of a new climate of trust".

REVERENCE FOR HUMANITY

« Peace must be born of mutual trust between nations rather than imposed on them through fear of one another's weapons » (GS, 82). The same need for a climate of trust holds true also within a given nation or people. In a special way it is incumbent upon "the leaders of nations" to promote a climate of sincere good will both within and without. And while they cannot ignore the complexity of international relations, they ought to feel themselves obliged to undertake the very grave task of peace-making. To serve the cause of peace: this is a work of supreme love for mankind. « Today it most certainly demands that leaders extend their thoughts and their spirit beyond the confines of their own nation, that they put aside national selfishness and ambition to dominate other nations, and that they nourish a profound reverence for the whole of humanity » (GS, 82).

"Reverence for humanity": this is indeed the nucleus of the whole question. If the human person is revered and respected in his or her inviolable dignity and inalienable rights, then injustice and aggression will be seen for what they are: an arrogance that conceals within itself a certain death wish because it subverts the balance of the natural order of fundamental equity of rights and duties, giving rise to a situation of moral chaos in which sooner or later "all" become victims.

The evangelical words, « Treat others the way you would have them treat you » (Mt 7:12), are the expression of a basic requisite for human co-existence, which applies equally to relations between individuals and to relations between nations.

CALLED TO FREEDOM

St Paul writes in the Letter to the Galatians: « For you were called to freedom, brethren; only do not use your freedom as an opportunity for the flesh, but through love be servants of one another. For the whole Law is fulfilled in one word: You shall love your neighbour as yourself » (Gal 5:13-14). Although the passage quoted refers above all to the subject of justification, here, however, the Apostle aims explicitly at driving home the ethical dimension of the « body-Spirit » opposition, that is, the opposition between life according to the flesh and life according to the Spirit. Precisely here, in fact, he touches the essential point, revealing, as it were, the very anthropological roots of the Gospel ethos. If, in fact, « the whole Law » (moral law of the Old Testament) « is fulfilled » in the commandment of charity, the dimension of the new Gospel ethos is nothing but an appeal to human freedom, an appeal to its fuller implementation and, in a way, to fuller « utilization » of the potential of the human spirit.

It might seem that Paul was only contrasting freedom with the Law and the Law with freedom. However a deeper analysis of the text shows that St Paul in the Letter to the Galatians emphasizes above all the ethical subordination of freedom to that element in which the whole Law is fulfilled, that is, to love, which is the content of the greatest commandment of the Gospel. « Christ set us free in order that we might remain free », precisely in the sense that he manifested to us the ethical (and theological) subordination of freedom to charity, and that he linked freedom with the commandment of love.

BAD USE OF FREEDOM

Paul warns us of the possibility of making a bad use of freedom, a use which is in opposition to the liberation of the human spirit carried out by Christ and which contradicts that freedom with which « Christ set us free ». In fact, Christ realized and manifested the freedom that finds its fullness in charity, the freedom thanks to which we are « servants of one another ». In other words: the freedom that becomes a source of new « works » and « life » according to the Spirit. The antithesis and, in a way, the negation of this use of freedom takes place when it becomes for man « a pretext to live according to the flesh ».

« AN OPPORTUNITY FOR THE FLESH »

Freedom then becomes a source of « works » and of « life » according to the flesh. It stops being the true freedom for which « Christ set us free », and becomes « an opportunity for the flesh », a source (or instrument) of a specific « yoke » on the part of pride of life, the lust of the eyes, and the lust of the flesh. Anyone who in this way lives « according to the flesh », that is, submits – although in a way that is not quite conscious, but nevertheless actual – to the three forms of lust, and in particular to the lust of the flesh, ceases to be capable of that freedom for which « Christ set us free »; he also ceases to be suitable for the real gift of himself, which is the fruit and expression of this freedom. He ceases, moreover, to be capable of that gift which is organically connected with the nuptial meaning of the human body, with which we dealt in the preceding analyses of the Book of Genesis (Gn 2:23-25).

THE FREEDOM OF CHRIST

« You brethren were called to freedom » (Gal 5:13). The Redemption places us in a state of freedom which is the fruit of the presence of the Spirit within us, because where the Spirit is, there is freedom (2 Cor 3:17). This freedom is at the same time a "gift" and a "duty"; a "grace" and an "imperative". At the same moment, indeed, when the Apostle reminds us that we have been called to freedom, he informs us also of the danger we run of putting it to bad use: « Do not use this freedom », he warns, « as an opportunity for living according to the flesh » (Gal 5:13). In the Pauline vocabulary the « flesh » does not mean the « human body », but the entire human person in so far as it is subjected to, and closed within, those false values which attract with the seductive promise of an apparently fuller life. (Gal 5:13 to 6:10).
The criterion for judging whether the use we make of our freedom is in conformity with our call to be

free or is, in fact, a relapse into slavery, is our subordination or lack of subordination to charity, that is, to the demands which derive from it. It is of fundamental importance to note that this criterion of judgement is provided for us in the life of Christ. The freedom of Christ is the true freedom, and our call to freedom is a call to share in the very freedom of Christ. Christ lived in full freedom because, in radical obedience to the Father, « he gave himself as a ransom for all. This is the message of salvation » (1 Tim 2:5). Christ is supremely free precisely in the moment of his supreme subordination and obedience to the demands of the salvific love of the Father: in the moment of his death.

FREEDOM AND LOVE

« You are called to freedom », says the Apostle. We have been made sharers in the very freedom of Christ: the freedom of giving ourselves. The perfect expression of freedom is communion in true love. Following upon this call there opens up before every human person the space for a decisive and dramatic alternative: the choice between a (pseudo) freedom of "self-affirmation", personal or collective, against God and against others, or a true freedom of "self-giving" to God and to others. He who chooses self-affirmation remains subject to the slavery of the flesh, alienated from God: he who chooses self-giving, is already living the eternal life. True freedom is that which is subordinated to love since, according to the teaching of the Apostle, « love is the fulfilling of the law » (Rom 13:10). From this teaching we can understand yet again that, for the Apostle, there is not, in the man who is justified, an opposition between freedom and the moral law. And the reason is precisely this, that the fulfilling of the law is love. The ultimate meaning of every moral law is love; every moral norm merely expresses an exigency of the truth of love. This is a very important point of the ethos of Redemption, indeed of the merely human ethos, which deserves to be investigated immediately. All of us, whatever be the culture to which we belong, define love as « desiring the good of the person loved ». Note well: of the person loved, for his own sake, and not merely for the sake of the one who loves. In this second case, indeed, love would actually conceal a relationship of utilitarian or hedonistic character with the other. The "good" of the person is that what the person "is": it is his "being". To will the good is to will that the other possess the fullness of his being.

THE NEW ETHOS OF THE REDEMPTION

To speak of « ethos » means to recall an experience that every man, not only the Christian, lives daily: it is at the same time simple and complex, profound and elementary. This experience is always connected with that of his own "freedom", that is, the fact that each one of us is truly and really the "cause of his own acts". But the ethical experience makes us feel free in an altogether singular way: it is an "obliged" freedom that we experience. Obliged not from « without » — it is not an exterior compulsion or constriction — but from « within »: it is the freedom "as such" that "must" act in one way rather than another.

This mysterious and wonderful « necessity » that exists within freedom without destroying it is rooted in the very force of "moral value", which man knows with his intellect: it is the expression of the normative force of the "truth" of good. Committing itself to « do » this truth, freedom is situated in the order that has been inscribed by the creative Wisdom of God in the universe of being. In the ethical experience, therefore, there is established a "connection between truth and freedom", thanks to which the person becomes ever more himself, in obedience to the creative Wisdom of God. « I do not do what I want to do, but what I hate... I do, not the good I will to do, but the evil I do not intend » (Rom 7:15-19). These words of Saint Paul describe the ethos of the man fallen into sin and therefore deprived of « original justice ». In the new situation man notices a contradiction between his intentions and his actions – « I do not do what I want to do » – though continuing to have in himself the perceptions of good and the tendency toward it.

THE HARMONY BETWEEN TRUTH AND FREEDOM

The harmony between "truth" and "freedom" has been broken, in the sense that freedom chooses what is contrary to the truth of the human person and the truth is smothered in injustice (Rom 1:18). Ultimately, from what does this interior division of man arise? He begins his history of sin when he no longer recognizes the Lord as his Creator and wants to be the one who, in absolute autonomy and independence, decides what is good and what is evil: « You will be like gods who know what is good and what is bad », says the first temptation (Gn 3:5). Man no longer wants the « measure » of his existence to be the law of God, he no longer receives himself from the creating hands of God, but decides to be the measure and principle of himself. The truth of his created being is denied by a freedom that has released itself from the law of God, the only true measure of man.

At first glance it would seem that the sinner's freedom is true freedom, inasmuch as it is no longer subordinated to the truth. In reality, however, it is only the truth that can make us free. Man is free when he submits to the truth.

GIFT FROM GOD

Charity is shown in all that the Apostle writes. What it is becomes almost visibly confirmed. So it is something greater than all its manifestations. It is "like their hidden heart", in which all originate. Charity is the interior life of this heart. To learn charity means to make one's own heart learn this interior life; make the heart learn, but also the intellect, the senses, the spirit, the body; make the whole man learn it. In order to practise charity, one must learn it. At times, it seems to us that this is not the case. Young people especially tend to believe that love is something immediate, something that we find in our hearts, especially as a "feeling". Yes. It is true that in our hearts, especially in the heart of a young person, the feeling of love is found ad seems to spring up by itself. All this is true. Such is the psychology of human love.

But let us not think that this sentiment alone is already that love about which St Paul writes in his First Letter to the Corinthians. Of course, "charity" that he talks about is "given" to man as a unique "gift from God". But at the same time it is "assigned to him as a task". It is enough to reflect on the Pauline description of charity in order to admit that it must be won by man through patient and constant work, so that it may mature in his heart and in his entire personality; so that it may permeate his character and his behaviour; so that it may become in man a mark and the foundation of his authentic holiness.

THE TRUE CHARITY

Above all, St Paul wishes to emphasize not so much what true charity is and is not, but rather the worthlessness of all that we might be able to do in life if we have not true charity.

His words speak for themselves.

Let us take only the last thought, in which the Apostle writes: « If I give everything I have to feed the poor and hand over my body to be burned, but have not love, I gain nothing » (1 Cor 13:3).

In this way, therefore, we must not judge charity by exterior works, but judge all our works according to charity.

Only by virtue of charity do these have supernatural value.

Without charity, every one of our actions may even amaze and surprise, but does not have "supernatural value".

The Apostle lets us suppose, on the other hand, that even modest and simple works can have a supernatural value if they derive from charity. The Apostle dedicates a good part of his text to emphasizing what are the fundamental characteristics of charity, by what signs and what attributes it can be recognized. So he writes: « Charity is patient; charity is kind. Charity is not jealous, it does not put on airs, is not snobbish... » (ibid., 13:4).

We should pause over each of these brief phrases and meditate individually on their meaning.

FORGIVENESS!

Forgiveness! Christ taught us to forgive. He spoke of forgiveness very often and in various ways. When Peter asked him how often he should forgive his neighbour, « as many as seven times? », Jesus answered that he should forgive « seventy times seven » (Mt 18:21 f.). That means, in practice, always: in fact, the number « seventy » times « seven » is symbolical, and it means, more than a given quantity, an incalculable, infinite quantity. Answering the question on how we must pray, Christ uttered those magnificent words addressed to the Father: « Our Father who art in heaven »; and among the requests that compose this prayer, the last one speaks of forgiveness: « And forgive us our debts, as we also have forgiven our debtors », those who are guilty towards us (« our debtors »). Finally Christ himself confirmed the truth of these words on the Cross, when, turning to the Father, he begged: « Father, forgive them; for they know not what they do » (Lk 23:34).

THE WORD OF THE HUMAN HEART

« Forgiveness » is a word spoken by the lips of a man to whom some evil has been done. It is, in fact, the word of the human heart. In this word of the heart each of us endeavours to go beyond the frontier of hostility, which can separate us from the other; he tries to reconstruct the interior space of understanding, contact, bond. Christ taught us with the word of the Gospel, and above all with is own example, that this space opens not only before the other man, but at the same time before God himself.

« This is your mother » (Jn 19:27).
Journey to Fatima.

« WHERE IS YOUR BROTHER? »

Cain rose up against his brother Abel, and killed him. Then the Lord said to Cain, « "Where is Abel your brother?" He said, "I do not know; am I my brother's keeper?" And the Lord said, "What have you done? The voice of your brother's blood is crying to me from the ground!" »... (Gn 4:2-10). In our time, in which this sin against man's life has become threatening again and in a new way, while so many innocent men are perishing at the hands of other men, the biblical description of what happened between Cain and Abel becomes particularly eloquent. Even more complete, even more overwhelming than the commandment itself « You shall not kill ». This order belongs to the Ten Commandments, which Moses received from God and which are at the same time written in man's heart as the interior law of moral order for all human behaviour. Does not that question of God's addressed to Cain: « Where is your brother? » speak to us even more than the absolute ban « not to kill? ». And following up closely on Cain's evasive reply, « Am I my brother's keeper? », come the other divine question: « What have you done? The voice of your brother's blood is crying to me from the ground! ».

FORGIVENESS IS INDISPENSABLE

Christ taught us to forgive. Forgiveness is indispensable also for God to put to human conscience some questions to which he expects an answer in complete interior truth.
At this time, in which so many innocent men are perishing at the hands of other men, there seems to be a special need to approach each of those who

kill, approach them with forgiveness in one's heart and at the same time with the same question that God, the Creator and Lord of human life, asked the first man who had made an attempt on his brother's life and had taken it from him — had taken what belongs only to the Creator and Lord of life.

« TO LAY DOWN ONE'S LIFE FOR ONE'S FRIENDS »

The Gospel is not only news which concerns the relationships between God and man, but it also concerns the relationships of men among themselves. Alongside and declared to be like the commandment to love God with all one's heart is that of loving one's neighbour as oneself (Mt 22:39). It is a love which must be realized in a mutual exchange and which goes beyond every human measure.

Jesus asks us to forgive and to love our enemies, placing before us as a model the Father's perfection (Mt 5:48); as a measure of mutual love between brethren, Jesus points out to us his own love, which led him to give his life: « This is my commandment: love one another as I have loved you. There is no greater love than this: to lay down one's life for one's friends » (Jn 15:12-13).

The Gospel, therefore, does not proclaim a reality which remains intimately locked up in the souls of believers, but is translated immediately into the radical tranformation of their interpersonal relationships, into a renewal of the network of social relations. The Gospel is not truly lived if it does not produce in the followers of Christ a radical change in their way of living in the concrete reality of society.

In revealing to man his divine sonship, the Gospel also reveals to man the response he must give to the Father's love in order to live as a son.

THE BROTHER OF THE POOR

The poor and those discriminated against identify more easily with Christ, for in him they discover one of their own. Right from the beginning of his life, at the blessed moment of his birth as Son of the Virgin Mary, Jesus was homeless, for there was no place for him in the inn (Lk 2:7). When his parents took him up to Jerusalem for the first time, to present their offering in the temple, they were numbered among the poor and they offered the gift of the poor (Lk 2:24). In his childhood he was a refugee, forced to flee the hatred that broke loose in persecution, to leave his own land and live in exile on foreign soil. As a boy, he was able to confound the learned teachers with his wisdom, but he still worked with his hands as a humble carpenter like his foster-father Joseph. After speaking out and explaining the Scriptures in the synagogue at Nazareth, « the carpenter's son » (Mt 13:55) was rejected (Lk 4:29). Even one of the disciples chosen to follow him asked: « Can anything good come out of Nazareth? » (Jn 1:46). He was also the victim of injustice and torture and was put to death without anyone coming to his defence. Yes, he was the brother of the poor; it was his mission — for he was sent by God the Father and anointed by the Holy Spirit to proclaim the Gospel to the poor (Lk 4:18). He praised the poor when he uttered this unsettling challenge to all who want to be his followers: « Blessed are the poor in spirit, for theirs is the kingdom of heaven » (Mt 5:3).

POOR IN SPIRIT

Being poor in spirit does not mean being unconcerned with the problems that beset the community, and nobody has a keener sense of justice than the poor people who suffer the injustices that circumstances and human selfishness heap upon them. Finding strength in human solidarity, the poor by their very existence indicate the obligation of justice that confronts society and all who have power, whether economic, cultural or political. And so it is the same truth of the first Beatitude that indicates a path that every person must walk. It tells those that live in material poverty that their dignity, their human dignity, must be preserved, that their inviolable human rights must be cherished and protected. It also tells them that they themselves can achieve much if they pool their skills and talents, and especially their determination to be the artisans of their own progress and development.

The first Beatitude tells the rich, who enjoy material well-being or who accumulate a disproportionate share of material goods, that man is great not by reason of what he possesses but by what he is – not by what he has but by what he shares with others.

THE CHURCH OF THE POOR

Poor in spirit is the rich man who does not close his heart, but faces up to the intolerable situations that perpetuate the poverty and misery of the many who are constantly hungry and deprived of their rightful chances to grow and develop their human potential, who lack decent housing and sufficient clothing, who suffer illness for want of even basic health care, who grow desperate for want of employment that would enable them to provide, through honest work, for the needs of their families. Poor in spirit indeed is the rich man who does not rest so long as a brother or sister is entrapped in injustice and powerlessness. Poor in spirit is the one who holds political power and remembers that it is given for the common good only, and who never ceases to devise means to organize all sectors of society according to the demands of the dignity and equality that is the birthright of every man, woman and child that God has called into existence. The Church herself, will heed the call of the Beatitudes and be the Church of the poor because she must do what Jesus did and proclaim the Gospel to the poor (Lk 4:18). But the preference that the Church shows for the poor and under-privileged does not mean that she directs her concern only to one group or class or category. She preaches the same message to all: that God loves man and sent his Son for the salvation of all, that Jesus Christ is the Saviour, « the way, and the truth, and the life » (Jn 14:6).

DEFENDING THE HUMAN DIGNITY OF THE POOR

Being the Church of the poor means that she will speak the language of the Beatitudes to all people, to all groups or professions, to all ideologies, to all political and economic systems. She does so, not to serve political interests, nor to acquire power, nor to offer pretexts for violence, but to save man in his humanity and in his supernatural destiny.

Defending the human dignity of the poor and their hope for a human future is not a luxury for the Church, nor is it a strategy of opportunism, nor a means for currying favour with the masses. It is her duty because it is God who wishes all human beings to live in accordance with the dignity that he bestowed on them. It is the mission of the Church to travel the path of man « because man – without any exception whatever – has been redeemed by Christ, and because with man – with each man without any exception whatever – Christ is in a way united, even when man is unaware of it » (RH, 14). The Church will therefore preach to the poor the whole Gospel; she will encourage them to be faithful to the divine life which they have received in Baptism, the life which is nourished in the Eucharist and which is revived and supported through the Sacrament of Reconciliation.

THE REDEMPTION RE-CREATES US

We can understand why the fruit of the Redemption in us is precisely the good deeds « which God prepared for us in advance ». The "grace" of the Redemption gives rise to an "ethos" of the Redemption.

Salvation truly renews the human person, who becomes created anew « in justice and in holiness ».

The grace of the Redemption restores to health and elevates the person's intellect and will, so that the person's freedom is enabled, by the same grace, to act with righteousness.

The human person is thus fully saved in his earthly life. Indeed, as I said before, it is in acting properly that the human person realizes the truth of his being, while, when he does not act properly, he does "himself" evil, destroying the order of his own being.

« IN JUSTICE AND IN HOLINESS »

The true and deepest alienation of man consists in the morally bad action: in this action, the person does not lose what he "has", but he loses what he "is", that is, he loses "himself". « What good is it for a man to gain the whole world, if he loses himself in the process? », the Lord tells us. The only true evil, "entirely" evil, for the human person is moral evil.

The Redemption re-creates us « in justice and in holiness » and enables us to act consistently with this state of justice and holiness of ours. It restores man to himself, makes him return from the land of his exile to his homeland: to his truth, to his freedom as a creature of God. And the sign, the fruit of this return, is good deeds.

THE ACT AND THE PERSON

In the light of the profound relationship between the person and his free acting we can understand what makes up the goodness of our acts, that is, the acts which are those good deeds « which God prepared for us in advance ». The human person is not the absolute master of himself. He is "created" by God. His being is a gift: what he is, and "his very being", here are a gift of God.

« We are truly his handwork », the Apostle teaches us, « created in Christ Jesus » (Eph 2:10). Continually receiving himself from the creating hands of God, man is responsible before him for all he does. When the act freely performed is in "keeping" with the person's being, it is good. It is necessary to emphasize this fundamental relationship between "the act" done by the person and "the person" who does it.

HARMONY BETWEEN PERSON AND ACTS

The human person is gifted with a truth of his own, with an intrinsic order of his own, with a make-up of his own. When his deeds are in harmony with this order, with the make-up proper to a human person created by God, they are good deeds « which God prepared for us in advance ». The goodness of our acting springs from a deep harmony between the person and his acts, while on the contrary, moral evil signals a break, a profound division between the person who is acting and his actions. The order inscribed in his being, that order which is his proper good, is no longer respected in and by his actions. The human person "is no longer" in his truth. Moral evil is precisely the evil of the person "as such"; moral good is the good of the person "as such".

« SLAVES OF JUSTICE »

The goodness of our acts is the fruit of the Redemption. Saint Paul therefore teaches that, by virtue of the fact that we have been redeemed, we have become « slaves of justice » (Rom 6:18). To be « slaves of justice » is our true freedom. In what does "the goodness" of human acting consist? If we pay attention to our daily experience, we see that among the various activities in which our person is expressed, some happen in us but are not fully ours, while others not only happen in us but are "fully ours". These are the activities that are born of our freedom: acts of which each one of us is the "author" in the true and proper sense of the term. They are, in a word, "free acts". When the Apostle teaches us that we are the handiwork of God, « created in Christ Jesus for good deeds », these good deeds are the acts which the human person, with God's help, does freely: goodness is a quality of our free acting, that is, that acting of which the person is the principle and the cause, and for which he is therefore responsible.

Through his free acting, the human person expresses "himself" and at the same time "fulfils" himself.

The Church's faith, based on divine revelation, teaches us that each one of us will be judged according to his deeds. Note: it is "our person" that will be judged on the basis of our deeds. It is understood from this that in our deeds it is "the person" who is expressed, who is fulfilled, and, so to speak, is formed.

Each one is responsible not only for his free actions, but through these actions he becomes responsible "for himself".

A CONVICTION OF FAITH

The Church is convinced that work is a fundamental dimension of man's existence on earth. She is confirmed in this conviction by considering the whole heritage of the many sciences devoted to man: anthropology, paleontology, history, sociology, psychology and so on; they all seem to bear witness to this reality in an irrefutable way. But the source of the Church's conviction is above all the revealed word of God, and therefore what is "a conviction of the intellect" is also "a conviction of faith". The reason is that the Church – and it is worthwhile stating it at this point – believes in man: she "thinks of man" and addresses herself to him "not only" in the light of historical experience, not only with the aid of the many methods of scientific knowledge, but in the first place in the light of the revealed word of the living God.

Relating herself to man, she seeks to "express" the eternal "designs" and transcendent "destiny" which "the living God", the Creator and Redeemer, has linked with him.

The Church finds "in the very first pages of the Book of Genesis" the source of her conviction that work is a fundamental dimension of human existence on earth. An analysis of these texts makes us aware that they express — sometimes in an archaic way of manifesting thought — the fundamental truths about man, in the context of the mystery of creation itself.

A « TRANSITIVE » ACTIVITY

Work understood as a « transitive » activity, that it so say an activity beginning in the human subject and directed towards an external object, presupposes a specific dominion by man over « the earth », and in its turn it confirms and develops this dominion. It is clear that the term « the earth » of which the biblical text speaks is to be understood in the first place as that fragment of the visible universe that man inhabits.

By extension, however, it can be understood as the whole of the visible world insofar as it comes within the range of man's influence and of his striving to satisfy needs.

The expression « subdue the earth » has an immense range. It means all the resources that the earth (and indirectly the visible world) contains and which, through the conscious activity of man, can be discovered and used for his ends. And so these words, placed at the beginning of the Bible, "never cease to be relevant". They embrace equally the past ages of civilization and economy, as also the whole of modern reality and future phases of development, which are perhaps already to some extent beginning to take shape, though for the most part they are still almost unknown to man and hidden from him.

THE DEVELOPMENT
OF TECHONOLOGY

This universality and, at the same time, this multiplicity of the process of « subduing the earth » throw light upon human work, because man's dominion over the earth is achieved in and by means of work.

There thus emerges the meaning of "work in an objective sense", which finds expression in the various epochs of culture and civilization.

Man dominates the earth by the very fact of domesticating animals, rearing them and obtaining from them the food and clothing he needs, and by the fact of being able to extract various natural resources from the earth and the seas.

But man « subdues the earth » much more when he begins to cultivate it and then to transform its products, adapting them to his own use.

Thus agriculture constitutes through human work a primary field of economic activity and an indispensable factor of production.

Industry in its turn will always consist in linking the earth's riches — whether nature's living resources, or the products of agriculture, or the mineral or chemical resources — with man's work, whether physical or intellectual.

This is also in a sense true in the sphere of what are

called service industries, and also in the sphere of research, pure or applied.

In industry and agriculture man's work has today in many cases ceased to be mainly manual, for the toil of human hands and muscles is aided by "more and more highly perfected machinery".

Not only in industry but also in agriculture we are witnessing the transformations made possible by the gradual development of science and technology.

THE ETHICAL NATURE OF WORK

Man has to subdue the earth and dominate it, because as the « image of God » he is a person, that is to say, a subjective being capable of acting in a planned and rational way, capable of deciding about himself, and with a tendency to self-realization. "As a person, man is therefore the subject of work". As a person he works, he performs various actions belonging to the work process; independently of their objective content, these actions must all serve to realize his humanity, to fulfil the calling to be a person that is his by reason of his very humanity.

The principal truths concerning this theme were recently recalled by the Second Vatican Council in the Constitution "Gaudium et Spes", especially in Chapter One, which is devoted to man's calling.

And so this « dominion » spoken of in the biblical text being meditated upon here refers not only to the objective dimension of work but at the same time introduces us to an understanding of its subjective dimension. Understood as a process whereby man and the human race subdue the earth, work corresponds to this basic biblical concept only when throughout the process man manifests himself and confirms himself "as the one who 'dominates'". This dominion, in a certain sense, refers to the objective dimension even more than to the objective one: this dimension conditions "the very ethical nature" of work.

MAN AS
THE SUBJECT OF WORK

There is no doubt that human work has an ethical value of its own, which clearly and directly remains linked to the fact that the one who carries it out is a person, a conscious and free subject, that is to say a subject that decides about himself.

This truth, which in a sense constitutes the fundamental and perennial heart of Christian teaching on human work, has had and continues to have primary significance for the formulation of the important social problems characterizing whole ages.

GOSPEL OF WORK

"The ancient world" introduced its own typical differentiation of people into classes according to the type of work done.

Work which demanded from the worker the exercise of physical strength, the work of muscles and hands, was considered unworthy of free men, and was therefore given to slaves.

By broadening certain aspects that already belonged to the Old Testament, Christianity brought about a fundamental change of ideas in this field, taking the whole content of the Gospel message as its point of departure, especially the fact that the one who, while "being God" became like us in all thing, devoted most of the years of his life on earth to "manual work" at the carpenter's bench.

This circumstance constitutes in itself the most eloquent « Gospel of work », showing that the basis for determining the value of human work is not primarily the kind of work being done but the fact that the one who is doing it is a person. The sources of the dignity of work are to be sought primarily in the subjective dimension, not in the objective one.

WORK AS A « MERCHANDISE »

In the modern period, from the beginning of the industrial age, the Christian truth about work had to oppose the various trends of "materialistic and economistic" thought.

For certain supporter of such ideas, work was understood and treated as a sort of « merchandise » that the worker — especially the industrial worker — sells to the employer, who at the same time is the possessor of the capital, that is to say, of all the working tools and means that make production possible.

This way of looking at work was widespread especially in the first half of the nineteenth century.

Since then, explicit expressions of this sort have almost disappeared, and have given way to more human ways of thinking about work and evaluating it.

The interaction between the worker and the tools and means of production has given rise to the development of various forms of capitalism — parallel with various forms of collectivism — into which other socioeconomic elements have entered as a consequence of new concrete circumstances, of the activity of workers' associations and public authorities, and of the emergence of large transnational enterprises.

Nevertheless, the "danger" of treating work as a special kind of "merchandise", or as an impersonal « force » needed for production (the expression « work-force » is in fact in common use) "always exists", especially when the whole way of looking at the question of economics is marked by the premises of materialistic economism.

WORKERS' SOLIDARITY

The development of human civilization brings continual enrichment in this field. But at the same time, one cannot fail to note that in the process of this development not only do new forms of work appear but also others disappear. Even if one accepts that on the whole this is a normal phenomenon, it must still be seen whether certain ethically and socially dangerous irregularities creep in, and to what extent.

It was precisely one such "wide-raging anomaly" that gave rise in the last century to what has been called « the worker question », sometimes described as « the proletariat question ». This question and the problems connected with it gave rise to a just social reaction and caused the impetuous emergence of a great burst of solidarity between workers, first and foremost industrial workers. The call to solidarity and common action addressed to the workers — especially to those engaged in narrowly specialized, monotonous and depersonalized work in industrial plants, when the machine tends to dominate man — was important and eloquent from the point of view of social ethics. It was the reaction "against the degradation of man as the subject of work", and against the unheard-of accompanying exploitation in the field of wages, working conditions and social security for the worker.

This reaction united the working world in a community marked by great solidarity.

WORKERS' RIGHTS

Workers' solidarity, together with a clearer and more committed realization by others of workers' rights, has in many cases brought about profound changes.

Various forms of neo-capitalism or collectivism have developed. Various new systems have been thought out.

Workers can often share in running businesses and in controlling their productivity, and in fact do so.

Through appropriate associations, they exercise influence over conditions of work and pay, and also over social legislation. But at the same time various ideological or power systems, and new relationships which have arisen at various levels of society, "have allowed flagrant injustices to persist or have created new ones". On the world level, the development of civilization and of communications has made possible a more complete diagnosis of the living and working conditions of man globally, but it has also revealed other forms of injustice, much more extensive than those which in the last century stimulated unity between workers for particular solidarity in the working world.

UNEMPLOYMENT OF INTELLECTUALS

Movements of solidarity in the sphere of work – a solidarity that must never mean being closed to dialogue and collaboration with others – can be necessary also with reference to the condition of social groups that were not previously included in such movements but which, in changing social systems and conditions of living, are undergoing "what is in effect" « proletarianization » or which actually already find themselves in a « proletariat » situation, one which, even if not yet given that name, in fact deserves it. This can be true of certain categories or groups of the working « intelligentsia », especially when ever wider access to education and an ever increasing number of people with degrees or diplomas in the fields of their cultural preparation are accompanied by a drop in demand for their labour. This "unemployment of intellectuals" occurs or increases when the education available is not oriented towards the types of employment or service required by the true needs of society, or when there is less demand for work which requires education, at least professional education, than for manual labour, or when it is less well paid. Of course, education in itself is always valuable and an important enrichment of the human person; but in spite of that, « proletarianization » processes remain possible.

TOIL IS UNIVERSALLY KNOWN

God's fundamental and original intention with regard to man, whom he created in his image and after his likeness, was not withdrawn or cancelled out even when man, having broken the original covenant with God, heard the words: « In the sweat of your face you shall eat bread » (Gn 3:19). These words refer to "the sometimes heavy toil" that from then onwards has accompanied human work; but they do not alter the fact that work is the means whereby man "achieves that" « dominion » which is proper to him over the visible world, by « subjecting » the earth. Toil is something that is universally known, for it is universally experienced.

It is familiar to those doing physical work under sometimes exceptionally laborious conditions. It is familiar not only to agricultural workers, who spend long days working the land, which sometimes « bears thorns and thistles » (Heb 6:8), but also to those who work in mines and quarries, to steel-workers at their blast-furnaces, to those who work in builders' yards and in construction work, often in danger of injury or death. It is likewise familiar to those at an intellectual workbench; to scientists; to those who bear the burden of grave responsibility for decisions that will have a vast impact on society. It is familiar to doctors and nurses, who spend days and nights at their patients' bedside. It is familiar to women, who, sometimes without proper recognition on the part of society and even of their own families, bear the daily burden and responsibility for their homes and the upbringing of their children.

AGAINST MAN

If one wishes to define more clearly the ethical meaning of work, it is this truth that one must particulary keep in mind. Work is a good thing for man – a good thing for his humanity – because through work man "not only transforms nature", adapting it to his own needs, but he also "achieves fulfilment" as a human being and indeed, in a sense, becomes « more a human being ».

Without this consideration it is impossible to understand the meaning of the virtue of industriousness, and more particularly it is impossible to understand why industriousness should be a virtue: for virtue, as a moral habit, is something whereby man becomes good as man.

This fact in no way alters our justifiable anxiety that in work, whereby "matter gains in nobility", man himself should not experience a "lowering" of his own dignity. Again, it is well known that it is possible to use work in various ways "against man", that it is possible to punish man with the system of forced labour in concentration camps, that work can be made into a means for oppressing man, and that in various ways it is possible to exploit human labour, that is to say the worker. All this pleads in favour of the moral obligation to link industriousness as a virtue with "the social order of work", which will enable man to become, in work, « more a human being » and not be degraded by it not only because of the wearing out of his physical strength (which, at least, up to a certain point, is inevitable), but especially through damage to the dignity and subjectivity that are proper to him.

FOUNDATION OF FAMILY LIFE

Work constitutes a foundation for the formation of "family life", which is a natural right and something that man is called to.

These two spheres of values — one linked to work and the other consequent on the family nature of human life — must be properly united and must properly permeate each other.

In a way, work is a condition for making it possible

to found a family, since the family requires the means of subsistence which man normally gains through work. Work and industriousness also influence the whole "process of education" in the family, for the very reason that everyone « becomes a human being » through, among other things, work, and becoming a human being is precisely the main purpose of the whole process of education. Obviously, two aspects of work in a sense come into play here: the one making family life and its upkeep possible, and the other making possible the achievement of the purposes of the family, especially education. Nevertheless, these two aspects of work are linked to one another and are mutually complementary in various points.

THE ETHICAL ORDER OF HUMAN WORK

It must be remembered and affirmed that the family constitutes one of the most important terms of reference for shaping the social and ethical order of human work. The teaching of the Church has always devoted special attention to this question, and in the present document we shall have to return to it. In fact, the family is simultaneously a "community made possible by work" and the first "school of work", within the home, for every person.

The third sphere of values that emerges from this point of view — that of the subject of work — concerns the "great society" to which man belongs on the basis of particular cultural and historical links. This society — even when it has not yet taken on the mature form of a nation — is not only the great « educator » of every man, even though and indirect one (because each individual absorbs within the family the contents and values that go to make up the culture of a given nation); it is also a great historical and social incarnation of the work of all generations.

A GREAT REALITY

Work is seen as a great reality with a fundamental influence on the shaping in a human way of the world that the Creator has entrusted to man; it is a reality closely linked with man as the subject of work and with man's rational activity. In the normal course of events this reality fills human life and strongly affects its value and meaning. Even when it is accompanied by toil and effort, work is still something good, and so man develops through love for work. This entirely "positive and creative, educational and meritorious character of man's work" must be the basis for the judgements and decisions being made today in its regard in spheres that include "human rights", as is evidenced by the international "declarations" on work and the many "labour codes" prepared either by the competent legislative institutions in the various countries or by organizations devoting their social, or scientific and social activity to the problems of work. One organization fostering such initiatives on the international level is the International Labour Organization, the oldest specialized agency of the United Nations Organization.

CONFLICT BETWEEN LABOUR
AND CAPITAL

Throughout this period, which is by no means yet over, the issue of work has of course been posed on the basis of the great "conflict" that in the age of, and together with, industrial development emerged « between "capital" and "labour" », that is to say between the small but highly influential group of entrepreneurs, owners or holders of the means of production, and the broader multitude of people who lacked these means and who shared in the process of production solely by their labour. The conflict originated in the fact that the workers put their powers at the disposal of the entrepreneurs, and these, following the principle of maximum profit, tried to establish the lowest possible wages for the work done by the employees. In addition there were other elements of exploitation, connected with the lack of safety at work and of safeguards regarding the health and living conditions of the workers and their families. This conflict, interpreted by some as a socio-economic "class conflict", found expression in the "ideological conflict" between liberalism, understood as the ideology of capitalism, and Marxism, understood as the ideology of scientific socialism and communism, which professes to act as the spokesman for the working class and the worldwide proletariat.

THE COMMUNIST SYSTEM

The real conflict between labour and capital was transformed into "a systematic class struggle" conducted not only by ideological means but also and chiefly by political means. We are familiar with the history of this conflict and with the demands of both sides. The Marxist programme, based on the philosophy of Marx and Engels, sees in class struggle the only way to eliminate class injustices in society and to eliminate the classes themselves. Putting this programme into practice presupposes "the collectivization of the means of production" so

340

that, through the transfer of these means from private hands to the collectivity, human labour will be preserved from exploitation.

This is the goal of the struggle carried on by political as well as ideological means. In accordance with the principle of « the dictatorship of the proletariat », the groups that as political parties follow the guidance of Marxist ideology aim by the use of various kinds of influence, including revolutionary pressure, to win "a monopoly of power in each society", in order to introduce the collectivist system into it by eliminating private ownership of the means of production. According to the principal ideologists and leaders of this broad international movement, the purpose of this programme of action is to achieve the social revolution and to introduce socialism and, finally, the communist system throughout the world.

THE VARIOUS RICHES OF NATURE

When we read in the first chapter of the Bible that man is to subdue the earth, we know that these words refer to all the resources contained in the visible world and placed at man's disposal. However, these resources "can serve man only through work". From the beginning there is also linked with work the question of ownership, for the only means that man has for causing the resources hidden in nature to serve himself and others is his work. And to be able through his work to make these resources bear fruit, man takes over ownership of small parts of the various riches of nature: those beneath the ground, those in the sea, on land, or in space. He takes all these things over by making them his workbench. He takes them over through work and for work.

READY FOR MAN

The same principle applies in the successive phases of this process, in which "the first phase" always remains the relationship of man with "the resources and riches of nature". The whole of the effort to acquire knowledge with the aim of discovering these riches and specifying the various ways in which they can be used by man and for man, teaches us that everything that comes from man throughout the whole process of economic production, whether labour or the whole collection of means of production and the technology connected with these means (meaning the capability to use them in work), presupposes these riches and resources of the visible world, riches and resources "that man finds" and does not create. In a sense man finds them already prepared, ready for him to discover them and to use them correctly in the productive process. In every phase of the development of his work man comes up against the leading role of "the gift made" by « nature », that is to say, in the final analysis, "by the Creator". At the beginning of man's work is the mystery of creation.

CAPACITY FOR WORK

All the means of production, from the most primitive to the ultra-modern ones – it is man that has gradually developed them: man's experience and intellect. In this way there have appeared not only the simplest instruments for cultivating the earth but also, through adequate progress in science and technology, the more modern and complex ones: machines, factories, laboratories, and computers. Thus "everything that is at the service of work", everything that in the present state of technology constitutes its ever more highly perfected « instrument », "is the result of work". This gigantic and powerful instrument – the whole collection of means of production that in a sense are considered synonymous with « capital » – is the result of work and bears the signs of human labour. At the present stage of technological advance, when man, who is the subject of work, wishes to make use of this collection of modern instruments, the means of production, he must first assimilate cognitively the result of the work of the people who invented those instruments, who planned them, built them and perfected them, and who continue to do so. "Capacity for work" – that is to say, for sharing efficiently in the modern production process – demands greater and greater "preparation" and, before all else, proper "training".

TWO INHERITANCES

Opposition between labour and capital does not spring from the structure of the production process or from the structure of the economic process. In general the latter process demonstrates that labour and what we are accustomed to call capital are intermingled; it shows that they are inseparably linked. Working at any workbench, whether a relatively primitive or an ultramodern one, a man can easily see that "through his work he enters into two inheritances": the inheritance of what is given to the whole of humanity in the resources of nature, and the inheritance of what others have already developed on the basis of those resources, primarily by developing technology, that is to say, by producing a whole collection of increasingly perfect instruments for work. In working, man also « enters into the labour of others » (Jn 4:38).

MASTER OF THE CREATURES

Guided both by our intelligence and by the faith that draws light from the word of God, we have no difficulty in accepting this image of the sphere and process of man's labour. It is "a consistent image, one that is humanistic as well as theological". In it man is the master of the creatures placed at his disposal in the visible world. If some dependence is discovered in the work process, it is dependence on the Giver of all the resources of creation, and also on other human beings, those to whose work and initiative we owe the perfected and increased possibilities of our own work. All that we can say of everything in the production process which constitutes a whole collection of « things », the instruments, the capital, is that it "conditions" man's work; we cannot assert that it constitutes as it were an impersonal « subject » "putting" man and man's work "into a position of dependence".

ECONOMISM

The error of thinking in the categories of economism went hand in hand with the formation of a materialist philosophy, as this philosophy developed from the most elementary and common phase (also called common materialism, because it professes to reduce spiritual reality to a superfluous phenomenon) to the phase of what is called dialectical materialism. However, within the framework of the present consideration, it seems that "economism had a decisive importance" for the fundamental issue of human work, in particular for the separation of labour and capital and for setting them up in opposition as two production factors viewed in the above-mentioned economistic perspective; and it seems that economism influenced this non-humanistic way of stating the issue before the materialist philosophical system did. Nevertheless it is obvious that materialism, including its dialectical form, is incapable of providing sufficient and definitive bases for thinking about human work, in order that the primacy of man over the capital instrument, the primacy of the person over things, may find in it adequate and irrefutable "confirmation and support". In dialectical materialism too man is not first and foremost the subject of work and the efficient cause of the production process, but continues to be understood and treated, in dependence on what is material, as a kind of « resultant » of the economic or production relations prevailing at a given period.

WORK AND OWNERSHIP

The Encyclical "Rerum Novarum", which has the social question as its theme, stresses this issue also, recalling and confirming the Church's teaching on ownership, on the right to private property even when it is a question of the means of production. The Encyclical "Mater et Magistra" did the same.
The above principle, as it was then stated and as it is still taught by the Church, "diverges" radically from the programme of "collectivism" as proclaimed by Marxism and put into practice in various countries in the decades following the time of Leo XIII's Encyclical. At the same time it differs from the programme of "capitalism" practised by liberalism and by the political systems inspired by it. In the latter case, the difference consists in the way the right to ownership or property is understood.

Christian tradition has never upheld this right as absolute and untouchable. On the contrary, it has always understood this right within the broader context of the right common to all to use the goods of the whole of creation: "the right to private property is subordinated to the right to common use", to the fact that goods are meant for everyone.

Furthermore, in the Church's teaching, ownership has never been understood in a way that could constitute grounds for social conflict in labour. As mentioned above, property is acquired first of all through work in order that it may serve work. This concerns in a special way ownership of the means of production. Isolating these means as a separate property in order to set it up in the form of « capital » in opposition to « labour » — and even to practice exploitation of labour — is contrary to the very nature of these means and their possession.

SOCIALIZATION

While the position of « rigid » capitalism must undergo continual revision, in order to be reformed from the point of view of human rights, both human rights in the widest sense and those linked with man's work, it must be stated that, from the same point of view, these many deeply desired reforms cannot be achieved by an "a priori elimination of private ownership of the means of production". For it must be noted that merely taking these means of production (capital) out of the hands of their private owners is not enough to ensure their satisfactory socialization. They cease to be the property of a certain social group, namely the private owners, and become the property of organized society, coming under the administration and direct control of another group of people, namely those who, though not owning them, from the fact of exercising power in society, "manage" them on the level of the whole national or the local economy.

THE MONOPOLY
OF THE MEANS OF PRODUCTION

This group in authority may carry out its task satisfactorily from the point of view of the priority of labour; but it may also carry it out badly by claiming for itself "a monopoly of the administration and disposal" of the means of production and not refraining even from offending basic human rights.

Thus, merely converting the means of production into State property in the collectivist system is by no means equivalent to « socializing » that property.

We can speak of socializing only when the subject character of society is ensured, that is to say, when on the basis of his work each person is fully entitled to consider himself a part-owner of the great workbench at which he is working with everyone else.

INTERMEDIATE BODIES

A way towards that goal could be found by associating labour with the ownership of capital, as far as possible, and by producing a wide range of intermediate bodies with economic, social and cultural purposes; they would be bodies enjoying real autonomy with regard to the public powers, pursuing ther specific aims in honest collaboration with each other and in subordination to the demands of the common good, and they would be living communities both in form and in substance, in the sense that the members of each body would be looked upon and treated as persons and encouraged to take an active part in the life of the body.

AN OBLIGATION

While work, in all its many senses, is an obligation, that is to say a duty, it is also a source of rights on the part of the "worker". These rights must be examined in the broad "context of human rights as a whole", which are connatural with man, and many of which are proclaimed by various international organizations and increasingly guaranteed by the individual States for their citizens. Respect for this broad range of human rights constitutes the fundamental condition for peace in the modern world: peace both within individual countries and societies and in international relations, as the Church's Magisterium has several times noted, especially since the Encyclical "Pacem in Terris".

The "human rights that flow from work" are part of the broader context of those fundamental rights of the person.

However, within this context they have a specific character corresponding to the specific nature of human work as outlined above. It is in keeping with this character that we must view them. Work is, as has been said, "an obligation", that is to say, "a duty, on the part of man". This is true "in all the many meanings of the word".

Man must work, both because the Creator has commanded it and because of his own humanity, which requires work in order to be maintained and developed.

Man must work out of regard for others, especially his own family, but also for the society he belongs to, the country of which he is a child, and the whole human family of which he is a member, since he is the heir to the work of generations and at the same time a sharer in building the future of those who will come after him in the succession of history. All this constitutes the moral obligation of work, understood in its wide sense.

When we have to consider the moral rights, corresponding to this obligation, of every person with regard to work, we must always keep before our eyes the whole vast range of points of reference in which the labour of every working subject is manifested.

For when we speak of the obligation of work and of the rights of the worker that correspond to this obligation, we think in the first place of the relationship between "the employer, direct or indirect, and the worker".

DIRECT AND INDIRECT EMPLOYER

Since "the direct employer" is the person or institution with whom the worker enters directly into a work contract in accordance with definite conditions, we must understand as "the indirect" employer many different factors, other than the direct employer, that exercise a determining influence on the shaping both of the work contract and, consequently, of just or unjust relationships in the field of human labour.

The concept of indirect employer includes both persons and institutions of various kinds, and also collective labour contracts and the "principles" of conduct which are laid down by these persons and institutions and which determine the whole socioeconomic "system" or are its result. The concept of « indirect employer » thus refers to many different elements.

The responsibility of the indirect employer differs from that of the direct employer – the term itself indicates that the responsibility is less direct – but it remains a true responsibility: the indirect employer substantially determines one or other facet of the labour relationship, thus conditioning the conduct of the direct employer when the latter determines in concrete terms the actual work contract and labour relations.

This is not to absolve the direct employer from his own responsibility, but only to draw attention to the whole network of influences that condition his conduct. When it is a question of establishing "an ethically correct labour policy", all these influences must be kept in mind.

A policy is correct when the objective rights of the worker are fully respected.

The concept of indirect employer is applicable to every society, and in the first place to the State. For it is the State that must conduct a just labour policy. However, it is common knowledge that in the present system of economic relations in the world there are numerous "links between" individual "States", links that find expression, for instance, in the import and export process, that is to say, in the mutual exchange of economic goods, whether raw materials, semi-manufactured or finished industrial products.

These links also create mutual "dependence", and as a result it would be difficult to speak, in the case of any State, even the economically most powerful, of complete, self-sufficiency or autarky.

« A man can have no greater love than to lay down his life for his friends » (Jn 15:13).

In the cell of Maximilian Kolbe.

Such a system of mutual dependence is in itself normal. However, it can easily become an occasion for various forms of exploitation or injustice and as a result influence the labour policy of individual States; and finally it can influence the individual worker, who is the proper subject of labour. For instance, the "highly industrialized countries", and even more the business that direct on a large scale the means of industrial production (the companies referred to as multinational or transnational), fix the highest possible prices for their products, while trying at the same time to fix the lowest possible prices for raw materials or semi-manufactured goods. This is one of the causes of an ever increasing disproportion between national incomes. The gap between most of the richest countries and the poorest ones is not diminishing or being stabilized but is increasing more and more, to the detriment, obviously, of the poor countries. Evidently this must have an effect on local labour policy and on the worker's situation in the economically disadvantaged societies.

Finding himself in a system thus conditioned, the direct employer fixes working conditions below the objective requirements of the workers, especially if he himself whishes to obtain the highest possible profits from the business which he runs (or from the business which he runs, in the case of a situation of « socialized » ownership of the means of production).

It is easy to see that this framework of forms of dependence linked with the concept of the indirect employer is enormously extensive and complicated.

It is determined, in a sense, by "all" the elements that are decisive for economic life "within a given

society and state", but also by much wider links
and forms of dependence.

The attainment of the worker's rights cannot
however be doomed to be merely a result of
economic systems which on a larger or smaller scale
are guided chiefly by the criterion of maximum
profit.

On the contrary, it is respect for the objective
rights of the worker – every kind of worker:
manual or intellectual, industrial or agricultural,
etc. – that must constitute "the adequate and
fundamental criterion" for shaping the whole
economy, both on the level of the individual society
and State and within the whole of the world
economic policy and of the systems of international
relationships that derive from it.

TO ACT AGAINST UNEMPLOYMENT

When we consider the rights of workers in relation
to the « indirect employer », that is to say, all the
agents at the national and international level that
are responsible for the whole orientation of labour
policy, we must first direct our attention to a
"fundamental issue": the question of finding work,
or, in other words, the issue of "suitable employment for all who are capable of it". The opposite of
a just and right situation in this field is unemployment, that is to say the lack of work for those who
are capable of it. It can be a question of general
unemployment or of unemployment in certain
sectors of work. The role of the agents included
under the title of indirect employer is "to act
against unemployment", which in all cases is an
evil, and which, when it reaches a certain level, can
become a real social disaster. It is particularly
painful when it especially affects young people,

who after appropriate cultural, technical and professional preparation fail to find work, and see their sincere wish to work and their readiness to take on their own responsibility for the economic and social development of the community sadly frustrated. The obligation to provide unemployment benefits, that is to say, the duty to make suitable grants indispensable for the subsistence of unemployed workers and their families, is a duty springing from the fundamental principle of the moral order in this sphere, namely the principle of the common use of goods or, to put it in another and still simpler way, the right to life and subsistence.

In order to meet the danger of unemployment and to ensure employment for all, the agents defined here as « indirect employers » must make provision for "overall planning" with regard to the different kinds of work by which not only the economic life but also the cultural life of a given society is shaped; they must also give attention to organizing that work in a correct and rational way. In the final analysis this overall concern weighs on the shoulders of the State, but it cannot mean onesided centralization by the public authorities. Instead, what is in question is a just and rational "coordination", within the framework of which the "initiative" of individuals, free groups and local work centres and complexes must be "safeguarded", keeping in mind what has been said above with regard to the subjective character of human labour.

MUTUAL DEPENDANCE

The fact of the mutual dependance of societies and States and the need to collaborate in various areas mean that, while preserving the sovereign rights of each society and State in the field of planning and organizing labour in its own society, action in this important area must also be taken in the dimension of "international collaboration" by means of the necessary treaties and agreements.

Here too the criterion for these pacts and agreements must more and more be the criterion of human work considered as a fundamental right of all human beings, work which gives similar rights to all those who work, in such a way that the living standard of the workers in the different societies will "less and less show those disturbing differences" which are unjust and are apt to provoke even violent reactions.

The International Organizations have an enormous part to play in this area.

They must let themselves be guided by an exact diagnosis of the complex situations and of the influence exercised by natural, historical, civil and other such circumstances.

They must also be more highly operative with regard to plans for action jointly decided on, that is to say, they must be more effective in carrying them out.

THE REAPPRAISAL
OF MAN'S WORK

In this direction it is possible to actuate a plan for universal and proportionate progress by all, in accordance with the guidelines of Paul VI's Encyclical "Populorum Progressio". It must be stressed that the constitutive element in this "progress" and also the most adequate "way to verify it" in a spirit of justice and peace, which the Church proclaims and for which she does not cease to pray to the Father of all individuals and of all peoples, is "the continual reappraisal of man's work", both in the aspect of its objective finality and in the aspect of the dignity of the subject of all work, that is to say, man.

The progress in question must be made through man and for man and it must produce its fruit in man.

A test of this progress will be the increasingly mature recognition of the purpose of work and increasingly universal respect for the rights inherent in work in conformity with the dignity of man, the subject of work.

JUST REMUNERATION

Just remuneration for the work of an adult who is responsible for a family means remuneration which will suffice for establishing and properly maintaining a family and for providing security for its future.

Such remuneration can be given either through what is called a "family wage" – that is, a single salary given to the head of the family for his work, sufficient for the needs of the family without the other spouse having to take up gainful employment outside the home – or through "other social measures" such as family allowances or grants to mothers devoting themselves exclusively to their families.

These grants should correspond to the actual needs, that is, to the number of dependents for as long as they are not in a position to assume proper responsibility for their own lives.

RE-EVALUATION OF THE MOTHER'S ROLE

Experience confirms that there must be "a social re-evaluation of the mother's role", of the toil connected with it, and of the need that children have for care, love and affection in order that they may develop into responsible, morally and religiously mature and psychologically stable persons. It will redound to the credit of society to make it possible for a mother — without inhibiting her freedom, without psychological or practical discrimination, and without penalizing her as compared with other women — to devote herself to taking care of her children and educating them in accordance with their needs, which vary with age. Having to abandon these tasks in order to take up paid work outside the home is wrong from the point of view of the good of society and of the family when it contradicts or hinders these primary goals of the mission of a mother.

IMPORTANCE OF UNIONS

In a sense, unions go back to the mediaeval guilds of artisans, insofar as those organizations brought together people belonging to the same craft and thus "on the basis of their work". However, unions differ from the guilds on this essential point: the modern unions grew up from the struggle of the workers — workers in general but especially the industrial workers — to protect their "just rights" vis-a-vis the entrepreneurs and the owners of the means of production. Their task is to defend the existential interests of workers in all sectors in which their rights are concerned. The experience of history teaches that organizations of this type are an indispensable "element of social life", especially in modern industrialized societies. Obviously, this does not mean that only industrial workers can set up associations of this type. Representatives of every profession can use them to ensure their own rights. Thus there are unions of agricultural workers and of white-collar workers: there are also employers associations. All, as has been said above, are further divided into groups or subgroups according to particular professional specializations. Catholic social teaching does not hold that unions are no more than a reflection of the « class » structure of society and that they are a mouthpiece for a class struggle which inevitably governs social life. They are indeed "a mouthpiece for the struggle for social justice", for the just rights of working people in accordance with their individual professions.

DIGNITY OF AGRICULTURAL WORK

Agricultural work involves considerable difficulties, including unremitting and sometimes exhausting physical effort and a lack of appreciation of the part of society, to the point of making agricultural people feel that they are social outcasts and of speeding up the phenomenon of their mass exodus from the countryside to the cities and unfortunately to still more dehumanizing living conditions.

Added to this are the lack of adequate professional training and of proper equipment, the spread of a certain individualism, and also "objectively unjust situations".

In certain developing countries, millions of people are forced to cultivate the land belonging to others and are exploited by the big landowners, without any hope of every being able to gain possession of even a small piece of land of their own. There is a lack of forms of legal protection for the agricultural workers themselves and for their families in case of old age, sickness or unemployment.

Long days of hard physical work are paid miserably. Land which could be cultivated is left abandoned by the owners. Legal titles to possession of a small portion of land that someone has personally cultivated for years are disregarded or left defenceless against the « land hunger » of more powerful individuals or groups.

But even in the economically developed countries, where scientific research, technological achievements and State policy have brought agriculture to a very advanced level, the right to work can be infringed when the farm workers are denied the possibility of sharing in decisions concerning their services, or when they are denied the right to free association with a view to their just advancement socially, culturally and economically.

In many situations radical and urgent changes are therefore needed in order to restore to agriculture – and to rural people – their just value "as the basis for a healthy economy", within the social community's development as a whole.

THE DISABLED PERSON AND WORK

Recently, national communities and international organizations have turned their attention to another question connected with work, one full of implications: the question of disabled people. They too are fully human subjects with corresponding innate, sacred and inviolable rights, and, in spite of the limitations and sufferings affecting their bodies and faculties, they point up more clearly the dignity and greatness of man. Since disabled people are subjects with all their rights, they should be helped to participate in the life of society in all its aspects and at all the levels accessible to their capacities. The disabled person is one of us and participates fully in the same humanity that we possess. It would be radically unworthy of man, and a denial of our common humanity, to admit to the life of the community, and thus admit to work, only those who are fully functional. To do so would be to practise "a serious form of discrimination", that of the strong and healthy against the weak and sick. Work in the objective sense should be subordinated, in this circumstance too, to the dignity of man, to the subject of work and not to economic advantage.

WORK AND EMIGRATION

Man has the right to leave his native land for various motives – and also the right to return – in order to seek better conditions of life in another country. This fact is certainly not without difficulties of various kinds. Above all it generally constitutes a loss for the country which is left behind. It is the departure of a person who is also a member of a great community united by history, tradition and culture; and that person must begin life in the midst of another society united by a different culture and very often by a different language. In this case, it is the loss of a "subject of work", whose efforts of mind and body could contribute to the common good of his own country, but these efforts, this contribution, are instead offered to another society which in a sense has less right to them than the person's country of origin.

A NECESSARY EVIL

Even if emigration is in some aspects an evil, in certain circumstances it is, as the phrase goes, a necessary evil. Everything should be done – and certainly much is being done to this end – to prevent this material evil from causing greater "moral harm"; indeed every possible effort should be made to ensure that it may bring benefit to the emigrant's personal, familial and social life, both for the country to which he goes and the country which he leaves. In this area much depends on just legislation, in particular with regard to the rights of workers. It is obvious that the question of just legislation enters into the context of the present considerations, especially from the point of view of these rights.

The most important thing is that the person working away from his native land, whether as a permanent emigrant or as a seasonal worker, should not be "placed at a disadvantage" in comparison with the other workers in that society in the matter of working rights. Emigration in search of work must in no way become an opportunity for financial or social exploitation.

WORK AND REST

Man, created to God's image, received a mandate to subject to himself the earth and all that it contains, and to govern the world with justice and holiness; a mandate to relate himself and the totality of things to him who was to be acknowledged as the Lord and Creator of all. Thus, by the subjection of all things to man, the name of God would be wonderful in all the earth (GS, 34).

The word of God's revelation is profoundly marked

by the fundamental truth that "man", created in the image of God, "shares by his work in the activity of the Creator" and that, within the limits of his own human capabilities, man in a sense continues to develop that activity, and perfects it as he advances further and further in the discovery of the resources and values contained in the whole of creation. We find this truth at the very beginning of Sacred Scripture, in the Book of Genesis, where the creation activity itself is presented in the form of « work » done by God during « six days », (Gn 2:2) « resting » on the seventh day. Besides, the last book of Sacred Scripture echoes the same respect for what God has done through his creative « work » when it proclaims: « Great and wonderful are your deeds, O Lord God the Almighty »; (Rv 15:3) this is similar to the Book of Genesis, which concludes the description of each day of creation with the statement: « And God saw that it was good » (Gn 1:4).

This description of creation, which we find in the very first chapter of the Book of Genesis, is also « in a sense the first "gospel of work" ». For it shows what the dignity of work consists of: it teaches that man ought to imitate God, his Creator, in working, because man alone has the unique characteristic of likeness to God. Man ought to imitate God both in working and also in resting, since God himself wished to present his own creative activity under the form of "work and rest".

CHRIST, THE MAN OF WORK

The truth that by means of work man participates in the activity of God himself, his Creator, was "given particular prominence by Jesus Christ" – the Jesus at whom many of his first listeners in

Nazareth « were astonished, saying "Where did this man get all this? What is the wisdom given to him?... Is not this the carpenter?" » (Mk 6:2-3). For Jesus not only proclaimed but first and foremost fulfilled by his deeds the « gospel », the word of eternal Wisdom, that had been entrusted to him. Therefore this was also « the gospel of work », because "he who proclaimed it was himself a man of work", a craftsman like Joseph of Nazareth. And if we do not find in his words a special command to work — but rather on one occasion a prohibition against too much anxiety about work and life — at the same time the eloquence of the life of Christ is unequivocal: he belongs to the « working world », he has appreciation and respect for human work. It can indeed be said that "he looks with love upon human work" and the different forms that it takes, seeing in each one of these forms a particular facet of man's likeness with God, the Creator and Father.

THE NORM OF HUMAN ACTIVITY

The teachings of the Apostle of the Gentiles obviously have key importance for the morality and spirituality of human work. They are an important complement to the great though discreet gospel of work that we find in the life and parables of Christ, in what Jesus « did and taught ». (Acts 1:1). On the basis of these illuminations emanating from the Source himself, the Church has always proclaimed what we find "expressed in modern terms" in the teaching of the Second Vatican Council: « Just as human activity proceeds from man, so it is ordered towards man. For when a man works, he not only alters things and society, he develops himself as well. He learns much, he cultivates his resources, he goes outside of himself and beyond himself.

Rightly understood, this kind of growth is of greater value than any external riches which can be garnered... Hence, the norm of human activity is this: that in accord with the divine plan and will, it should harmonize with the genuine good of the human race, and allow people as individuals and as members of society to pursue their total vocation and fulfil it » (GS, 35).

« IN THE SWEAT OF YOUR FACE »

There is yet another aspect of human work, an essential dimension of it, that is profoundly imbued with the spirituality based on the Gospel. All "work", whether manual or intellectual, is inevitably linked with "toil". The Book of Genesis expresses it in a truly penetrating manner: the original "blessing" of work contained in the very mystery of creation and connected with man's elevation as the image of God is contrasted with the "curse" that "sin" brought with it: « Cursed is the ground because of you; in toil you shall eat of it all the days of your life » (Gn 3:17). This toil connected with work marks the way of human life on earth and constitutes "an announcement of death": « In the sweat of your face you shall eat bread till you return to the ground, for out of it you were taken » (Gn 3:19).

Almost as an echo of these words, the author of one of the Wisdom books says: « Then I considered all that my hands had done and the toil I had spent in doing it... » (Eccl 2:11).

There is no one on earth who could not apply these words to himself.

TO MAKE ITS LIFE MORE HUMAN

Christ, « undergoing death itself for all of us sinners, taught us by example that we´too must shoulder that cross which the world and the flesh inflict upon those who pursue peace and justice »; but also, at the same time, « appointed Lord "by his Resurrection" and given all authority in heaven and on earth, Christ is now at work in people's hearts through the power of his Spirit... He animates, purifies and strenghtens those noble longings too by which the human family strives "to make its life more human" and to render the whole earth submissive to this goal » (GS, 38).

The Christian finds in human work a small part of the Cross of Christ and accepts it in the same spirit of redemption in which Christ accepted his Cross for us. In work, thanks to the light that penetrates us from the Resurrection of Christ, we always find a "glimmer" of new life, of the "new good", as if it were an announcement of "the new heavens and the new earth" (2 Pt 3:13) in which man and the world participate precisely through the toil that goes with work. Through toil — and never without it. On the one hand this confirms the indispensability of the Cross in the spirituality of human work: on the other hand the Cross which this toil constitutes reveals a new good springing from work itself, from work understood in depth and in all its aspects and never apart from work.

NEW GOOD

Is this "new good" — the fruit of human work — already a small part of that « new earth » where justice dwells? If it is true that the many forms of toil that go with man's work are a small part of the

Cross of Christ, what is the relationship of this new good to "the Resurrection of Christ"? The Council seeks to reply to this question also, drawing light from the very sources of the revealed word: « Therefore, while we are warned that it profits a man nothing if he gains the whole world and loses himself » (Lk 9:25), the expectation of a new earth must not weaken but rather stimulate our concern for cultivating this one. For here grows the body of a new human family, a body which even now is able to give some kind of foreshadowing of the new age. Earthly progress must be carefully distinguished from the growth of Christ's kingdom. Nevertheless, to the extent that the former can contribute to the better ordering of human society, it is of vital concern to the Kingdom of God » (GS, 39).

« ...HAS DONE GREAT THINGS FOR ME »

On the feast of the Assumption, the Church's liturgy places on the lips of Mary the same words: « The Almighty has done great things for me ». She who had been chosen from eternity as the Mother of the Word Incarnate; she, in whom God himself lived in the person of the Son, begins in a particular manner to live in God – the Father, Son and Holy Spirit.

She, in whom the same God in the Person of the Son, chose a dwelling-place, was conceived immaculate: she was free from the taint of original sin. Because of this she was also preserved from the law of death, which entered into the history of mankind together with sin.

St Paul writes (and we read these words in today's liturgy): « For as by a man came death, by a man has come also the resurrection of the dead. For as in Adam all die, so also in Christ shall all be made alive. But each in his own order: Christ the first fruits, then at his coming those who belong to Christ » (1 Cor 15:21-23).

FREE FROM ORIGINAL SIN

Free – by the power of Christ – from original sin; redeemed in a particular and exceptional way, Mary was also included in a particular and exceptional way in his resurrection. The resurrection of Christ had already overcome in her the law of sin and death through her immaculate conception. At that moment there was already accomplished in her the victory over sin and the law of death, the penalty of sin.

It was necessary that she, who was the Mother of the Risen Christ, would be the first among men to participate in the full power of his resurrection.

It was necessary that she, in whom dwelt the Son of God as author of the victory over sin and death, would also be the first to live in God, free from sin and the corruption of the grave:

– from sin, through her immaculate conception
– from the corruption of the grave, through the assumption.

SHE IS THE « SIGN »

Let us contemplate in a special way the Mother of God. Let us fix our gaze on her definitive dwelling in God. On her glory.

She is that great « sign » which, according to the words of St John in the Apocalypse appeared in the heavens (Rv 12:1).

This sign is at the present time closely connected with the earth. It is first of all the sign of the struggle « with the dragon » (Rv 12:4), and in this struggle we read again the whole story of the Church on earth: the struggle against Satan, the struggle against the forces of darkness, which never cease to attack the Kingdom of God.

This is, at the same time, the sign of the definitive victory. In the mystery of her Assumption Mary is the sign of this definitive victory, of which the author of the Apocalypse speaks: « Now the salvation and the power and the kingdom of our God and the authority of his Christ have come » (Rv 12:10).

ALL THE BOOKS
OF THE OLD AND NEW TESTAMENT

OLD TESTAMENT

Gn	Genesis
Ex	Exodus
Lv	Leviticus
Nu	Numbers
Dt	Deuteronomy
Jos	Joshua
Jdg	Judges
Rth	Ruth
1 Sam	1 Samuel
2 Sam	2 Samuel
1 Kgs	1 Kings
2 Kgs	2 Kings
1 Chr	1 Chronicles
2 Chr	2 Chronicles
Ezr	Ezra
Neh	Nehemiah
Tb	Tobit
Jdth	Judith
Esth	Esther
1 Mac	1 Maccabees
2 Mac	2 Maccabees
Jb	Job
Ps	Psalms
Prv	Proverbs
Eccl	Ecclesiastes
Song	Song of Solomon
Wis	Wisdom
Sir	Ecclesiasticus
Is	Isaiah
Jer	Jeremiah
Lam	Lamentations
Bar	Baruch
Ez	Ezekiel
Dn	Daniel
Hs	Hosea
Jl	Joel
Am	Amos
Ob	Obadiah
Jon	Jonah
Mic	Micah
Na	Nahum
Hab	Habakkuk
Zep	Zephaniah
Hag	Haggai
Zec	Zechariah
Mal	Malachi

NEW TESTAMENT

Mt	Matthew
Mk	Mark
Lk	Luke
Jn	John
Acts	The Acts
Rom	The Romans
1 Cor	1 Corinthians
2 Cor	2 Corinthians
Gal	Galatians
Eph	Ephesians
Phil	Philippians
Col	Colossians
1 Thes	1 Thessalonians
2 Thes	2 Thessalonians
1 Tim	1 Timothy
2 Tim	2 Timothy
Ti	Titus
Philem	Philemon
Heb	To the Hebrews
Jas	Epistle of James
1 Pt	1 Peter
2 Pt	2 Peter
1 Jn	1 John
2 Jn	2 John
3 Jn	3 John
Jud	Jude
Rv	Revelation

REFERENCES

SEASON OF ADVENT

9 The expectation of Christ: O R, 48.'83   **10** Harmony between man and Christ: O R, 48.'83   **11** The book of Emmanuel: O R, 52.'83   **12** The new earth, in which justice will dwell: O R, 50.'81   **12** The advent of meeting   **13** Behold, the Lord God comes: O R, 50.'81   **14** The Lord keeps faith forever: O R, 52.'83   **15** The source of our joy: O R, 52.'83   **16** Messianic promises: O R, 52.'83   **17** Let us venerate the redemption which was accomplished in you: O R, 50.'82   **18** The exalted Daughter of Sion: O R, 51.'83   **18** Temple and spouse: O R, 51.'83   **19** The Immaculate One is the first marvel of the Redemption: O R, 50.'83   **20** Full of grace: O R, 51.'83   **21** Mary, mother and virgin: O R, 51.'83   **22** The theological dimension of Mary's Immaculate Conception: O R, 50.'83   **23** M. Kolbe, an apostle of a new « Marian era »: O R, 50.'82   **24** Immaculate because Mother of God: O R, 50.'82   **25** There is love everywhere: O R, 50.'82   **26** The duty of « acceptance »: O R, 50.'83   **27** Mission of the Messiah: O R, 50.'83   **28** Intermediary Advent: O R, 52.'82   **29** Advent: a time of conversion: O R, 49.'83   **30** A clean heart create for me: O R, 49.'83   **31** You know the time: O R, 49.'83   **33** Salvation comes from God: O R, 51.'83   **34** Salvation is man's great aspiration: O R, 51.'83   **34** The first experience of salvation: O R, 51.'83

SEASON OF CHRISTMAS

39 For that Word who was made flesh: O R, 1-2.'84   **40** We thank you for the Child laid in a manger...: O R, 1-2.'84   **40** God and man: O R, 1-2.'84   **41** Nothing is lost in man: O R, 1-2.'84   **42** Christmas: O R, 1.'81   **43** Let us recover the truth of Christmas: O R, 1.'81   **44** The « power » of the New-born: O R, 1-2.'83   **45** Christ is our peace: O R, 1-2.'84   **46** To be blessed by God is to be happy: O R, 52.'83   **47** Mary « our mother » in the faith: O R, 50.'83   **48** « Not knowing man »: O R, 1-2.'84   **49** Mary and the Church, living temples: O R, 3.'84   **50** Mary: « Theotokos »: O R, 1-2.'84   **51** Mary, the « servant » of the Lord: O R, 52.'82   **52** The Mother of the Redeemer: O R, 52.'84   **53** Peace on earth is proclaimed: O R, 1-2.'84   **54** From a new heart peace is born: O R, 1-2.'84   **54** Epiphany means manifestation: O R, 3.'84   **55** The inner strength of the Epiphany: O R, 3.'84   **56** The attitude of St. John the Baptist: O R, 4.'84

SEASON OF LENT

61 You are dust: O R, 9.'82   **62** « Put to death whatever in your nature is rooted in earth: O R, 11.'84   **63** Jealous love: O R, 9.'82   **64** Metanoeite: O R, 8.'83   **65** The work of conversion: O R, 8.'83   **66** The Kingdom of God is at hand: O R, 10.'82   **66** « Away with you, Satan! »: O R, 13.'84   **67** « I am the light of the world »: O R, 16.'84   **69** « Lord, if you had been here, my brother would never have died »: O R, 16.'84   **70** The root of death: O R, 16.'84   **71** The sacrifice as the means of the liberation: O R, 16.'83   **72** The solidarity of suffering: S D, 8   **73** The world of suffering: S D, 8   **73** Why does evil exist: S D, 9   **75** The moral justice of the evil: S D, 10   **76** The sin of the world: S D, 15   **77** The dominion of sin: S D, 16   **78** He gave himself for me: S D, 16   **79** « Let this cup pass from me »: S D, 18   **80** « It is finished »: S D, 18   **82** Sharing in the Cross: S D, 21   **82** Worthy of the Kingdom of God: S D, 22   **83** « Fellow heirs with Christ »: S D, 22   **84** « Father, forgive them... »: S D, 23   **85** The salvific power of God: S D, 24   **86** Call to the virtue: S D, 24   **87** The creative character of suffering: S D, 24   **88** Christ's redemptive suffering: S D, 25   **89** Mary's suffering: S D, 25   **90** « Let him take up his cross »: S D, 25   **91** « For Christ » and « for the sake of Christ »: S D, 26   **92** The Gospel of suffering: S D, 26   **93** The power of suffering: S D, 26   **94** A new kind of motherhood: S D, 27   **95** The meaning of suffering: S D, 27   **96** The real neighbour: S D, 28   **98** The apostolate of « the good Samaritan »: S D, 29   **99** « The Spirit of the Lord is upon me »: S D, 30   **100** A civilization of love »: S D, 30   **101** The Messiah's exaltation: O R, 16.'82   **102** The beginning of the exaltation: O R, 16.'82   **103** Sacrament of love: O R, 18.'84   **105** The Lamb of God: O R, 16.'82   **106** The sign of the universal redemption: O R, 16.'82   **107** The Cross, a guarantee of life: O R, 14.'83   **108** In the Cross of Christ, the foundation of our hope: O R, 14.'83

SEASON OF EASTER

113 Peace be with you: O R, 18.'81   **113** The empty tomb: O R, 16.'82   **114** « I am the resurrection and the life »: O R, 15.'83   **115** Passover: the passage from death to life: O R, 18.'84   **116** Easter joy must be steeped in thanksgiving: O R, 21.'83   **117** The third day he rose from the dead: O R, 16.'81   **118** « I am with you always, to the close of the age »: O R, 14.'83   **119** « I came that they may have life! »: O R, 20.'81   **120** The inner life of man: O R, 20.'81   **121** Joseph, a just man: O R, 14-15.'82   **122** Hoping against every hope: O R, 14-15.'82   **123** Witness of the Divine Mystery: O R, 14-15.'82   **124** Kekaritoméne: O R, 13.'81   **125** The son of God: O R, 13.'81   **126** Prototype and model of the Church: O R, 13.'81   **127** « Behold »: O R, 13.'81   **127** I have come to do your will: O R, 13.'81   **128** He dwelt among us: O R, 13.'81   **129** Only hope: O R, 15.'83   **130** Redemption come from the Cross: O R, 15.'83   **131** Intellectual and moral formation: O R, 19.'82   **132** Christ is the cornerstone: O R,

ORDINARY TIME

ABBREVIATIONS

A A	Apostolicam actuositatem
C C L	Code of Canon Law
Div. in mis.	Dives in misericordia
E N	Evangelii nuntiandi
F C	Familiaris consortio
G S	Gaudium et Spes
H V	Humanae vitae
L E	Laborem exercens
L G	Lumen Gentium
O R	Osservatore Romano
O T	Optatam Totius
R H	Redemptor hominis
S D	Salvifici doloris
U R	Unitatis redintegratio

Stampa: Industrie Grafiche di G. Zeppegno - Torino